Imagining Scotland

For Iain and Jennifer

Imagining Scotland

Tradition, Representation and
Promotion in Scottish Tourism since
1750

JOHN R. GOLD and MARGARET M. GOLD

SCOLAR PRESS

Published by
SCOLAR PRESS
Gower House
Croft Road
Aldershot
Hants GU11 3HR
England

Ashgate Publishing Company
Old Post Road
Brookfield
Vermont 05036
USA

British Library Cataloguing in Publication Data

Gold, John R.
    Imagining Scotland: Tradition,
    Representation and Promotion in Scottish
    Tourism since 1750
    I. Title   II. Gold, Margaret M.
    941.1

Library of Congress Cataloging-in-Publication Data

Gold, John Robert.
    Imagining Scotland: tradition, representation, and promotion in
    Scottish tourism since 1750/by John R. Gold and Margaret M. Gold.
        p. cm.
    Includes bibliographical references and index.
    ISBN 1–85928–059–5
    1. Tourist trade—Scotland.   I. Gold, Margaret M.   II. Title.
    G155.G7G65   1995   95–7887
    338.4'7914104—dc20   CIP

ISBN 1 85928 059 5

Typeset in Sabon by Poole Typesetting (Wessex) Ltd, Bournemouth and printed in Great Britain by Biddles Ltd, Guildford.

Contents

List of figures and tables   *vii*
Preface and Acknowledgements   *xi*

1   Introduction   1

2   Tourism, place promotion and the cultural frame   16

3   Travellers' tales   36

4   Sir Walter Scott and the propagation of the highland myth   60

5   The coming of the railways   86

6   The rhetoric of the open road   116

7   Selling highland Scotland: the role of heritage   140

8   Selling industrial Scotland: tourism and the workplace   160

9   Cities of culture   176

10 Conclusion   194

Bibliography   *203*
Index   *224*

List of figures and tables

List of figures

1.1 A scene from Brigadoon (MGM, 1954). *Source*: BFI Stills, Posters and Designs   3

2.1 Cairngorm scene: crag, loch, pinewood, capercailzie and roe deer. *Source*: Edlin (1969, 37)   30

3.1 Prospect of the west view of the City of Edinburgh (T. Culeth, *c*. 1770). *Source*: authors' collection   37

3.2 Johnson and Boswell's tour of the Hebrides. *Source*: drawn by the authors   46

3.3 Early traveller's map, Edinburgh to Dunkeld. *Source*: authors' collection   51

3.4 The Falls of Foyers (D.O. Hill, RSA and W. Forrest, *c*. 1840). *Source*: authors' collection

4.1 Paper-covered editions of Scott's novels. *Source*: authors' collection   66

4.2 'Balmoral – HM The Queen's Highland Home' (James Cassie, RSA, 1858). *Source*: City of Aberdeen Art Gallery and Museums Collections   82

5.1 Castle Hill, Edinburgh. *Source*: Stevenson (1889, 13)   88

5.2 Stereoscopic photographs. *Source*: authors' collection   92

5.3 'Growing popularity of the Highlands'. *Source*: Hammerton (n.d., 129)   94

5.4 Comparison of the Scottish railway networks, 1852 and 1914. *Source*: drawn by the authors   95

5.5 *Cook's Tours in Scotland*. *Source*: Thomas Cook Travel Archive   105

5.6 'A Little Holiday in Scotland'. Source: *Punch*, 1 September 1888. Reproduced by permission of *Punch*   113

6.1 The rhetoric of the open road. *Source*: Stephenson (1946, 13)   117

6.2   *Whisky Galore!* (Ealing Studios, 1949). *Source*: BFI Stills,
      Posters and Designs   121
6.3   Motoring and touring map. *Source*: authors' collection   129
6.4   *The Face of Scotland* (Brian Cook, 1933). *Source*: dust-
      jacket for Batsford and Fry (1933)   134

7.1   Crieff Highland Games leaflet. *Source*: Crieff Highland
      Gathering Ltd   143
7.2   Dunrobin Castle, Golspie, Sutherland. *Source*:
      photograph by the authors   148
7.3   The Loch Ness Monster Trail. *Source*: Inverness, Loch
      Ness and Nairn Tourist Board   157

8.1   The New Lanark Heritage Trail. *Source*: Arnold
      (1993, 223)   166
8.2   The Malt Whisky Trail, Speyside. *Source*: tourist brochure   173

9.1   Programme, Edinburgh Festival Fringe (Anna Landucci,
      1993). *Source*: Edinburgh Festival Fringe Society   183
9.2   Glasgow: Cultural Capital of Europe, 1990. *Source*:
      Glasgow City Council   188
9.3   'Glasgow's Alive' advertising campaign. *Source*: Glasgow
      City Council   190

10.1 Storyboard for 'When Will You Go?' advertisement.
      Source: video recording, Faulds Advertising Agency,
      Edinburgh   198

List of tables

2.1   Elements and actors in the communication process   23

5.1   Golf clubs in Scotland and England   107

Studies in the History of Travel and Tourism

General Editors' Preface

In recent years – and more particularly since the publication of Edward Said's pathbreaking *Orientalism* – there has been a growth of interest in cultural, intellectual and historical aspects of travel and tourism. Thus far, however, literary theorists, sociologists and anthropologists, as well as those concerned with cultural and critical studies, have contributed more to this field than historians. This series seeks to rectify this situation by encouraging the publication of scholarly work in relation to the historical and social construction of distinctive 'foreign' destinations; the origins and development of resorts; the complex processes of transnational interaction and stereotyping; and the social and cultural aspects of new modes of mass travel and communication. Simply because it is predominantly social-historical in approach, however, the series will not necessarily exclude consideration of individual travellers and travel writers from a wide range of periods and cultures.

Over the last two decades, social historians have become increasingly expert at devising methodologies which capture and explain the behaviour of 'typical' aggregates. But they have shown themselves to be altogether less comfortable in relation to the reconstruction of the life patterns and experiences of individuals – whether 'normal', 'deviant' or plain eccentric. For this reason, our series will also encourage work which, moving beyond conventional narrative biography, attempts to explain the culturally determined motives of explorers and travellers who confronted the 'unknown' and the 'other' at specific, and not infrequently tragic, historical junctures.

In his two masterpieces, *Silence* and *The Samurai*, Shasaku Endo has shown that 'alien cultures' are simultaneously and confusingly transparent and utterly unknowable. By drawing on techniques and approaches from the mainstream of social and cultural history and historical geography, contributors to the series will no doubt reflect upon, and critically qualify that cryptic generalization. Simultaneously, they will provide valuable background material for the very large numbers of teachers, researchers and students now engaged in the booming fields of leisure and tourism studies.

Bill Luckin
Pyrs Gruffudd

Preface and Acknowledgements

This book stems from our shared interests in Scotland as a place and as an imaginative construction. We were interested in the way that Scotland has been imagined and represented in the years since the defeat of the 1745 uprising initiated the process of integrating that country into the wider British and international economies. We were particularly fascinated by the imagery conveyed to potential travellers and tourists with the intention of attracting them to Scotland. The book that you see before you is an attempt to follow through many of the overlapping themes that have emerged and to draw together common elements in the presentation of Scotland to the outside world.

At the outset, it is as well to clarify our position in writing this book. We are not Scots, nor was our experience and upbringing Scottish. Insofar as either of us has specific memories of the matter, our childhood knowledge of Scotland was very scanty. As children growing up in the South of England, our respective families never seriously thought about visiting Scotland for annual holidays. It was 'too wet', 'too cold' and 'much too far' to contemplate. Some of the more serious gaps in our knowledge have been filled over the last twenty years by extensive visits; sometimes to do research, sometimes with students, sometimes with the children on what passes for family holidays, and most often as part of an obsession with the Edinburgh Festival. Nevertheless, we remain outsiders and the processes and imagery discussed here to some extent constitute our experience as consumers of that imagery. At times this book may consider the relationship between portrayals of Scotland and the Scottish identity, but when doing so we are emphatically not reflecting on our own identity.

As with any book, there are many accumulated debts which it is a pleasure to acknowledge. The School of Social Sciences at Oxford Brookes University and the School of European and International Studies at Thames Valley University have provided finance and other assistance to facilitate our work. Colleagues and students have provided ideas and encouragement. Steve Ward brought various sources on heritage tourism to our attention. In particular we should like to thank Heather Croall and George Revill for supplying us with visual materials. John Gold would like to express his sincere thanks to the Department of Geography, Queen Mary and Westfield College (University of London) for their generous hospitality. This book was written there while on sabbatical as Visiting

Professor in the Christmas Term of 1994. Philip Ogden, Murray Gray, Jenn Page and Roger Lee all contributed to making the book possible in one way or another.

Thanks must also be recorded to the following libraries and their staff for their assistance: the British Library, National Library of Scotland, Senate House (University of London), Dalhousie University, the Queen Elizabeth II Library of the Memorial University of Newfoundland, the LIbrary of Congress, the British Film Institute, Queen Mary and Westfield College, Oxford Brookes University and Thames Valley University. The Stills Library of the British Film Institute and the Thomas Cook Travel Archive assisted in locating illustrations that accompany this text. We are particularly grateful to Philip Bigg who prepared the photographs and to John Williamson who drew the maps.

Formal acknowledgement is made to the following for permission to reproduce copyright material: Glasgow City Council, Crieff Highland Gathering Ltd, City of Aberdeen Art Gallery and Museums Collection, the Scotch Whisky Association, Crown Copyright and the Forestry Commission, Thomas Cook, the Official Loch Ness Monster Exhibition, Garamond Publishers Ltd, B.T. Batsford Ltd, the Edinburgh Fringe Society, Lumiere Pictures, Turner Entertainments, the Inverness, Loch Ness and Nairn Tourist Board, the *Punch* Library and the New Lanark Conservation Trust. Other items come from the authors' own collection or are photographs taken by the authors. All reasonable efforts have been made to trace whether copyright exists on older items. If anything should have been missed, we should be grateful if the copyright holders would contact us, whereupon we shall be pleased to settle matters.

Finally, this volume is dedicated to our children, Iain and Jennifer, who insisted that it should be.

West Ealing
December 1994

CHAPTER ONE

Introduction

'The stark beauty of the Scottish landscape awakens the poetry in most visiting souls, and it generates plenty of creativity amongst the locals.'

Andrew Eames, *Summer in Scotland*

RUSTIC. 'This cottage is on the Glenfalloch Estate. Take the first turn off by the Ministry of Defence road, hard left at the nuclear bunker in the mountain and on past the Wowee Marina and Leisure Complex on the hillside.'

Ian Pattison, *More Rab C. Nesbitt Scripts*

Representations of Scotland

For a small nation, Scotland holds a remarkably deep fascination for people in many parts of the world. This partly reflects the history of emigration. People of Scottish descent in North America, Africa, Australasia and elsewhere keep alive what they regard as their heritage through participation in Burns and Caledonian Societies, sponsorship of pipe bands, clan gatherings and the holding of highland games, even if that heritage may often be a recent invention. Yet the fascination with Scotland is not just a question of ancestry. There is an awareness, even a familiarity, with Scottish artefacts, products and landscapes that is truly international and not solely confined to areas containing Scottish migrants. The poetry of Robert Burns thrives in Russia, to the extent that the Russians have assimilated Burns Night customs. Scientific teams from North America come in pursuit of the Loch Ness Monster. Pipe band competitions draw a strong international entry.

Representations of the Scottish countryside have an interesting place in this wider consciousness. Scottish landscapes, for example, are well represented as settings for artistic works. The paintings by Turner and Landseer, the poetry and songs of Robert Burns, the novels of Sir Walter Scott and Robert Louis Stevenson with their myriad translations, the nineteenth-century operas of Donizetti and Rossini, and the music of Felix Mendelssohn and Malcolm Arnold are just a few of the many artistic ventures set in Scotland, particularly in the Highlands and Islands. Popular culture tells the same story. Illustrators of children's books, the writers and cover-designers of Mills and Boon romances, photographers of the

National Geographic and newspaper travel writers routinely concentrate on two specific aspects of Scotland: Edinburgh's striking topography and architectural treasures or the seemingly timeless Scotland of the Highlands and Islands, with their dramatic scenery, scattered communities and feudally-based society.

Such settings are also a staple of the production strategies employed by the international film industry. Colin McArthur's (1982b) study of films on Scotland shows that films with traditional settings had already appeared during the era of the silent cinema, accompanied by associated themes of tartan and sentimental narrative forms. Ealing Studios comedies such as *Whisky Galore!* (1949) and *The Maggie* (1953) placed their action in the landscapes and society of the Scottish islands. A series of classic costume dramas from Walt Disney Productions (for example, *Rob Roy*, 1953; *Kidnapped*, 1960; and *Greyfriars Bobby*, 1961) brought Hollywood's inter-pretations of an idealized historic Scotland to family audiences worldwide.

Perhaps the most revealing aspects of the portrayal of Scotland were conveyed by the planning for MGM's musical *Brigadoon* (1954, MGM). The story involved the clash of tradition and modernity when two Americans, lost in the mists, come across an enchanted highland village that only stirs for three weeks each century. Its producer, Arthur Freed, had looked for suitable Scottish locations for the village of Brigadoon and its surrounding countryside, but eventually gave up the search. Scotland, he remarked, no longer looked like Scotland (Borley, 1994, 3). The chosen alternative was to construct studio sets of a highland village in a glen, with painted backdrops illustrating the loch and the heather on the hills (Figure 1.1). These were more in line with the makers' predilections.

This same rich repository of readily accessible and advantageous cul-tural associations is actively exploited by product advertising and market-ing, since it has proven commercial value. The key selling proposition often employs the splendour of the surroundings as an attractive backdrop against which to show the versatility or elegant durability of the product concerned. Hence, luxury four-wheel drive motor vehicles are set against the rugged grandeur of the Scottish Highlands (the Isuzu Trooper 3.1 Turbo Diesel – 'Monarch of the Glen'). Fashion models pose against back-drops of loch and mountain to advertise designer knitwear or expensive waxed jackets. An American computer company runs an advertisement showing a busy executive sitting in a stationary car while waiting for a train to pass at a road crossing on the West Highland line (never a frequent event at the best of times). Impatient to make the best use of his time, he checks the impressive three-dimensional bar chart on his lap-top computer.

Perhaps the most relentless use of highland scenery as an adjunct to the selling process is seen in the packaging and marketing of Scottish food exports. Walker's Pure Butter Shortbread Rounds, for instance, arrive in

1.1 A scene from *Brigadoon* (MGM, 1954). The official captions to the film stills contain such statements as: 'A wee bit of Scotland comes to life inside a Hollywood sound stage'.

tins bearing portraits of key figures in the 1745 uprising and carry the caption that the contents are 'baked to a generations' old recipe ... in the secluded village of Aberlour, Strathspey, in the heart of the Scottish Highlands'. Baxter's Soups have labels that display tartan and scenes of misty mountains, lochs and glens, with a typical version noting how the firm has been making soups in Speyside since 1868 'using old family recipes and the superb natural produce of their native Scottish Highlands'. Glen Grant malt Scotch whisky, also from Speyside, boasts that the area is famed for 'the wild grandeur of its mountains, the purity of the highland air ... and the wonderful softness of the water'. The Famous Grouse, a blended whisky from Perth, has a label bearing a red grouse perched on a boulder and surrounded by heather. With a game bird that symbolizes upper-class sporting pursuits, the advertiser tries to gain the cachet of status when declaring that both bird and whisky are 'raised in the Highlands'. Many new varieties of Scottish spring water, launched to gain a share of the rapidly growing European market for bottled table waters, employ the same imagery. Bearing names such as Strathmore and Highland Spring, they have labels which feature soft-focused watercolour sketches of their mountainous sources and captions that praise the purity of water created by years of percolation through such rocks. The supermarket chain Waitrose sell their biscuits in wrappings with period-style paintings of full-antlered stags grazing by the lochside or on the slopes of mist-shrouded mountains. The carton designs for Scott's Piper Oatmeal and Old Fashioned Porage Oats respectively bear portraits of tartaned pipers and participants in highland games, with labels proclaiming that the products within are made exclusively from 'pure fresh oats'.

Purity, freshness, tradition and quality, then, are freely associated with specific depictions of highland scenery and society as part of the selling process. Collectively, these and similar representations provide a ready supply of colourful and distinctive images that many would argue fuel the geographies of the mind of those in the outside world, not least because, as high value-added commodities, they are a common sight at airport shops and delicatessens throughout the world. Yet they supply as selective an imagery as did the set-designers of *Brigadoon*; a fantasy world of misty mountains and sunlit glens filled with smiling, tartan-wearing countryfolk going about their simple but wholesome lives.

Landscapes of tourist promotion

So far we have dealt with the way that these representations of highland landscapes and society are used in the selling of commodities, but it must be stressed that they are commodities that are bought and sold in their own right. Despite widespread disparagement of the characteristic representations of Scotland commonly found in the media and elsewhere (McArthur, 1982a; MacLean and Carrell, 1986; Pittock, 1991; Daly, 1994), those concerned with selling Scotland to tourists living outside the boundaries of that country readily avail themselves of this rich seam of familiar imagery. One powerful reason is that it is immediately recognized by an international audience.

That impression is sustained by an overview of a sample of brochures circulating at travel agents in North America, Europe and Asia in the summer of 1994.[1] If the words in a brochure (BTA, 1994, 34) produced for potential North American tourists are to be believed, in the popular imagination:

> Scotland conjures up images of dramatic mountains, shimmering lochs, tartans, bagpipes and fine malt whisky. Scotland is all of this and more besides ... it is a land rich in romantic baronial castles, Highland Games and the historic towns and cities. Explore the beautiful Highlands, the wooded glens, meandering salmon rivers and traditional fishing villages ...

That impression could indeed be sustained by the touring itineraries, that, by dint of extraordinary skills in route creation, contrive to take the visitor through even the Central Lowlands seeing only castles, hills, waterfalls and craft shops on the way (e.g. STB, 1993, 12–19). Only Edinburgh, the cultural heart of Glasgow and the Old Town of Stirling are offered as counter-attractions.

Perhaps the most accessible index of selectivity, however, lies in the content of the glossy colour photographs contained in these publications. Often taken to be the most important element in travel brochures, the photography contained eight specific, clichéd shots that were used in at least one-quarter of those considered here. These shots were:

- Photographs of hills and distant mountains, invariably in warm summer colouring. Although there may be mists or striking cloud effects, the scenery usually seems accessible to the casual hill-walker rather than that which would challenge the dedicated mountaineer. The terrain is inviting, never menacing.
- Two walkers, one male and one female, admiring a sunlit panorama of mountain and glen. In line with the theme of accessibility, they look more like car-travellers than serious hikers or ramblers. Although both are wearing suitable clothing (light walking boots, sweaters), they are not unduly encumbered by rucksacks or waterproofs. The male, who is the dominant figure in the composition, clutches binoculars or, somewhat incongruously for the 1990s, a walking stick. He stands slightly in front of his companion and points authoritatively at an item

of interest in the far distance. She gazes appreciatively in the appropriate direction. Some thistles in full bloom in the foreground are an optional extra.

- A solitary kilted piper, in full regalia, either playing the bagpipes or with the pipes resting on his shoulder. He stands on the brow of a hill, knee-deep in purple heather or a thick textured grass. A light breeze is sufficient to cause the vegetation to undulate gently but is clearly not strong enough to disrupt proceedings.

- A building (normally a highland castle or white-walled thatched croft-house), situated by the lochside. A rowing boat is usually moored at the water's edge to give foreground interest, but the view lacks any other sign of human habitation. The scene is usually illuminated by a bright shaft of sunlight, but dark-toned skies suggest shelter and warmth in the face of an imminent storm.

- Deserted Hebridean shore pictures, which come in two versions. The first type are wide angle shots taken from a low angle of regard. They reveal endless strands of shimmering white sands lapped by gentle waves. Some strands of kelp, shells or a small rock in the foreground help to lend a sense of scale. The other version consists of higher-elevation, contre-jour pictures of rock- and island-strewn coasts shot against a vivid west coast sunset.

- Golfers on a coastal links course. Driving off from a tee adjacent to the ocean, they stare intently into the distance to watch the flight of a ball driven impeccably by one of their number. Tartan trousers or tartan fabrics on a golf bag are a common additional referent.

- A 'fishing picture', either a solitary angler dressed in waders fishing in a Borders salmon river or the brightly painted prows of fishing boats moored in line at the quayside of a highland fishing village. The latter normally shows a clutter of fishing tackle lying on the quay and often hints at the bounty of the sea (e.g. a lorry being loaded with crates or a fisherman showing a live lobster to an admiring tourist).

- The profile of Edinburgh's Castle and Old Town, taken either from the Prince's Street Gardens or from Calton Hill. Unwanted detail, such as the roofs of Edinburgh's Waverley railway station and its associated tracks, is normally filtered out by choice of lens, camera angle, or careful foreground screening.

Other views that appeared less frequently include highland cattle grazing in a sunlit glen, whisky distilleries, pipe bands, highland games, Scottish country dancers, Caledonian-MacBrayne ferries leaving west coast harbours and vintage steam-hauled excursion trains crossing the spectacular 21-arch curved rail viaduct at Glenfinnan at the head of Loch Shiel on the West Highland line.

Even from this small sample it is readily apparent that, aside from the urban charms of Edinburgh, the potential tourist is presented with images that primarily show the landscapes of the Highlands and Islands in summer. It is a view of Scotland that is highly selective in three senses. First, it portrays landscapes of highland and rural areas that are inhabited by only a tiny fraction of the Scottish population. Secondly, it depicts a society with a social and occupational structure that is quite different from elsewhere in Scotland. Finally, it shows a country that masquerades as being timeless and unchanging. In all three senses, there is precious little attempt to show the 'other Scotland' that is the demographic and economic heart of the nation. Indeed, the rest of the nation remains nigh invisible as part of the enterprise of selling Scotland.

Image and promotion

This continuing use of the traditional imagery of Scotland is testimony to its tenacious grip on the imaginations of those who promote tourism. Yet having said this, there is now evidence of powerful trends that are actively injecting new styles into promotional work that supplement the dominant depiction of Scotland. The stimulus is economic. Within the last twenty years tourism has changed from an informally-organized sector to a multi-million pound industry operating on a global basis. It is vitally important to Scotland in general, but its significance is disproportionately great for rural regions such as the Highlands and Islands, Dumfries and Galloway, Borders and parts of Tayside. Tourism contributes around 5 per cent of the total Scottish gross domestic product and supports around 185,000 jobs.[2] The estimated 9.8 million tourists who visited Scotland in 1991 spent around £1.7 billion. Overseas visitors are particularly significant. Although they generated only 1.5 million tourist visits (around 15 per cent of the total) compared with 8.2 million from the United Kingdom, their spending amounted to around 30 per cent of the total (STCG, 1992).

Much therefore is at stake, and competing in a global but rapidly-changing and fickle market has its problems. Holiday decisions represent the largest single allocation of resources made annually by most households and many now contemplate second holidays and short-breaks. There are various competing choices of destination and even the patronage of nostalgic expatriates and their descendants wishing to 'return to Scotland' cannot be taken for granted in times of recession. The business sector, too, is unpredictable. Globalization and the growing international competition between potential tourist destinations has transformed the way in which corporate and learned society treasurers set about making their choices of venue for seminars and conferences. Faced with these changing external circumstances, Scottish national, regional and civic authorities have increasingly turned to professional publicity and marketing agencies to improve their prospects of winning customers.

This has served not just to dilute the engaging amateurism of Scottish promotional endeavours, but has also altered the content of what is communicated in two important respects. First, while continuing to draw on the traditional commodified view of Scotland, the introduction of professional agencies has brought in new imagery borrowed from other spheres of publicity, most notably product advertising and marketing. Given their involvement in this wider field, professional agencies are prone to treat tourism like any other activity and extend the best ideas developed for selling other commodities to tourism. The resulting convergence of the central selling propositions used for tourism with those employed in advertising other commodities is, therefore, hardly surprising (see Wernick, 1991).

Secondly, involvement of professional agencies tends to heighten awareness of the actions taken by perceived competitors. As Schudson (1984, 5) points out, the power of advertising rests more in its repetition of obvious exhortations than in its subtle transmission of values. Awareness of a particularly effective piece of campaign by a rival often leads to rapid replication. In part, this can be attributed to the hope of sharing in their success or, more negatively, the wish to neutralize any special advantage that this competitor is enjoying. However, it also reflects growing accord within the industry about the icons of desirability for promoting tourism. Professional journals and a growing number of practical manuals (e.g. Witt and Moutinho, 1989; Ashworth and Goodall, 1990; Gren, 1992; Kotler et al., 1993) have served to codify a consensus about good practice and strategy that transcends the local or even national context. In addition, there are more defensive factors working to produce the same result. Whatever their inherent charms, Scottish resorts and cities often contend with an unenviable reputation for antiquated facilities, poor service and difficult communications. Aping the style and message of perceived competitors is a simple mechanism by which one can argue that Scotland contains and can match the best of what is available elsewhere.

Examples are easy to find. Scottish hotels, once legendary for their quirky individuality, now employ images of quality and refinement indistinguishable from those found in the brochures of large hotel chains anywhere in the western world. The former industrial towns of central Scotland vie with one another in repackaging dereliction into heritage. The whisky and food industries offer guided works tours and create 'tourist experiences' on a pattern initiated in the USA. Marine life centres offer a package of experiences (children's touch pools, walk-through aquaria, recovery ponds for injured seals) and facilities (adventure playgrounds, gift shops and restaurants) that mirror the contents of many such schemes elsewhere around the coasts of the British Isles. The Cairngorm ski centres represent themselves as offering ski and après-ski facilities that are the equal of Alpine resorts. Taken as a whole, these strategies inject a style of imagery into promotional work that is different from previous practice. Rather than simply revelling in attributes held to be quintessentially and uniquely Scottish, they re-create and reproduce a set of images that are an intrinsic part of tourist promotion throughout the world (Gold and Ward, 1994).

Aims and scope

This book is concerned with the origins, anatomy and propagation of these different styles of imagery and with the operation of the creative imaginations that produced them. Its subject matter is the development of Scottish tourism from around 1750 to the present. However while it aims to provide a representative overview of its history, the specific focus is less of a study of patterns and trends than of an inquiry into the way that Scotland has been represented to tourists over this period. As such, this book comprises an essay in what may be termed 'place promotion' (Gold and Ward, 1994), which can be defined as the purposive shaping of written, visual or broadcast materials to communicate selective images of specific geographical localities or areas to a target audience for the purpose of increasing those places' income and prosperity.[3] There is detailed consideration of representations of Scotland taken from historic and contemporary posters, pamphlets, guidebooks and other media used in publicity and marketing. We ask how these representations came about and what was the thinking behind them; who produced these materials, what messages were incorporated, and how those messages were communicated to the potential audience of travellers and tourists. In this connection, considerable attention is paid not just to those aspects of Scotland and Scottish life that were depicted, but also those that were omitted.

Taken as a whole, this book has three main aims. The first is to present a history of *Scottish* tourism since 1750. In the process, we seek to fill a gap in the literature that is camouflaged by those who claim to have written histories of British tourism. Almost inevitably, when viewed analytically, these are histories of English travel and tourism with a few Scottish issues mentioned in passing. Secondly, we attempt to understand this history through the lens of the thinking and actions of those who participated in its development. Whenever possible, the analysis proceeds with documentation that is contemporary to the times with which we are dealing. Thirdly, we aim to throw light on sets of images of place and landscape worthy of study in their own right as a historical record of the ways in which Scotland has been conceived and portrayed to the outside world over the past 250 years.

At the outset, it is worth making four points that help to define the scope of this book and its central arguments. The first concerns the definitions of 'travel' and 'tourism'. In his lengthy discussion of the origin and usage of these terms, Buzard (1993, 1–17) indicated both how these terms have overlapped and how they have developed different connotations. Although nowadays treated as a synonym for all purposive movement, *travel*, the older of the terms, is etymologically related to the word 'travail'. Travel carries the positive connotations of hard-won experience achieved despite difficulty. Travellers are people who experience things fresh and travel at the most in small groups. By contrast *tourism* often has negative associations in popular parlance. Tourism deals with travellers en masse, with all that is implied by large-scale movements of people regarding the demands placed on host destinations. The word 'tourist' commonly conjures up mental pictures of 'a personality profile, a life-style, perhaps a class classification, and a host of scenarios in which "the tourist" performs some characteristic act. The tourist is the dupe of fashion, following blindly where authentic travellers have gone with open eyes and free spirits' (ibid., 1).

In this text, 'travel' is taken to be a specialized word with two distinct meanings. Historically it relates to an antecedent of modern tourism; when applied to present-day tourism, 'travel' emerges as a niche market that appeals to those who seek vacations embodying independence and originality (in whatever way that may be packaged). 'Tourism' is taken to be a more general term that includes travel. It is defined here in a non-pejorative and behavioural manner as 'the temporary short-term movement of people to destinations outside the places where they normally live and work, and activities during their stay at these destinations' (Holloway, 1988, 2; quoted in Squire, 1994a, 2). To qualify as tourism, trips should involve staying away from home for at least 24 hours but less than a year (Shaw and Williams, 1994, 5). This, therefore, includes trips for business as well as social and recreational purposes. It incorporates both domestic tourism (within the same country) and international tourism (between different countries), even though our focus here is almost exclusively on the latter.[4]

The second point in clarifying the scope of this study concerns the nature of promotional activity. The promotion of tourism has, at its heart, communication between a disparate set of agencies and equally disparate, far-flung and heterogeneous audiences. The complex and multifaceted problems involved in attempting even to identify audiences when considering historical instances of communication, let alone trying to distinguish audience response or impact, means that there is no systematic attempt in this text to cover the full cycle of communication from production of messages through to their consumption by the audience.[5] Instead, our focus is primarily on the production and characteristics of messages about Scotland conveyed in promoting tourism, examining the characteristics of the producers (or communicators) who shaped those messages, the nature of the content produced and the media chosen to communicate that content. In doing so, of course, it is recognized that place promotion has never been solely the province of those with a direct financial interest in, or administrative responsibility for, the effective development of a town or region. Enthusiastic amateurs, acting out of perceived self-interest or local pride, have always played their part in championing the cause of tourism. Indeed, their word may seem to carry more weight given that it is not linked to a specific selling effort. Eulogistic accounts of walking in the Scottish mountains, hobbyist guides to Scotch whisky and glossy coffee-table books on outstanding architecture, therefore, also have their place in the pattern of communication that will be examined.

The third point extends this argument further. Since the imagery found in literature aimed at potential tourists is embedded in a wider set of cultural representations of Scottish landscapes and society, it is not possible to confine the analysis solely to publications or other media content explicitly created to promote commercial tourism. The representations of Scotland found in such literature are frequently drawn from and reinforced by the representations found in a wide range of other media. Hence allusion is made here to the published notebooks of travellers as readily as to the publicity brochures of tourist resorts, to the writings of regional and historical novelists as well as to brochures produced by tourist boards, to landscape paintings as well as the poster art of the railway companies, and to feature films as well as television advertising.

Finally, communication takes place in a cultural frame. Tourism itself is not just an economic activity but is also an integral part of modern culture (Leiss et al., 1990, 5). The expression and meaning of promotional imagery and messages, therefore, can be seen as constructed and mediated within the wider cultural context. Those who promote tourism avail themselves of a vast range of symbols and ideas that they can recycle and transform when communicating with their potential audience. These, as Chapter 2 notes, can be understood as part of a culturally-constructed discourse that bonds together images of people, landscape and well-being.

Structure and organization

This text contains ten chapters. Chapter 2 provides a discussion of the historical and theoretical background to place promotion to gain a sense of context for this study. It begins by considering the origins of place promotion and its development regarding four spheres of activity: colonization, boosterism, urban and regional development and tourism. Then, drawing on media and advertising research, it discusses the elements and processes involved in promoting tourism. There is discussion of the organizations involved, the chosen media, and the way in which the message is fashioned. Chapter 2 ends by introducing three notions that are valuable in understanding the form of communication involved, namely: discourse, ideology and rhetoric.

From this point the book may be conveniently divided into two broad groups of chapters. The first, Chapters 3 to 6, are arranged chronologically, although there is inevitable overlap at the margins. Collectively they illustrate the origins, consolidation and propagation of the traditional imagery of Scotland, its towns and regions. The starting point lies in the eighteenth century with the aftermath of the '45 uprising – the last serious attempt to re-establish the Stuart[6] monarchy in Great Britain. In its wake came a series of social, economic and political upheavals that quickened the absorption of Scotland into the new British State and opened up opportunities for travellers and tourists to visit in ever increasing numbers.

Improvements in transport and accommodation were of particular significance. Scotland had been a remote and difficult country for travel. The lack of roads and bridges, the mountainous terrain, poor or non-existent accommodation and the absence of maps and guides for the traveller made exploration of the land difficult. As Chapter 3 shows, improvements in these elements during the late eighteenth century helped to encourage growing numbers of travellers to visit Scotland and to write enthusiastically, sometimes fancifully, about the wonders they had seen. Their tales played a large part in establishing an agenda not only of places and things to see, but also the ways in which the visitor should experience them. The emergence of the first recognizable guidebooks and maps is traced, before turning to examine an issue that aroused the curiosity of contemporary travellers, namely the quest to verify the authenticity or otherwise of the poetry of the ancient Celtic bard, Ossian.

Chapter 4 continues the story into the nineteenth century, containing background to much of what occurred subsequently. After dealing with the rise of literary tourism, particularly in relation to the localities associated with Robert Burns in Ayrshire, it deals with the invention and propagation of the highland myth, primarily by Sir Walter Scott. Through his writings and activities as the pageant-master of Scotland, Scott re-invented Scottish traditions and brought them to the notice of a public far beyond the nation's borders. Chapter 4 traces these developments and shows how new ways of looking at the landscape, and indeed new types of valued landscapes, evolved.

Later rounds of social and infrastructural developments in turn created the opportunity for the growth of mass tourism in the nineteenth and twentieth centuries, an opportunity turned into commercial reality by the organizational and promotional endeavours of a growing tourist industry. Chapter 5 takes tradition and modernity as its theme. After outlining trends in literary and narrative forms, it considers the new directions taken by tourism because of the transport revolution brought about by the growth of the steamship network and, in particular, by the spread of railways. After considering the way in which the railways themselves set about attracting tourists, the growth of organized travel is analysed, with particular emphasis on the role played by Thomas Cook in developing organized tours of Scotland – the first recognizable steps towards mass tourism. The final sections of the chapter consider the emergence of niche markets consisting of particular hobbyist interests, including photography, mountaineering, hunting and shooting and golf.

Chapter 6 continues the historical account into the motor age. The opening section supplies background in an overview of changing tastes and media, examining trends in participation in Scottish tourism and the representation of Scotland in the new visual media. The next section provides a brief historical survey of continuing trends in accessibility, pointing to the development of the road network, the decline in significance of the railways and steamship lines, and the growth of mixed-media tourism as exemplified by fly-drive holidays. This is followed by discussion of issues concerned with motor tourism, dealing in turn with organized group travel and private motoring. Early efforts to create maps and guidebooks for the private motorist are then considered, with examples taken including the *Shell County Guides* and the *Face of Britain* series produced by Batsford. Finally, there is brief analysis of the explosion in published material for the tourist from public, private and commercial bodies that has occurred in the post-1945 period.

The second group of chapters (7 to 9) is arranged thematically and deals with the way that modern Scotland is being sold primarily through the activities of the heritage industry. Chapter 7 begins this discussion by considering the selling of Highland Scotland. It defines the meaning of heritage and interpretation and then examines a series of issues relating to the operations of the heritage industry. The first concerns the question of authenticity in representing the past-in-the-present. We then consider the geographical and thematic packaging of particular regions in promoting tourism. The ensuing section considers the contested interpretations of highland history made available to tourists, as revealed by the contrasting standpoints of the landed family and the dispossessed. The formal activity of representing folk-life and tradition is tackled by looking at the interpretive policies of folk-life museums of greatly differing scales. This chapter ends by discussing the interpretive centres devoted to exploitation of international interest in the Loch Ness Monster, which constitute one of the most popular and most commodified of Scotland's tourist attractions.

Chapter 8 provides a parallel theme by investigating the way in which Scotland's industrial past is recycled into heritage. It examines the rise of interest in industrial archaeology as a sphere of study and a leisure pursuit, but notes the imbalance and uneven representation of Scotland's industrial heritage. After a case study of the way that New Lanark, the scene of Robert Owen's model community experiments at the turn of the nineteenth century, is now interpreted for visitors, we consider how two traditional industries, food-processing and whisky, have converted the notion of the works tour into a leading tourist activity. Particular attention is drawn to the way in which the whisky industry has crafted an imagery, steeped in highland tradition, which is applied at all levels from individual distilleries, through regional heritage trails to the purpose-built Scotch Whisky Heritage Centre located next to Edinburgh Castle.

Chapter 9 tells a tale of the marketing of two cities. It notes how Edinburgh, long internationally recognized as a centre of learning and the arts, has marketed itself as a 'city of culture' – most notably through the Edinburgh Festival and its associated Fringe events. It then examines how the authorities in Glasgow, a city that long had a poor reputation in the outside world, have attempted to give it a new image of culture as part of a general 're-imaging' process. In particular, it shows how Glasgow revived its old tradition of arranging major festivals and exhibitions to publicize itself as a city of culture. By so doing, the city is attempting to graft on a new imagery of postmodern urbanism to extricate itself from the legacy of the past and sell itself in the wider marketplace.

The concluding chapter (10) provides a short summary of the key themes to emerge from this book before reflecting on a television advertising campaign run by the Scottish Tourist Board in August 1994. Although representing a state-of-the-art assembly of fleeting glimpses of Scottish scenery and society into a montage of colourful imagery, its predominantly nostalgic message underlines the continuing prevalence of tradition and nostalgia in representations of Scotland to the outside world. The chapter closes by indicating the lasting problems for Scottish tourism of these limited, and limiting, representations of Scotland.

Notes

1. The following comments are based on a sample of 25 such brochures informally gathered both at first hand in Canada and from colleagues in the USA, Germany, Norway, Japan and Israel.

2. That compares with 4 per cent in the electronics industry, 3 per cent in food and drink, and 2 per cent in the whisky industry (STCG, 1992).

3. Strictly speaking, place promotion overlaps the fields of both publicity, which involves use of media, and public relations, which centres on face-to-face communication in dealing with the press or broadcasting media. Given our emphasis on written and visual representations of Scotland in this text we will primarily be dealing with publicity, but there is no strict exclusion applied.

4. In making this point, we recognize the vexed problem of what constitutes 'domestic' in the Scottish context: whether Scotland as defined by its national borders or Scotland as a component part of the United Kingdom. In terms of examining how Scotland is represented to the outsider, however, it makes much greater sense to view tourist trips starting and ending within the borders of Scotland as domestic tourism and all movements into Scotland for tourist purposes from elsewhere, including other parts of the United Kingdom, as international tourism.

5. For more on the general question of audience impact or response that results from cycles of communication, see Gold (1974). For literature that is specifically related to tourism, see Urry (1990), Hughes (1992) and Squire (1994a).

6. Although the spelling 'Stewart' is employed by some writers, the family name was altered to the French-influenced 'Stuart' by Mary, Queen of Scots (Wormald, 1991, 18), and is the version used in this book.

CHAPTER TWO

Tourism, place promotion and the cultural frame

'That is certainly what advertising does. Instead of presenting a
private argument or vista, it offers a way of life that is for everybody
or nobody. It offers this prospect with arguments that concern only
irrelevant and trivial matters.'

Marshall McLuhan, *Understanding Media*

Advertisements and other materials promoting tourism are an unexceptional part of daily life. The walls of underground stations and poster hoardings in London carry advertisements for India (INDIAhhh – only nine hours away), Israel (HAV'A Stroll in the Moonlight), Alpine resorts (Slope Off For Less) and Cyprus (The Unforgettable Island). Newspapers, keen to generate advertising revenue, carry holiday supplements and thinly disguised editorial 'puffs' masquerading as editorial content. Their televisual counterparts draw large audiences for 'holiday programmes' which show suave presenters smiling their way through a week's free hospitality at resorts around the world. Travel agents in every high street and in many shopping malls carry shoals of colour brochures on their display shelves. Images of elsewhere are everywhere, but familiarity does not necessarily breed understanding. Only in recent years has a substantial body of literature appeared which attempts to analyse these taken-for-granted representations of place and landscape and locate them in their historical and cultural settings (e.g. Williamson, 1978; Wernick, 1991; Goldman, 1992; Gold and Ward, 1994; O'Barr, 1994).

This chapter sketches something of that background in order to place the ensuing material on promotional representations of Scotland, past and present, in its wider context. The focus is an analysis of promotion as communication, with brief comment on the characteristics of the producers or communicators, the media they use and the messages that are shaped. Three notions helpful in conceptualizing such activity are then considered, namely discourse, ideology and rhetoric. We begin, however, with a survey of the nature and origins of place promotion.

Place promotion

There are as yet no systematic surveys of where and when place promotion first emerged. Its roots lie in many different motives and spheres of activity since, broadly speaking, place promotion is an inviting proposition whenever towns or regions are trying to improve their own prospects or status often in relation to competitors. Place promotion can, therefore, be variously linked to civic rivalries, imperial expansion, regional policy, land and housing speculation, post-industrial urban change, leisure and recreational developments. Historically these different forms have overlapped and interacted to such an extent that it is impossible to create a typology with watertight categories. Nevertheless for discussion purposes we can identify four types of place promotion, connected respectively with colonial schemes, civic boosterism, urban and regional development, and tourism.

Colonial schemes

Place promotion was an accepted activity throughout the colonial era. Sir Richard Whitbourne (1623), one of the earliest promoters of colonies on Newfoundland, wrote a tract on the opportunities and potential that was available. Its lengthy title expresses both the hopes and problems of the enterprise: 'A discourse and discovery of New-found-land. With many reasons to prove how worthy and beneficial a plantation may there be made, after a better manner than it was. Together with the laying open of certain enormities and abuses that trade to that country, and the means laid downe for reformation of'. Hence the task was not only to inform but also to persuade. As with so many other subsequent schemes, persuasion inevitably involved a two-edged strategy. First, promoters needed to tempt sponsors to invest in risky schemes on the very margins of the Empire or to induce migrants to take their families into the unknown. To do so, place promoters resorted to a predictable litany of advantages to show that such colonies offered unparalleled opportunities. Climates were always mild and benevolent, droughts had no precedent, land was uniformly fertile and waiting for the plough, and rivers and coastal waters teemed with fish. Native peoples were placid, friendly and emphatically made no claims on ownership.[1] Secondly, a long history of extravagant claims and consistent failures to live up to expectations meant that promoters needed to counter the 'enormities and abuses' often heaped on such developments in case they seriously dented the potential viability of the colony. If that meant embroidering the truth, inventing favourable dispatches, or selectively presenting the reports of explorers or surveyors, then so be it (Jones, 1946; Cameron, 1974).

Place promotion of this type continued to play a significant role in the development of the North American continent throughout the nineteenth and even into the twentieth century in less populated regions (e.g. Holcomb, 1990, 5–15; Zube and Kennedy, 1990, 188–90). In parts of the British Empire and the Dominions, it persisted rather longer. The Uganda Railways devised a poster with cartoons of wild animals to convince potential upper-class migrants that the East African Highlands were a winter playground for 'aristocrats'. Rather more down-to-earth promotional publications by the Australian Information Service seeking skilled workers and families of child-bearing age remained available to potential migrants in Britain and elsewhere until the early 1960s.

Boosterism

'Boosterism', the marketing of a town or city in an attempt to gain a greater share of finite national prosperity (Sadler, 1993, 176), supplies another variant of place promotion. Although some claim that boosterism originated in the rivalries of the mercantile city-states of the Hanseatic League or medieval Italy (Goodwin, 1993, 145), a more convincing root lies in the nicknaming of US towns and cities in the nineteenth and twentieth centuries.

These were important in shaping and communicating identity. For instance, before the fire of 1871, Chicago termed itself the Garden City and the Gem of the Prairies. Later, as its self-conception altered, other names were adopted. While it might have been known to others as the Windy City, City of Big Shoulders and the Crime Capital, city boosters in Chicago stressed its new economic role by calling it the Metropolis of the West, Hogopolis, Cornopolis, the Hub of American Merchandising and the Country's Greatest Rail Centre. San Francisco, by contrast, emphasized its site and elegance in titles such as the Bay City, the City of a Hundred Hills, the Queen City and the Paris of America. Smaller towns plumped for more specific epithets. Hence Las Vegas is the Broadway of the Desert, Indio (California) became the Desert Wonderland and, with its space connections, Titusville (Florida) titled itself the Gateway to the Galaxies (Tuan, 1974, 202–3).

Urban and regional development

Over time this activity took on a sharper edge as place promotion was drawn into broader strategies of urban and regional development. In his survey, Ward (1994; see also 1996) examined the comparative progress of locally-based place promotional activity in Britain, the USA and Canada from 1870 onwards. He noted that differing economic, institutional and political circumstances have shaped promotional policies in different ways. Thus, while campaigns to attract investors and visitors became a regular and accepted part of local economic policy in the Northeastern states of the USA in the 1840s, the same policy only spread to Canada in the later decades of the nineteenth century, and to Britain in the 1930s. In Britain, for example, place promotion was primarily oriented towards tourism (see the ensuing section) and residential developments (e.g. Gold and Gold, 1991, 1994) until that stage.

Nevertheless economic and industrial place promotion progressively became a ubiquitous part of urban and regional policy in the postwar period. Connected initially to the management of growth and planned expansion (e.g. Gold, 1974), place promoters subsequently responded to the needs of the recession-hit 1970s and 1980s. Place promotion aimed at the industrial market became a widespread activity, even if it was undertaken in many cases without conviction that it would achieve much (Burgess, 1982, 6). It also became enmeshed in the agenda of the 'New Right'. In other words, against a political climate that stressed individualism and enterprise, cities and regions were seen as bundles of social and economic opportunities competing against one another in the open market for a share of capital investment (Philo and Kearns, 1993, 18).

In these new circumstances attraction of inward industrial investment, particularly in the manufacturing sector, became of paramount importance. Its urgency is measured by the fact that cities and regions throughout the western world now employ specialist staff or agencies with the sole function of attracting corporate investors. Publicity budgets remain much higher in relative as well as absolute terms. A wider range of media are employed than previously, with the normal staples of place promotion – brochures, posters and press advertising – now supplemented by television advertising and promotional videos. New tasks have also been set. For example, a recent trend seen on both sides of the Atlantic links place promotion to 're-imaging policy', which aims to counter a city's erstwhile poor image by building a new identity based on good quality services, leisure facilities and expressions of high culture (see also Chapter 9). Another trend links it to the regeneration of inner city districts, either by attempting to rebuild their economic base (see Burgess and Wood, 1988; Holcomb, 1994; Brownill, 1994) or by attracting tourists (Law, 1993; Barke and Harrop, 1994).

Tourism

Promotional activities to encourage tourism began in the nineteenth century. There were, of course, antecedents. Shrines and towns on pilgrimage routes are one such example from medieval Europe. The spa resorts of Britain began to boast the efficaciousness of their waters in the early eighteenth century through broadsheets and similar tracts. Around the same time, substantial numbers of upper-class travellers were making their way round the sights of Europe on the Grand Tour. By the end of the century plentiful numbers of guidebooks were available to assist their passage, providing them not only with things to see but also with instructions on how they should be seen (Towner, 1985; see also Chapter 3).

These developments, however, impinged only on a small segment of the community. It was not until the mid-nineteenth century that mass tourism developed in earnest, particularly through the activities of firms such as Thomas Cook (see Chapter 5). With this development of tourism came gradual adoption of promotional activity. British seaside resorts began to advertise their wares to take advantage of the day excursion and short-stay market. Gradually they competed with one another in a promotional rhetoric that invoked invigorating climates, flawless sandy beaches, sparkling waters, and superior accommodation (Ward, 1988; Yates, 1988). The resorts on Scotland's Ayrshire coast and the Clyde islands, for example, boasted of their fine sands, good hotels, proximity to noted golf courses, mild climates and sundry amusements. Expanding rapidly after the introduction of bank holidays in the 1870s, they vied with one another to encourage tourists to come 'doon the watter' for day trips and, later, for annual holidays. Dunoon on the Firth of Clyde championed its claims as 'the Watering Place for a Happy Holiday' and the 'best centre for the far-famed steamer excursions ...'. Its rival Rothesay, on the Isle of Bute, claimed with typical rhetorical flourish to be the 'Madeira of Scotland' with 'the most equable climate in Scotland'.

The railway companies, too, began publicity to increase traffic within their catchment areas. At first, as we shall see in Chapter 5, this was done on a haphazard basis but many of the more ambitious companies began to adopt systematic practices in the late nineteenth century. Wilson (1970), for instance, traced the way in which the Great Western Railway gradually became involved in publishing tourist line guides and holiday brochures from the 1870s onwards. He demonstrated how initial sporadic efforts were superseded by an integrated approach that extended from custom-written guides and booklets to pictorial posters, folders and promotional letterheads.

In the USA similar developments were taking place. Articles and books expressing awe at the natural beauties of areas such as Yosemite and Yellowstone were circulated widely in American newspapers and journals. With the completion of the first transcontinental railway in 1869 came the start of rapid growth in tourism, which was primarily promoted by the railways themselves. Zube and Galante (1994), for example, showed how mid-nineteenth century colonial-style place promotion for the Four

Corners States (Arizona, Colorado, New Mexico and Utah) progressively embraced tourism, with tourist handbooks being produced from the 1880s onwards. By the end of the nineteenth century, such activity was sufficiently commonplace to be regarded as a norm.

Space does not permit a comprehensive account of the development of the tourist industry during the twentieth century and the parallel challenge that was posed for place promotion. Four points about the changing nature of the tourist market, however, are important with a view to the content of later chapters of this book.

The first point concerns the size of the market. Those seeking to promote tourism are increasingly playing for high stakes, given the rapid rise in the numbers participating in tourism. The combination of paid holiday time, shorter working hours, higher disposable income and greater personal mobility for those in work established a mass market for tourism. Shaw and Williams (1994, 178–80) traced the growth of this market in a movement which began in the USA in the interwar years, continued in Europe in the 1950s, and ended with the globalization of the tourist industry. Simply in terms of international tourism, this represented an increase from 25 million tourists in 1950 to 405 million in 1989.[2]

Secondly, those promoting tourism are dealing with a market that is concentrated spatially and at particular times of year. In 1989, 64 per cent of all tourist trips worldwide were to destinations in Europe, with a small handful of historic cities and resorts absorbing a disproportionate share. Moreover, visitors arrived predominantly during a few peak months of the year, leading to overcrowding for those months and over-capacity for the rest of the year. The challenge, as shown in the next section, is to find strategies by which to spread the load spatially and temporally.

Thirdly, place promoters have had to come to terms with greater consumer choice in the market for tourism. Demand has diversified away from the once standard pattern of summer beach holidays and winter sports. Growing competition has created the need to repackage existing tourist opportunities as well as creating new ones. Even the most traditional seaside resorts or holiday camp chains employ advertising and marketing consultants to update their image and provide new unique selling propositions to try to retain their market share.

This is necessitated by the constant appearance of new attractions in the market. A good example is provided by leisure and theme parks. These were pioneered in the USA by Walt Disney Productions with the creation of Disneyland at Anaheim, California (1956) and Disney World, Florida (1965) and were subsequently copied by smaller variants in both the USA and Europe.[3] Together they have established a mass market for short-day and day-excursion tourism that scarcely existed twenty years ago. Similar arguments apply to the business conference market. Having grown in

direct response to changes in the business environment,[4] business conferences and associated tourism generate a voracious demand for new
venues. Cities in many developed and some developing countries have
invested heavily in creating new conference centres and associated infrastructure which are then promoted as part of a package that includes
existing features of the city's cultural life.

Finally, one aspect of increased consumer choice, the search for authenticity, deserves comment in its own right as part of the challenge for tourist
place promotion. Tourism is an activity that allows individuals to sample
other cultures and ways of life. Travel writing and televised holiday
programmes recognize that many tourists would regard seeing buildings,
social customs and artefacts in their authentic settings as a key element in
successful holidaymaking. Whether this in turn says anything significant
about tourists or their relationships with their own cultures is debatable.[5]
What is important is that there is tangible advantage to be gained by marketing places as, say, the scenes of famous battles, traditional agricultural
or fishing settlements, the castle in which a queen was imprisoned or
the point from which Bonnie Prince Charlie sailed to France (after
MacCannell, 1976, 14). Verification may well be of secondary concern.[6]

Together these developments have brought about qualitative change in
the nature and composition of the tourist market by the 1990s. Faced with
such change, towns and regions wanting to gain, expand, or just retain a
share in that market have increasingly turned to formal place promotion
to do so. This trend became more prevalent in the early 1970s when resorts
and other tourist destinations found themselves also faced with the same
economic problems of recession and structural change facing those
engaged in place promotion for urban and regional development. It is
scarcely surprising, therefore, that there has been increasing convergence
in the strategies and content of these two types of place promotion since
that time (see Chapter 9).

Promotion as communication

In the previous chapter we argued that there was a process of communication at the heart of promotional activity. As with any act of communication involving media to transmit messages to their audience, the process
contains four separate elements: the producers, or communicators, who
create the content (or message); the content itself; the media they employ
to communicate it; and the audience who are its consumers. In saying
this, there is no suggestion of any linear chain of cause-and-effect linking
production to consumption, since there are feedbacks at many levels. For
example, those who produce material for tourists are invariably them-

selves consumers of such materials at other times and feed that experience into their promotional work. Moreover, any act of communication takes place against many other acts which may reinforce, countermand or even neutralize the impact of the specific message (Gold, 1980). Any typology of elements, therefore, should be considered as no more than useful categories by which to divide up and study the process.

Table 2.1 summarizes the basic elements and actors involved. To avoid the added complication of differences in institutional structures, this table relates primarily to the Scottish context. Nevertheless, even here the lists are indicative rather than comprehensive. Given our focus on the production and nature of promotional messages, there is no further discussion in this section of audience characteristics[7] but some brief comment is worthwhile at this stage about the organizations responsible for promotional activity, the media they use and how the message is shaped.

Table 2.1 Elements and actors in the communication process

Producers	Content	Media	Audiences
Local authorities	Written/print	Brochures	Day trips
Regional authorities	Graphic	Posters	Short-stay weekend
State-appointed agencies, e.g. tourist boards, Forestry Commission	Moving image Spoken	Radio Television Film Video Gifts	Summer or winter vacation National International
Interest groups			Private travel
Charitable trusts			Business travel
Private businesses			
Advertising agents			
Marketing agents			
Travel writers			

Producers (Communicators)

The 'producers' in the present discussion are those individuals or organizations that have taken an active role in communicating material about Scotland to potential travellers and tourists since 1750. For almost all this period they comprise two distinct elements: an informal grouping comprising supportive travel writers and unpaid local propagandists; and a bewildering array of bodies with official responsibility for the task.

With regard to the latter, the traditional pattern was for tourist promotion to be handled by the town clerk's or publicity departments of municipal authorities. The former typically lacked any specialist knowledge of promotional work; the latter tended to be more proficient in public relations rather than any form of publicity work. The result was that tourist promotion was treated as a low-level task to be undertaken by anyone with sufficient time on their hands or else was contracted out to firms specializing in the production of town guides.[8] Little attention was paid to either a creative strategy (designing and shaping the message) or to media strategy (decision making as to media choice, the appropriate balance of different media and frequency of usage) so long as they did not exceed the available budget.

This pattern lasted until the early 1970s with little debate, even though it was clear that Scottish towns and resorts lagged far behind the levels of promotional effort and expenditure invested by competitors elsewhere, particularly in England and Wales. Matters started to change with recession and growing realization of the growth and economic importance of the tourist industry to the future of Scotland.

The response came from various quarters. Scotland's regional and district councils, especially in the major cities and the golfing and ski resorts, began to employ advertising and marketing agencies in the hope of improving the cutting edge of their efforts at tourist promotion. Whether or not these approaches were more 'effective' than the previous home-spun efforts is something about which even the advertising industry is unclear (e.g. see Schudson, 1984, 87). What is certain is that this step introduced qualitatively different approaches to targeting audiences, selecting media, shaping messages and planning and coordinating campaigns and, significantly, to identifying the 'product'.

There was also an institutional response. State-appointed authorities that previously espoused only incidental interest in tourism took a more active promotional role. The Forestry Commission provides a good example. The Commission had been involved with forest parks in Scotland from 1935, but these were places that permitted rather than actively encouraged visitors and had little physical provision of facilities apart from camp sites. The Commission also produced a guidebook series, but these were middle-class in outlook and effectively put forward the views of the park rangers and wardens (Revill and Watkin, 1994). After critical reviews in the late 1960s, important changes occurred. Physical provision of facilities for visitors increased dramatically accompanied by extensive new interpretive literature designed particularly for the passing motorist and general-interest tourist.

More significant was the establishment of bodies specifically created to handle the promotion of tourism. The 1969 Development of Tourism Act created the British Tourist Authority and tourist boards for England, Scotland and Wales. These were directly funded by Government and have specialist staff working in-house on promotional activities. They were to work alongside other authorities in order to attract tourists to their territories, to redistribute tourists within those territories, and take a hand in developing new niche markets (e.g. Reid, 1994, x).

In the case of Scotland, this has proved a daunting task. The Scottish Tourist Board (STB) works against the background of a 'kaleidoscopic web' (Patmore, 1983, 24) of different institutions and powers.[9] Central Government, in the shape of the Scottish Office, has attempted to promote greater harmony and achieve greater cost-effectiveness by reorganizing the relevant bodies,[10] but progress has been slow. As Derek Reid, the Chief Executive of the STB, almost despairingly noted in June 1994:

> For too long, one of Scotland's most substantial industries has suffered, to put it plainly, from a lack of focus. No one doubted its potential, but equally, we had failed to discover the means of bringing together a fragmented business to maximise that potential. ... Over the next few years, we must concentrate all our efforts on a highly co-ordinated approach to developing the industry, and to the messages we send to the outside world. Have no doubt about it, Scotland faces increasingly intense competition from several neighbouring countries, and these competitors are promoting themselves internationally with clearly defined and powerful images of what they have to offer the visitor.
>
> To match their efforts and achieve the same degree of impact, we need to develop our tourism profile so that it bears the universally recognisable stamp of Scotland. But we can only do this effectively if we are far more co-ordinated as an industry than we have ever been before. (Reid, 1994, ix)

In many respects, this is a strange argument. As the previous chapter showed, few countries bear a more 'universally recognizable stamp' than Scotland. Yet Reid was probably correct in arguing that promotional messages aimed at potential tourists emanate from bodies with different purposes and points of view. For the period that we are considering here, there is no doubt that promotion of Scottish tourism has been consistently characterized by many voices.

Media

Like everywhere else, tourist promotion in Scotland has rested on two staple media, the brochure and the poster. Surprisingly, given their significance in the development of travel and tourism, there is very little research available on their origins and development.

Brochure

Brochures have their antecedents in the handbooks and guides produced for travellers in the late eighteenth and early nineteenth centuries.
They were of two main types: some intended simply to promote places in
advance of travel; others were descriptive guides to be carried and used
to interpret the sights. In neither case was there any notion of a standard
format other than the need to be portable. Over time this changed
radically. By the 1960s the advent of packaged holidays and the expansion
of travel agency networks created a demand for a more standardized
product that consumers could take away and examine in their own homes
before reaching decisions. The result was the familiar A4-sized glossy
brochure, intended to fit on the regularly-spaced display shelves of travel
agents.

At first these brochures were simple listings of accommodation and
prices accompanied by snapshot photographs, but gradually they developed a new standard style. Its most distinctive element was the colour
photography that was integral to the selling message. Normally the work
of professionals, it rivalled food and architectural photography in its
ability to glamorize and mislead. Camera angle and technique create vivid
expectations of the elegance of tourist accommodation and the wonders
of the scenery. In the process, as seen in the previous chapter, brochure
editors employ a restricted range of depictions that, through repetition
and familiarity, have become emblematic of Scotland and Scottish holidaymaking. Such depictions may well be a powerful filter on subsequent
experience, as several writers have suggested (e.g. MacCannell, 1976;
Buck, 1977).

Posters

Posters also have a lengthy pedigree. A form of advertising that relies
on clear and striking visual content for its impact, the use of posters was
transformed in the nineteenth century by technological innovation. The
invention of the powered printing press was followed by colour lithography and typography and later by the development of offset rotary
presses (Constantine, 1986, 4). These technological developments ensured
that posters for display on public hoardings became a common sight. The
arrival on the scene of professional poster artists improved the standard
of depictions and layout, such that by the 1890s high-quality posters competed for attention at railway stations and other public places frequented
by the travelling public.

The poster was essentially an instrument of awareness, conveying a
basic theme and providing addresses where one could write for brochures
that would supply more information. Many other advertising media have
now been added as ways of achieving that awareness, including press
advertising, video recordings, and television commercials and gifts, such
as inscribed book-matches and pens. The pattern, however, remains the
same. Although those responsible for promoting tourism have progres-

sively had to address an increasingly complex and diverse market, it is still the ubiquitous brochure, supplemented by the poster, that presents the main selling message.

Shaping the message

The content of the various materials used to represent Scotland to tourists will emerge in the course of the ensuing chapters and do not require overview at this stage. It is worth noting here the role of the creative imagination in shaping the message of place promotion.

At the outset it must be recognized that this is an inherently conservative art. Imagination in the sense of the source and business of original thought (Warnock, 1976) has never been a strong feature in devising tourist promotional materials or indeed in place promotion generally. Practice has always been led by a handful of brilliant, and often rather simple, advertisements and slogans that have achieved lasting fame. These act as landmarks in the development of the art; once seen, they are quickly assimilated by others.

An instructive example is found in the case of New York's 1977 'I ♥ New York' campaign. New York City, like many other industrial metropolises, lost much of its manufacturing base during the postwar period and has suffered from a growing list of social, economic and political problems. The 'I ♥ New York' campaign used advertising and other promotional techniques to create a positive feeling about the city that was directed at residents and tourists alike. Its enormous success was alleged to have helped the city avoid bankruptcy. Perhaps understandably it spawned many imitations, indeed so many that Holcomb (1993, 136) felt able to commend Pittsburgh's slogan ('We're #1') primarily on the grounds that it was not another 'I ♥ X' slogan.[11]

Once seen, the process of imitation spreads the same message far and wide, progressively denting the likely impact of subsequent campaigns (Ward and Gold, 1994, 4–5). Yet in many ways, imitation is a perfectly logical strategy in a world characterized by the constant pressures of competition from rivals. It takes an accepted theme and recasts the image of a place into that mould. At a stroke it supplies a creative strategy that seems up to date and matches the promotional efforts of rivals. These ideas will then be worked and reworked into new variants, until something strikingly new arrives. At that point the whole cycle starts again.

Nevertheless the conservatism that constrains and channels the creative imagination is not only a consequence of the similarity of the product and the intrinsic limitations of the creative process. There are also factors in the wider cultural matrix which have a constraining impact on promotional imagery.

The cultural frame

The rise in interest in cultural studies, an area of critical theory and practices that has developed in the humanities and social sciences over the last two decades (Johnson, 1983; Turner, 1990; Grossberg et al., 1992), has supplied insight into a series of variables and processes that influence the way in which acts of communication take place.[12] At the same time, the freewheeling experimentation and plurality of cultural studies has meant that almost all the key notions are hotly contested. At the outset, therefore, it is important to define the key terms to be used, and none more so than 'culture' itself.

The problem with defining culture is that it carries a variety of meanings in academic discourse and popular parlance, having both artistic and social connotations (Burgess and Gold, 1985, 2–3). Although traditional criticism assumed that expositions of culture were only found in literature and the arts, the term 'culture' embodies a complex relationship between general human development and particular ways of life. Proper use of the term needs to take into account the fact that each culture also involves the material and symbolic forms that characterize those ways of life. Culture is the 'social heritage' of a group of people (Fletcher, 1988). It includes a group's material practices and customs, along with their expression in places and landscapes and production of symbolic systems of representation. A definition of culture therefore requires an understanding of these practices, customs and expressions.

From the perspective of this book it is important to emphasize two points. First, popular media, such as tourist brochures, guidebooks and posters, are as legitimate an expression of culture as literature, classical music and the theatre. Secondly, representations of Scotland are widely diffused and embedded in many different cultures. It is as justifiable to relate interpretation of such representations to the needs and beliefs of those cultures as it is to relate them to Scottish culture, even if the two diverge considerably. Indeed, culture clash is a common, often inevitable, part of the discourse of tourist promotion.

'Discourse' is another term that needs careful definition in view of the wide variety of meanings attached to the word (Purvis and Hunt, 1993). It is a notion that has recently helped to reshape conventional analysis of human communication. Most theorists follow Michel Foucault (e.g. 1970) in reserving the term 'discourse' for ideas that involve society in some way. Foucault himself was interested in how ideas at any point in time are related to a body of other ideas that have preceded them. Conventions and social practices have histories. To Foucault those flows of ideas over time that depict society and its order could be regarded as discourse (O'Barr, 1994, 3).[13]

Several advertising theorists have indicated how this notion could be extended to promotional activity. Cook (1992), for example, regards discourse as involving two elements: the *text*, the material that is communicated, and the *context* which surrounds the act of communication. Discourse is text and context together, interacting in a way perceived as meaningful and unified by those who participate in the process of communication. O'Barr (1994, 3) adds a further dimension, implicitly recasting a familiar distinction made in media research between manifest content (objective, directly measurable messages) and latent content (messages that are interpreted). His distinction is between primary and secondary discourse. 'Primary discourse' relates to the messages that advertising openly purports to convey; 'secondary discourse' refers to ideas about society and culture that are contained in advertisements.

The notion of 'discourse' used here shares certain features with the work of these theorists but differs in its relationship to the social realm. Discourse is regarded in this book as the act of communication, including the text that is communicated and the context in which that text is communicated. Its particular persuasive force and the relationship of the discourse to society are provided by two other notions which interact with discourse – 'ideology' and 'rhetoric'. However, to understand fully the meaning and operation of these various terms and their relationship to one another, it is helpful to work by stages through an illustration (Figure 2.1) and to define key terms in the process.

Figure 2.1 shows a drawing taken from a booklet produced by the Forestry Commission to explain its forest parks to the general public. It shows an artist's representation of a scene in Glen More Forest Park in Scotland's Cairngorms (Edlin, 1969, 37). Drawn by a regional artist, Conrad McKenna, it depicts a forest and moorland scene rendered as a wood-cut illustration. At a superficial level it portrays a scene of the wildlife and vegetation awaiting the visitor. The foreground is occupied by a capercailzie, two roe deer and a patch of indeterminate woodland flowers. A Scots pine dominates the middle distance. A male and a female hiker, dressed in tartan clothing, occupy left-centre. Their posture suggests they are enjoying the view of the loch, its wooded shores and the distant hills that complete the composition.

Yet beneath the surface of this inviting picture are a wealth of other hidden meanings that comprise the 'secondary discourse'. Drawn in the early 1960s, the illustration can be read as an indication of contemporary assumptions about, inter alia, power, politics, aesthetics and gender. There are power and political implications of the capercailzie and the red deer. Both are actively hunted and, for some, would symbolize the perpetuation of a social order in Highland Scotland. The inclusion of regularly spaced stands of conifers besides the native Scots pine depicts the

2.1 Cairngorm scene: crag, loch, pinewood, capercailzie and roe deer.

Forestry Commission's planting policy at that time, a policy that, as we will see below, was far from uncontentious. The portrayal of the hikers in their tartan clothing can be interpreted from the standpoint of gender relationships, especially in terms of posture, and also in class terms, with regard to who is depicted. To go further with this analysis, however, requires consideration of ideology and rhetoric.

Ideology

Ideology is a contentious term embracing a 'family of concepts' including ideas, beliefs, political philosophies, *Weltanschauungen* and moral justifications (Plamenatz, 1970, 27; Eagleton, 1991). In Marxist discourse the word ideology had pejorative overtones, referring to a 'limited material practice which generates ideas that misrepresent social contradictions in the interest of the ruling class' (Larrain, 1983, 27–8). From this viewpoint ideologies are justifications which mask specific sets of interests (Bell, 1977, 298). By contrast, other schools of thought have revived the term in a non-pejorative manner. Cultural anthropologists (e.g. Geertz, 1973) identify ideology in terms of the structure of values and interests that inform any representation of reality, a meaning that leaves untouched the question of whether or not the representation is false or oppressive (Mitchell, 1986, 4).

The definition adopted here is in line with the second type. An ideology is taken to be a pervasive set of ideas, beliefs and images that a group employs to make the world more intelligible to itself. Ideology is thus viewed as an essential part of the process by which people come to terms with the world around them. It is sometimes conceived as being part of a conscious process of manipulation, but others (e.g. Hall, 1977) point out that ideology operates by being embedded in commonsense wisdom. As such it is a frame which helps to make sense of and rationalize experience. Whether or not it distorts depends both on the ideology and the values applied to judge it.

Viewed in these terms the expression and meaning of promotional imagery and messages are therefore seen as being constructed and mediated within the framework of ideology. The impact of ideology is invariably conservative. Representations constructed in line with ideology tend towards conformity, even among those who, like place promoters, are each seeking to obtain a competitive advantage relative to rival schemes. Ideology also serves to legitimize the status quo and often, but not invariably, the interests of the dominant group in society.

In applying this analysis to Figure 2.1 it is worth recalling MacCannell's remark that tourism is not just an aggregate of merely commercial activities: 'it is also an ideological framing of history, nature, and tradition;

a framing that has the power to reshape culture and nature to its own needs' (MacCannell, 1992, 1). The drawing embodies the ideology of the dominant group in society. The tourist is invited to visit the Glen More Forest Park, but is invited to do so by a guidebook which tells the history of the area in a particular way. It also suggests how the park should be used, fitting within the rights of access given and valuing the landscape that has been created. The drawing notably presents symbols of hunting as a perfectly normal part of the scene. It does not draw attention to the fact that the presence of the stag and capercailzie are a product of an unequal system of land ownership that was responsible in many areas for driving the indigenous occupants off the land.[14] It does not draw attention to the severe limitations of public access to the hills and mountains of Scotland compared with the rights given to private landowners to enjoy hunting and shooting undisturbed. In the process, therefore, it provides a portrait of the Scottish Highlands that is ahistorical, apolitical and implicitly supports the status quo. The alternative construction, which views these landscapes as the end product of dispossession and exploitation, does not figure in this example of tourist promotion.[15]

Rhetoric

A further dimension is added to the analysis by the concept of rhetoric, another notion that traditionally has had a bad press. Defined as 'the use of discourse, either spoken or written, to inform or persuade or move an audience' (Corbett, 1971, 3), rhetoric is essentially a symbolic language by which the speaker, author or copy-writer addresses a target audience about an object, product or service and tries to convince them of its worth. As such it was long considered as a distortion by philosophers (Baynes et al., 1987, 423). It is only recently that critical theorists have argued that rhetoric is a perfectly normal and rational way of coming to terms with complex reality (Blumenberg, 1987; Simons, 1988; Enos and Brown, 1993). Indeed, even though it was traditional to contrast the value-neutral objectivity of science with rhetoric and ideology, in practice even scientific writing incorporates these dimensions (Kipps, 1994, 53).

This approach is helpful since it allows rhetoric to be treated in a non-pejorative manner as a normal part of everyday discourse rather than as a distortion. Rhetoric is part and parcel of ideologically-constructed discourse. It involves presentation of an argument to persuade the audience that a particular scheme or project is worth considering further, even at the expense of changing their previous position on the matter. That argument is designed to further the interests of the producer, but to be effective it requires that the audience are convinced that the communicator is worthy of belief and that the communicator has an accurate sense of the audience and their needs.

As noted elsewhere (Gold and Gold, 1994), one of the most interesting application of notions of rhetoric to promotional messages was supplied by Jarvis (1987). Drawing on advertising research by Raymond Williams (1980) and Dyer (1982), he analysed the environments used in a wide range of product advertising. Concentrating on advertisements for cars, alcoholic drinks and electrical goods, Jarvis noted that designers of posters, television commercials and journal advertisements used a restricted array of settings in creating copy. These included such staples as palm-fringed desert island beaches, thatched cottages, the warm and inviting interiors of the modern offices or apartments. To Jarvis, these stylized settings are an expression of an 'environmental rhetoric'. The frequency with which they appear strongly suggests that the language is shared by both the communicators and audience, even if in many cases 'there is no descriptive or functional need' (Jarvis, 1987, 14) to employ such environmental settings as part of an advertisement.

Jarvis illustrated the nature of this rhetoric with regard to the city, but the theme and the analysis can be extended well beyond urban settings and the context of product advertising. We have already implicitly demonstrated the power of rhetoric in the previous chapter with its discussion of brochure photography, but further points can be made by again considering Figure 2.1. The artist has constructed a rhetoric that does not just invite the visitor to participate in the experience of the forest park, but also to experience that environment in a particular way. The two figures in the middle distance are part of the view but are in no way intrusive. The illustration invites visitors to place themselves in the position of these hikers and to enjoy the countryside in a similar manner. Much of the countryside that they are invited to enjoy displays the standard features of majestic mountain and wooded glen, an environment that remains heavily overladen by nineteenth century romanticism and by more recent preferences for moorland, wilderness and solitude.

Nevertheless the rhetoric breaks with the dominant ideology in one important respect. Reflecting the interests of his sponsors, the artist has added the stands of coniferous trees mentioned above. This represents a statement of aesthetics. The trees are shown as an apparently natural part of this environment; a view intended to challenge popular distaste at the Forestry Commission's policy of planting regimented lines of non-native trees to cover the untamed open spaces of the Highlands. By merging these trees into the background alongside other symbols of nature, the artist effectively invites the visitor to reconsider them as a legitimate part of the Scottish countryside.

Conclusion

This chapter has examined historical and theoretical perspectives that supply background to the current inquiry. The initial survey indicated the long-standing roots of place promotion in the fields of colonial expansion, civic boosterism, urban and regional development, and tourism. After identifying significant trends, we highlighted the process of communication that lies at the heart of tourist promotion. The discussion focused around the nature of three elements in the communication process, namely producers (or communicators), media and content. We briefly considered the various private and public agencies, at all scales, involved in tourist promotion, the media they use and the message that is shaped. This section concluded by noting the constrained nature of the creative imagination involved in place promotion. In order to understand this process better, the final part of the chapter considered the cultural frame of such activity. After considering the nature of culture itself, three notions were introduced that are valuable in conceptualizing such activity – discourse, ideology and rhetoric. In this study discourse is regarded as the act of communication, including the text that is communicated and the context in which it is communicated. Ideology is the framework within which that act takes place; a framework that rationalizes the particular to the general and generally serves as a conservative force. Rhetoric is the force that gives communication its persuasive edge.

Notes

1. The relationship between colonial promotion and the ideological construction of history to exclude the claims of native peoples has still to be fully explored. Useful insights and a valuable bibliography, however, are provided by Hulme (1986).
2. Figures for Scotland were supplied in the previous chapter. Further discussion of the global development of tourism in either qualitative or quantitative sense lies necessarily beyond the scope of this book. For more information, see Burkart and Medlik (1981), Pearce (1987), Urry (1990), WTO (1991), Shaw and Williams (1994).
3. For more on the general principles involved, see Lyon (1987), Winsberg (1992) and Boniface (1994).
4. For instance, the rise of the service and information sectors, new working patterns, new forms of managerial structure and the rise of consultancy.
5. A style of thought that has its antecedents in the reaction of those who believed that modern life was inherently anguished and alienating (see Berman, 1983). MacCannell (1976, 1992), for example, sees tourism as a vehicle by which people try to repair the damage that modernity has wrought upon their lives by going in search of those 'unspoiled' cultures that are authentically rooted in the places where they are found.

6. Full discussion of the ways in which other cultures are represented, an important undercurrent here, lies beyond the scope of this text. For more on this matter, see the brilliant analysis of Orientalism by Said (1978), as well as Jackson (1989) and O'Barr (1994).
7. See the discussion of this point in Chapter 1.
8. A good example being Berrow and Sons, a Worcester-based firm which has long designed guides for many British towns on the basis of a standard size and format.
9. For example, the Highlands and Islands Development Board was established in 1965 to promote economic and social development north and west of the Great Glen. This remit included tourism. Now, as Highlands and Islands Enterprise, it continues to discharge this duty.
10. The most recent attempt occurred in July 1994, with a proposal by the Scottish Office to merge local Scottish Tourist Boards into 14 new tourism marketing authorities.
11. Although when first encountered, Scotland's own versions – 'I ♥ Skye', 'I ♥ Harris' and the rest – do have the advantage of an amusing double entendre.
12. For an alternative view of the process of communication in tourist promotion, see Squire (1994a, 6–8), who in turn draws on Jakobson (1960), Johnson (1986) and Burgess (1990).
13. It is impossible to do justice to the debate over Foucault's ideas on discourse within the scope of this text. For more information see Reiss (1982), Shields (1991) and Barnes and Duncan (1992).
14. See the discussion in Chapters 5 and 7. Although few people were driven off the land to make way for deer forests, capercailzie or grouse, these activities took over on estates where proprietors had over-optimistically cleared their tenants to make way for sheep.
15. That alternative construction does occur in the discourse of radical interpreters of the highland question. Chapter 7 contains much fuller discussion of this point.

CHAPTER THREE

Travellers' tales

'Travel is one of the most complex forms of self-indulgence, and ideally is undertaken for its own sake. At its goal it dies.'

Colin Thubron, *Journey into Cyprus*

Although not always recognized at the time, Scotland in mid-eighteenth century was poised on the edge of a period of social and economic transformation. At first glance, the copper-plate prospect of the Edinburgh of around 1770 (Figure 3.1) looks very similar to views drawn at the end of the seventeenth century (e.g. Cavers, 1993, 18–19). The tranquillity of the scene is apparently underpinned by the depictions of the gentry conversing or taking leisurely walks in the surrounding countryside. Nevertheless change is on the way. Edinburgh had started to overcome the constrictions of its crag-and-tail site. Implementation had begun of principles for reform contained in the pamphlet 'Proposals for Carrying on Certain Public Works in the City of Edinburgh' (1752). The Nor' Loch, which was formerly situated at the foot of the Castle Hill, has already been drained as a prelude to the construction of the New Town. In addition a small, barely visible figure on the road in the middle distance tramps towards the city with a bundle of possessions tied to a stick over his shoulder. He is an important symbol. Migration into the Central Lowlands grew steadily, especially from 1780 onwards, pointing to wider structural social and economic adjustments taking place within the nation.

This chapter juxtaposes its account of the representations of Scotland in travellers' tales against this background. It reviews published tales of journeys to and through Scotland in the late eighteenth and early nineteenth centuries, noting the reasons why Scotland first engaged the interest of travellers in the second half of the eighteenth century. Particular emphasis is given to the search for evidence of the authenticity or otherwise of the works of the ancient poet Ossian. Before tackling these subjects, however, it is important to gain an impression of the state of the nation at the start of our study period.

After Culloden

It is difficult to overemphasize the significance of the events of 1745–6 in the study of modern Scottish history. In July 1745 the arrival of the Young

3.1 Prospect of the west view of the City of Edinburgh (T. Culeth, *c.* 1770).

Pretender heralded the last attempt to re-establish the Stuart monarchy in Great Britain. Charles Edward Stuart's army, consisting primarily of Highlanders, marched south and reached Derby in the English East Midlands by December. The subsequent retreat and defeat at Culloden brought material change to the social, economic and political order in Scotland, as well as changes in its relationship to the wider British State. It would in time also have a profound impact on Scottish culture. The escape of Bonnie Prince Charlie and the aura of heroic failure engendered by the '45 all became an important part of the myth handed on and exploited by nobility and tourist boards alike. Its full cultural impact, however, awaited the attentions of Sir Walter Scott and other nineteenth-century iconographers (see Chapter 4); its socio-economic and political impact was immediate, especially for the Highlands and Islands.

This needs to be placed in context. In 1750 Scotland as a whole was predominantly rural. Dr Alexander Webster, a leading member of the Church of Scotland, estimated the Scottish population in 1755 at 1,265,000, of which 652,000 (51 per cent) lived north of the Central Lowlands. Levels of urbanization were low. Only four towns contained more than 10,000 people: Edinburgh with 57,000; Glasgow 31,900; Aberdeen 15,600; Dundee 12,400. Inverness, the only town of any size in the Highlands, had a population of just 9700 (Smout, 1969, 243).

During the next 50 years major changes occurred. The first stirrings of the urban and industrial economy were seen alongside transformation in the nature, organization and output of agriculture. As elsewhere in Great Britain these changes were accompanied by demographic increase. The 1801 census recorded a population of 1,608,000, a 27 per cent increase on Webster's estimate. The highest growth occurred in the towns and cities of the Central Lowlands. A portion of this was due to Irish immigration, but was augmented by a steadily increasing outflow from north and western Scotland, due primarily to the Highland Clearances. Edinburgh reached 81,600 people in 1801 but it had already been overtaken by Glasgow (83,700), steadily developing as the cradle of Scottish industry. Larger proportional increases were recorded in the industrial towns of the Clyde Valley. Paisley and Greenock each grew by more than 450 per cent, with their populations rising to 31,200 and 17,400 respectively. The northern population declined relative to that of the central belt. By 1821, for example, the population living north of the Central Lowlands stood at 873,000 or 41 per cent of total (Smout, 1969, 242). Besides internal migration to the Central Lowlands, there was also emigration, especially to North America. Even the population of Inverness had fallen to 8700, 10 per cent less than Webster's estimate.

This change in relative fortunes merits further comment. There had long been marked contrasts between highland and lowland Scotland. The phrase 'beyond the Highland line' was commonly used to describe the abrupt change to be found in terms of social organization, culture, economy and modernity (Youngson, 1974). Highland society contrasted sharply with its lowland counterpart. Predominantly Gaelic-speaking, it was organized along clan lines and dominated by a feudal system of land ownership.

The hold of tradition in the Highlands was irrevocably loosened by the vicious aftermath of the Jacobite defeat at Culloden. Having experienced two pro-Stuart uprisings in thirty years, the Hanoverian administration moved quickly to remove the capacity of the Highlanders to foment and join revolt (Gold and Gold, 1985). Initial disarmament measures were quickly followed by a conscious longer-term policy that sought to remove the area's quasi-independence and, in particular, to integrate it into the national economy. Measures adopted for this purpose included confiscations and attempts to destroy the cultural identity of rebel clans. Perhaps the most effective were those measures that attacked the system of land ownership and tenure. Private ownership was now instituted in place of the previous feudal pattern. Instead of joint ownership of the land, highland estates were now subject to their new owners' extensive powers of management and disposal over their lands. The atrophy of kinship links between the owners of estates and their tenantries meant that the former were prone to view their tenants primarily in economic terms as either a resource or a hindrance to development. This type of thinking contributed to widespread estate reorganization. The old structure was swept away and replaced by commercial livestock farms (and later sporting estates). Around 500,000 tenants in all were displaced. Some were forced to accept single passage on emigrant ships, some drifted south to the Central Lowlands, others were allocated diminutive smallholdings ('crofts') on the littoral margins with access to common grazing land.[1]

Another direct response to the defeat at Culloden lay in road construction. The Hanoverians' need for a military infrastructure to subjugate the Highlands required the building and renovation of forts and the stationing of larger numbers of troops in the region. Given the poor quality of roads in rural Scotland, it became essential to create a good network for logistic and strategic reasons. This process had begun after the 1715 uprising, with 250 miles of road and 40 new bridges constructed in the central Highlands between 1725 and 1736 on routes surveyed by General Wade. After Culloden Wade's chief surveyor, Major William Caulfield, supervised the building of 750 further miles including a road across the treacherous peat-bogs of Rannoch Moor and from Perth to Fort George (near Inverness) and to Aberdeen (Whyte and Whyte, 1990, 126).

Mapping was another activity stimulated by military needs, with the most notable contribution supplied by the military survey produced under the direction of General William Roy. Between 1747 and 1755 Roy created a detailed military map at a scale of approximately two miles to the inch. This not only supplied a basis for further road construction, it also provided a reliable inventory of the countryside that was unequalled in scope in Great Britain until the publication of the first edition of the Ordnance Survey maps in England in the early nineteenth century.

These developments had important consequences. The coastal areas and islands of the west had long been accessible by sea, as shown by the extensive travels of Martin Martin in 1695. By contrast the interior of Scotland was remote and difficult country. The lack of roads and bridges, the mountainous terrain, the dearth of accommodation, and the absence of maps and information for the traveller made exploration of the land difficult. Construction of roads and availability of maps and information gave travellers some basis on which to make their journeys. The stationing and constant relocations of large numbers of troops gave precedent for large numbers of visitors to move round even remote regions. Sequestration of land and use of income generated for building inns provided some accommodation for visitors from the leisured classes.

Yet while qualitative changes had been initiated, much remained to be done. Accessibility improved with the advent of new roads, bridges and the growth of stage-coach services, but the coverage was patchy. By 1800 it still took four days to travel from Edinburgh to Inverness. There were no public coaches or post horses. A lack of ferries to cross sea lochs and firths necessitated long detours. Roads in areas like Caithness and Sutherland scarcely existed. The Reverend Charles Cordiner on his journey in 1776 describes travelling into a wilderness with increasingly rugged paths: 'for several miles the best road which the guides could take, was in the channel of a rivulet, and its bed was far from being smooth: nothing to be seen around but a wilderness of rocks' (Cordiner, 1780, 95). Certainly, the north coast remained inaccessible until well into the nineteenth century. The seventh edition of *Duncan's Itinerary* (Duncan, 1805 et seq.: quote from 1830) informed travellers heading westwards along the northern coast that: 'There is no made road farther than two miles beyond Reay Kirk ... The traveller will also do well to fill his flask, and supply his scrip at Reay Kirk Inn, as he may rest assured he will require their aid before he reaches Tongue. This has become more necessary since the country has been depopulated.' Similarly Botfield (1829, 132) wanted to travel westwards to Cape Wrath, but upon enquiry found that 'roads though traced out and progressively advancing towards completion, were still unfinished, and consequently quite impassable for carriages of any description'.

Information for the traveller in the form of guidebooks and maps remained deficient. This was particularly true the further north one travelled. In another observation on the difficulties of travelling in the far north, Cordiner (1780, 115–16) noted: 'I am convinced the interior parts of this country are very inadequately laid down in the maps of Scotland, and the names of places are often either altogether wanting, or at an amazing distance from where they ought to be'.

Horses posed their own set of problems. Cordiner (1780) had to change horses in the far north because his own large animal could not cope with the rough terrain. He also found it hard to obtain supplies of horse feed. Another horse traveller, Mary-Anne Hanway, encountered considerable problems with horses being unwilling to climb hills. At Loch Geary, for example, she had to sit decorously for half an hour while a boy, an old man and three old women dragged the carriage up the hill: 'all the human creatures this dismal place afforded' (Hanway, 1775, 105).

Accommodation also remained problematic. Many areas offered little hospitality beyond that which was available from the local people. While there was a cultural tradition of affording hospitality to strangers, this was steadily eroded both by depopulation in certain areas and by social change. As one writer (Botfield, 1829, 128) commented, the obligation of hospitality 'has decayed under the influx of strangers and the influence of modern manners'. Even where inns were available, their quality was sometimes deplorable. The notorious King's House in Glen Coe was a case in point. In 1785 Newte wrote that there was 'not a bed in it fit for a decent person to sleep in' nor any provisions. It was, he argued, 'a cursed place' (Newte, 1791, 119). Visiting it in 1792, Lettice (1794) castigated its 'coarsest most ill-dressed fare' and his dirty room, but above all feared catching a dread disease from the landlord's sick son. Dorothy and William Wordsworth, who stayed there in 1803, observed the diversity of their fellow guests, who included drovers, carriers, horsemen and other travellers. They also commented on their 'poor and miserable' long rooms with beds so damp that they could not retire to bed until the sheets could be dried.

The winding road

In spite of these potential discomforts, visitors were more than willing to come to Scotland. Part of the reason lay in the impossibility of visiting 'Grand Tour' destinations on the war-torn European continent. Pre-occupation with the 'Grand Tour' as a framework for travel had led to neglect of Britain (Ousby, 1990). The search for domestic locations for travel reinforced a new interest in exploring Britain as a suitable pastime for the upper classes. Scotland joined the Lake District and rural Wales as suitable locations for self-enriching travel. The new travellers could be said to be influenced by a mixture of three sets of motives: curiosity, scientific and otherwise; national pride; and aesthetic experience.

Curiosity took many forms. Mary-Anne Hanway (1775) wrote that her main aim was to travel critically rather than casually, 'to accommodate my friends with information than merely to gratify the greediness of vacant curiosity'. For some, the goal was to see and experience primitive societies whose language and culture were already felt to be disappearing fast. In some cases this was overlain by interest in the supernatural, especially in the gifts of second sight and prophesy which was thought to be a trait of those living in the Highlands and Islands (Keay and Keay, 1994, 861). Others, as we shall see later, set themselves the specific goal of learning more about the fabled poet Ossian and finding out whether or not the poems attributed to him were genuine.

Dr Johnson in his *Journey to the Western Islands of Scotland* (1775; see Chapman, 1924) shared that objective and an interest in second sight, but added scientific curiosity. He argued that reading accounts is insufficient and that 'ideas are always incomplete, and that at least, till we have compared them with realities, we do not know them to be just. As we see more we become possessed of more certainties, and consequently gain more principles of reasoning, and found a wider basis of analogy.' Not to have seen wild mountainous, thinly inhabited regions meant that one's intellect remained unacquainted 'with much of the face of nature, and with one of the great scenes of human existence'. Putting it another way, his companion James Boswell declared that it was to see 'a system of life almost totally different from what we had been accustomed to see; and, to find simplicity and wildness, and all the circumstances of remote time or place, so near to our great island, was an object within reach of reasonable curiosity'.[2]

Pride in the emerging British identity also played its part. In the preface to his six-volume collection of travel writings Mavor (1798, 1) provided a typical version of this genre:

> Yet in whatever light we regard the British islands; whether as the cradle of liberty, the mother of arts and sciences, the nurse of manufactures, the mistress of the sea; or whether we contemplate their genial soil, their mild climate, their various natural and artificial curiosities, we shall find no equal extent of territory on the face of the globe, of more importance, or containing more attractions, even in the estimation of those who cannot be biased by native partiality.

Patriotic Britons would find much pleasure and utility in their domestic travels, enlarging their own ideas and thereby benefiting and informing their compatriots. For instance, reporting on a tour undertaken in 1792, Lettice states that he wished to contribute to the 'moral union' between the English and Scots and to make it as complete as the 'civil union'. He felt that the presence of travellers and gentlemen in the autumn for the

shooting and the chase were all part of the civilizing process of the Highlands (Lettice, 1794). Travelling in the same year, Robert Heron, the
biographer of Robert Burns, claimed to be an honest Briton jealous of the
honour and prosperity of his country, keen to discern the bases of its
affluence and to suggest improvement (Heron, 1793).

These motives were undoubtedly complemented by changing landscape
tastes. In the early eighteenth century élite taste favoured the ideal classical
landscapes of Claude and Poussin, with the value of native British beauty
judged by how it compared with Italy or Italian paintings. By mid-century
the rise of the more vernacular Picturesque movement made the rugged
terrain of regions like Highland Scotland attractive to travellers (Gruffudd,
1994, 247–8). Picturesque travel was an activity undertaken in a specific
and structured manner, with its own vocabulary of terms and chosen ways
of imagining the countryside. Landscapes were seen through the filter of
aesthetic theory and its peoples were viewed as noble, sturdy peasants. In
doing so, picturesque tourists generally avoided the products of the
industrial age, but without entirely embracing nostalgia. Exceptions could
always be made if stimulating contrasts were offered. One writer, confronted by a Scottish aqueduct, remarked that 'where objects of art enter
into a direct rivalship, as it were, with the objects of Nature, and are of
sufficient magnitude, and importance, to maintain the composition, the
suspense in which the mind is held, is of the most pleasing kind' (from
Andrews, 1989; quoted by Gruffudd, 1994, 248).

Drawn by these three main objectives, the numbers of visitors to
Scotland slowly increased. While the numbers were minuscule by modern
standards, their activities are likened by Butler (1985) to the actions of
explorers, gradually mapping out routes and establishing foci of interest.
Most confined their journeys to the Borders or to the attractions of the
Central Lowlands, with the remoter parts of the Highlands left to the more
hardy and determined. Yet as the century progressed people gradually
ventured further afield. In letters to his daughter, for example, the Earl of
Breadelbane provided interesting comments on the growth and nature of
tourism (quoted in Holloway and Errington, 1978). In 1759 he wrote that
it was the fashion to travel into the Highlands due to difficulties of
travelling abroad. By 1773 he wrote that the Tour through the Highlands
was 'le bon ton' and complained that his house was always '16 at table
several days together', overflowing with people who he had never met
previously but to whom he had extended hospitality because they had
arrived with a personal recommendation. By the end of the century,
Robert Heron (1793) observed the arrival of various carriages containing
a party from England about to leave for the Highlands: 'This has, indeed
become, from various circumstances, a very fashionable summer tour
within these last ten or twelve years'.

Perhaps the key to the behaviour of travellers was the activities of their predecessors. When returning home, the latter often assembled their journals and jottings into formal memoirs of their travels, sometimes circulated to friends and acquaintances and sometimes formally published. By doing so they acted as models for others who subsequently toured Scotland clutching copies of these travellers' tales which, in turn, they would replicate and embellish.

The first guides

This point about guidance to the traveller requires discussion in its own right. The early traveller to Scotland, as elsewhere, relied on human guides, since the modern 'guidebook' or its equivalent did not exist.[3] Human guides were necessary in Scotland for other reasons too, including the lack of proper roads in some areas, the erratic nature of accommodation and refreshment and the difficulty of relying on locally provided information when few people spoke English. This gave many travellers the feeling that they were indeed in foreign parts. Cordiner, for example, employed two Gaelic-speaking guides to take him across the north coast. Johnson (Chapman, 1924, 25) employed two Highlanders at Inverness 'partly to shew us the way'. At Auknasheals (Glensheals): 'We were at a place where we could obtain milk ... The people of this valley did not appear to know any English, and our guides now became doubly necessary as interpreters' (ibid., 37). In more difficult terrain on Skye, Boswell noted: 'A guide, who had been sent with us from Kingsburgh, explored the way (much in the same manner as, I suppose, is pursued in the wilds of America) by observing certain marks known only to the inhabitants' (Chapman, 1924, 297).

This practice continued into the nineteenth century even after the proliferation of written guides. *Duncan's Itinerary* advised travellers that they 'should endeavour to procure a guide, as they may otherwise deviate from the path, which is what Highlanders call a Bridle road, and there are few houses to be met with' (Duncan, 1805 et seq.: seventh edition, 1830, 84). Further south in the Trossachs, the *Itinerary* also recommended hiring James Stewart of Ardhenacrochkan Farm ('a very intelligent person'), who had servants and owned boats for trips on Loch Katrine.

The prime source of written guide material in the early days, as noted above, were travellers' tales. Johnson and Boswell carried a copy of Martin Martin's *Description of the Western Islands* (1695) with them on their tour and had read both ancient and recently published travel writings, for example, by Thomas Pennant and William Sacheverall (Chapman, 1924, 273; Curley, 1976). In turn many others would later carry a copy of Johnson's tome on their own travels.

Travelling with Johnson and Boswell

Of all the travellers' tales produced in the late eighteenth century, Johnson's *Journey to the Western Islands of Scotland* (1775) had the greatest impact on subsequent travellers.[4] That it should have received this status is in some respects surprising. According to Boswell (Chapman, 1924, 172), Johnson was strongly prejudiced against Scotland and substantial parts of his account consist of scornful statements about the land and its people. His strong interest in the disappearing culture of the Western Isles and the epic nature of the journey undertaken, however, captivated his contemporaries and invited emulation of parts, if not all, of Johnson's travels. Moreover those wishing to travel with Johnson could take advantage of a dual perspective. Shortly after Johnson's death Boswell published *The Journal of a Tour to the Hebrides with Samuel Johnson, LLD* (Boswell, 1785; Chapman, 1924). By perusing Johnson's *Journey*, travellers could learn how one of the major literary figures of his day reacted as he roamed around rural Scotland. By reading Boswell's *Journal* they could also visualize Johnson in the landscape, talking to local dignitaries and producing the usual stream of aphorisms. From Boswell the visitor also gained more sustained descriptions of the landscapes and places through which Boswell and Johnson were passing.

Consisting of a travelogue with lengthy commentaries, the *Journey* covers an expedition that extended over almost three months (18 August–9 November 1773).[5] Although its title stressed the trip's main destination, Johnson and Boswell also took in the east coast from Edinburgh to Inverness, the Highlands and the west coast as well as the Hebrides (see Figure 3.2). The key to Johnson's representation of place and landscape lay in his attention to wider social themes. As Selwyn (1979, 357) pointed out, the *Journey* chronologically falls between two of the major works of the Scottish Enlightenment – Adam Ferguson's *An Essay on the History of Civil Society* (1767) and Adam Smith's *The Wealth of Nations* (1776) – and shared with them the Enlightenment interest in the transition from pre-commercial societies (e.g. Hampson, 1968, 155–7). Johnson's motive for travel to the Hebrides stemmed primarily from fascination with a society which was being subjected to pressures for change likely to lead to its demise. Despite his broad faith in the value of civilization Johnson conveyed a sentimental attachment to the old feudal order which bordered on idealism (Selwyn, 1979, 347): 'Civility is part of the national character of Highlanders. Every chieftain is a monarch and politeness, the natural product of royal government, is diffused from the laird through the whole clan.'

By contrast, wild scenery or Picturesque surroundings were of little interest. The landscapes of the central Highlands were dismissed as having

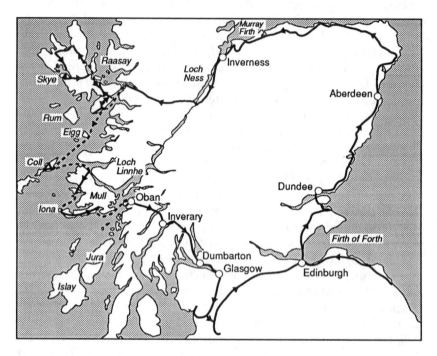

3.2 Johnson and Boswell's tour of the Hebrides.

little to detain the traveller: 'An eye accustomed to flowery pastures and waving harvests is astonished and repelled by this wide extent of hopeless sterility' (ibid., 34). The wonder of walking through a natural arch in the rock was lightly cast aside: '(it) might have pleased us by its novelty, had the stones, which encumbered our feet, given us leisure to consider it' (ibid., 67). The sight of a once-occupied landscape on the Isle of Mull gave rise to outright melancholy (ibid., 126):

> We travelled many hours through a tract, black and barren, in which, however, there were the reliques of humanity; for we found a ruined chapel in our way.
> It is natural, in traversing this gloom of desolation, to inquire, whether something may not be done to give nature a more cheerful face, and whether those hills and moors that can afford heath cannot with a little care and labour bear something better?

At times the narrative even seems to question the point of travel itself in such environments: 'It will very readily occur, that this uniformity of barrenness can afford very little amusement to the traveller; that it is easy to sit at home and conceive rocks and heath, and waterfalls; and that these journeys are useless labours, which neither impregnate the imagination, nor enlarge the understanding' (ibid., 35). Yet there is no mistaking the sense of exploration that permeated the book. There is a strong feeling that there is a world of which people living further south have little conception or understanding, but which can be learned by travel: 'To the southern inhabitants of Scotland, the state of the mountains and the islands is equally unknown with that of *Borneo* and *Sumatra*: Of both they have only heard a little, and guess the rest'.

It was this crucial sense of exploration and discovery that, in turn, appealed to later travellers. As Robert Heron (1793, 40) remarked, Dr Johnson made the English curious with his account of 'a scene in which he might contemplate nature in her grandest, wildest aspects, and human society in its rudest, simplest form'.

Gilpin and Picturesque tourism

Other travellers' tales paid much greater attention to the landscape as the object of the journey. The Reverend William Gilpin, one of the key arbiters of English landscape tastes, undertook a number of journeys commenting on and sketching British scenery, and offering the rhetoric of the Picturesque as a filter for experiencing landscape. In 1776, he took a short tour of Scotland which he was 'obliged to perform, for want of time in little more than a fortnight' (Gilpin, 1789, 110). By and large few scenes completely fulfilled for him the requirements imposed by application of Picturesque principles. Scottish landscapes for him were more suited to painting than sketching. Despite this, he declared that they possessed qualities that led them to be valued in their own right in that they represented examples of the sublime: 'Indeed these wild scenes of sublimity, unadorned even by a single tree, form in themselves a very grand species of landscape' (ibid., 122).[6] He also mused on the nature of beauty in Scotland:

> A vast range of mountains, the lines of which are simple; and the surfaces broad, grand, and extensive, is rather sublime than beautiful. Add trees upon the foreground tufted woods creeping up the sides of the hills, a castle upon some knoll, and skiffs upon the lake (if there be one) and the landscape will still be sublime, yet with these additions (if they are happily introduced) the beautiful will predominate. This is exactly the case of the Scotch views. The addition of such furniture would give them beauty. At present, unadorned grandeur is their characteristic; and the production of sublime ideas, the effect.

The idea that landscape could or even should be improved to produce greater effect and true beauty was quite acceptable to the cultivated eighteenth-century traveller. Landscape gardeners and others had remodelled English estates on the basis of images and ideas received from the arts, even if they strove hard to conceal their handiwork (Lowenthal and Prince, 1965). Those principles would be extended to Scotland, as demonstrated by the Falls of Bruar. Situated on the Duke of Atholl's estate near Blair Atholl, the Falls had cut into the mountainside, sculpting the rock into shapes that included an arch. Gilpin visited the Falls after a recommendation to do so, but was scathing in his comments (1789, 145): 'They were scarce worth so long and perpendicular a walk. One of them indeed is a grand fall; but it is so naked in its accompaniments, and seen from so bad a point, that upon the whole it is of little value.' The prime cause of his disgust was the lack of any vegetation around the Falls.

His comments attracted others. Eleven years later Robert Burns visited the Falls and responded by writing a poem entitled 'The Humble Petition of Bruar Water to the Duke of Atholl'. This appealed to the Duke to improve the scene by the addition of trees (Robert Burns: quoted in PKDC, n.d.):

> My Lord, I know, your noble ear
>   Woe ne'er assails in vain;
> Embolden'd thus, I beg you'll hear
>   Your humble slave complain
> How saucy Phebus' scorching beams,
>   In flaming summer-pride,
> Dry-withering, waste my foamy streams,
>   And drink my crystal tide.
>
> ...

Would, then, my noble master please
  To grant my highest wishes?
He'll shade my banks wi' tow'ring trees,
  And bonie spreading bushes.
Delighted doubly then, my Lord,
  You'll wander on my banks,
And listen mony a grateful bird
  Return you tuneful thanks.

This act invited and received further imitative responses from later travellers. Despite the fact that the fourth Duke of Atholl did start planting trees shortly after Burns' visit,[7] later visitors chose to see the Falls through Burns' eyes and exercise their own poetic skills. James Cririe (1803), for example, was still complaining of the naked glen, even though improvements were clearly in hand:

Neglected Bruar, in his naked glen,
  Impet'ous rushes down from steep to steep
Progressive, threat'ning those who dare approach
  His headlong foaming course, and thund'ring falls.'

Ironically, the appearance of the Falls today conforms to the ideas of eighteenth-century taste.

Maps and itineraries

By the close of the eighteenth century conscious reference to previous travellers' tales was firmly established as a way for travellers to mediate their landscape experiences. Over time the number of available tales built up considerably, with later travellers slavishly writing journals that recorded thoughts, observations and landscape details in the style of Johnson, Gilpin or whatever other mentor they admired. Their accounts began to add advice to other travellers, consciously constructing what can now be recognized as prototypes of fully-fledged guidebooks.

James M'Nayr (1797), for instance, published a tour guide to the Highlands of Scotland and to the falls of the Clyde. Although written in the same spirit as the other travellers' accounts, it added information for those wanting to follow in his footsteps with advice about when to travel, roads, suitable inns, viewing points and walks to take. In the same manner, the Honorable Mrs Murray of Kensington (1799) prefaced her guide with the words: 'This is a book designed to be taken with the traveller. It gives information about distances, inns (good or bad), the state of the roads, roads fit for carriage and those not.' Mrs Murray's advice reached new levels of minutiae, including ferry prices and guidance as to the appropriate type of carriage, tools, bedlinen and provisions that the traveller required.

This development presaged more formal maps and guides. The map shown in Figure 3.3 provides an example of a traveller's map dating from 1775. Part of a map covering the route from Edinburgh to Thurso on the north coast, it shows the first 65 miles from Edinburgh through to Dalnacardoch (Perthshire) rendered in three linear strips.[8] Besides the road itself, wayfarers were supplied with basic information about towns and country-houses (with the names of their owners), and a minimal amount of information about topography and notable features. It was intended purely as a guide to travelling between given places. At a time when alternative routes were few and deviations from the set route were potentially hazardous and time-consuming, there was little need to offer much more.

Gradually this situation changed, as can be seen by considering the travel guides which came to be known as *Duncan's Itinerary* (Duncan, 1805 et seq.). These were pocket-sized volumes designed to accompany the traveller. The first edition was 1.5 centimetres in thickness and measured 20 centimetres long and 9 wide. It contained a single map marking only the most important mountains or lochs. The information was presented road by road, briefly indicating objects to be seen to the left or right. Particular emphasis was given to the houses belonging to the gentry.

By 1830 *Duncan's Itinerary* had reached its seventh edition. While still pocket size, it was altogether thicker with fuller information and map details, with no less than eighteen appendices of statistical information about topography, demography, climate and a variety of other features of interest, notably: 'Romantic scenery, deserving of the traveller's notice'. In part this reflects increasing economic development in tourist regions, with new roads and buildings and greater possibility of profitably deviating from set routes. Yet it also mirrors efforts to improve and embellish interpretation for travellers.

A good example is supplied by Appendix I which refers to the Falls of Foyers (or Fyers). The Falls were located at the point at which the River Foyers tumbles down the mountainside into Loch Ness and were a popular subject for romantic illustrators (Figure 3.4). Wade's military road passed close to this point, so they were accessible to those tourists who managed to travel as far north as Inverness. As in other appendices, travellers' descriptions are used to emphasize the delights of the scenery. After giving the height of this waterfall as 212 feet, the words of a Dr Garnett are quoted:

> Down this precipice the river rushes with a noise like thunder into the abyss below, forming an unbroken stream as white as snow. From the violent agitation arises a spray that envelops the spectator, and spreads a considerable distance. This is undoubtedly one of the highest falls in the world, and the quantity of water is sufficient to give it

3.3 Early traveller's map, Edinburgh to Dunkeld.

3.4 The Falls of Foyers (D.O. Hill, RSA and W. Forrest, c. 1840).

consequence. The scene is awful and grand. Though an immense quantity falls down the celebrated cascade of Niagara in North America, yet its height is not much more than half the height of this, being only 150 ft.

This was a sight that any tourist who had come to Scotland for the sublime and horror would not want to miss.

In search of Ossian

Before leaving the subject of the travellers' tales, it is worth considering an issue that brought so many travellers to Scotland in the late eighteenth century – the search for knowledge of Ossian, a legendary Gaelic poet. This may be linked to the Celtic revival, which replaced an interest in Roman antiquities and Latin poetry with a pride in the indigenous British past. In such circumstances, the publication of three volumes of ancient bardic poetry purported to be from the third century AD caused a literary sensation. In 1819, more than half a century later, William Hazlitt (quoted in Stafford, 1988, 1) was to place the works of Ossian alongside Homer, the Bible and Dante as 'four of the principal works of poetry in the world'.

Responsibility for publishing these works rested with James Macpherson, a Gaelic-speaking highlander who had attended Aberdeen University. Although a minor poet in his own right,[9] Macpherson's literary career only took off after a meeting in 1759 with the playwright John Home. Home was interested in the Gaelic verse that Macpherson had collected, but not being a Gaelic speaker, needed to see it in translation. Macpherson refused but eventually showed him a work entitled 'The Death of Oscur', purported to be epic poetry passed down by oral tradition from the blind bard and harpist Ossian. Home showed this to friends including Hugh Blair, Professor of Rhetoric and Belles Lettres at Edinburgh University. Blair pressed Macpherson for more poetry.

Reluctantly Macpherson obliged and the first of Macpherson's Ossianic poems was published in the shape of a slim volume entitled 'Fragments of Ancient Poetry' (Macpherson, 1760). Despite being very short, just fifteen pieces of prose, the 'Fragments' met with huge success and Macpherson was immediately fêted and befriended by some of the leading figures of eighteenth-century Scottish society. It also whetted the public and academic appetite for more poetry. Blair organized a subscription to finance Macpherson on a tour through the Highlands to collect more original material, resulting in a lengthy epic poem, 'Fingal' (Macpherson, 1762). Another journey, financed this time by the Earl of Bute, resulted in publication of a further epic poem entitled 'Temora' (Macpherson, 1763).

Two years later a collected 'Works of Ossian' also appeared (Macpherson, 1765).

The combination of Celtic heroes, highland scenery, chivalry and fine emotions and sensibility displayed in such ancient breasts was an irresistible combination. It also led to new ways of seeing and representing the Scottish landscape. Leneman (1987), for example, claimed that the Ossianic poetry had a threefold effect. First, it gave people a new way of looking at sublime, wild and desolate scenery. Secondly, it encouraged them to view landscapes in association with Ossian, peopling the landscape with their imagination. Finally, it supplied a new way of seeing the highlander. If the landscape had not changed over the centuries, then the highlander must be the same noble creature as of yore.

It was not just the British public that responded to these ideas, since the poems also caught the mood of nascent European Romanticism. Parts or all of the poems were translated into 26 other languages (Stafford, 1988). Ossian was Napoleon's favourite poet. He carried a copy of his poems on his campaigns and commissioned an opera 'Les Bardes' by Leseur, which includes Ossian's dream. Mehul wrote the opera 'Uthal' (Colgan, 1987). Balzac, Manzoni, Tolstoy and many others imitated him (Scott, 1994, 366). Interest was notably high among German writers and scholars. Herde wrote an essay 'On Ossian and the Songs of Ancient Peoples'. Goethe, Schiller and Lessing agreed with Hazlitt in the assessment that Ossian was the equal of Homer. Beethoven named Ossian and Homer as among his favourite poets and wanted to write settings for Scottish songs (Fiske, 1983, 33, 73; Scott, 1994). The lure of Ossian was still strong in the 1820s when Felix Mendelssohn visited Scotland and wrote both his *Hebridean Symphony* and the *Fingal's Cave Overture*. In fact Macpherson's writings played a part in the emerging sense not only of British identity but of growing sense of nationalism in Europe.

At the same time heated controversy surrounded the authenticity of Macpherson's poetry. A substantial body of opinion dearly wanted the poems to be authentic because of the boost this would have given to ancient Celtic (and British) culture. Sceptics wanted to see firmer evidence. They asked for publication of the original manuscripts from which Macpherson transcribed the poems, but Macpherson prevaricated. His promise to publish the originals was never fulfilled.[10]

While lengthy exploration of this debate lies outside the scope of this book,[11] it is important to recognize the influence that the published poetry and quest for its verification gave to travel in the Highlands and Islands. Ossian was the focus of the first wave of 'literary tourism' – the search for places celebrated for associations with books or authors (Squire, 1994b). Travellers such as Samuel Johnson, sceptical about Ossian from the outset, went to Scotland partly to prove that the poems were forgeries. Others also went to prove the authenticity of the poems and see the landscapes which had inspired Ossian and to tread in his footsteps. In doing so their actions were strongly influenced by the myth of the golden age. For them there was another landscape to be found beneath the veneer of modern Scotland; a world untouched by forces of modernity, where simplicity, peace and the culture of antiquity still reigned. Heron (1793, 157), for instance, felt the spell of Ossian as he left Perth and approached Dunkeld: 'I began to reflect that I was entering the land of Ossian's heroes; the land which preserved those few simple, grand, and gloomy objects which gave a melancholy cast to the imagination of the poet, and supplied that sublime, but undiversified imagery which forms one of the most peculiar characteristics of the ancient gaelic poetry.'

Moreover, given the lack of specific place information contained in Ossian's poetry, there was free range for the imagination. Gilpin, travelling in 1776, construed the landscapes of Glencoe and Morven in terms of the saga of Fingal (Gilpin, 1789). Charles Cordiner interpreted the circular stone-built brochs[12] of Highland Scotland in terms of Ossianic myth. They may not necessarily have had sacred significance, but he felt that they had indubitably had spiritual value for Celtic society: 'If we allow the authenticity of Ossian's poem wind coming down in eddies through these openings may have made harps hung upon the wall produce a wild aeolian tune and utter those alarming sounds in the night, that supernatural music ...' (Cordiner, 1780, 107).

Others pored over the poems for clues as to the setting of key sites and then actively searched for them in the field. Particular attention was devoted to finding human relics of Fingal (e.g. Murray, 1799) and viewing Fingal's Cave (generally taken to be on Staffa in the Inner Hebrides: Murray, 1799; Botfield 1829). Another popular quest concerned Ossian's burial place, thought to have been found in the Narrow Glen (Sma' Glen). During the construction of the military road, a tomb and gravestone had been discovered that many felt could be the last resting place of Ossian. Robert Burns had visited the site in 1787 (Mackay, 1992, 336). Dorothy and William Wordsworth later travelled south to Crieff along the road without realizing the significance of the spot. As if to rectify matters, William Wordsworth (see 1916, 288–9) composed a poem ('Glen Almain; or the Narrow Glen') in its honour:

> In this still place, remote from men,
>   Sleeps Ossian, in the Narrow Glen;
> In this place, where murmurs on
>   But one meek streamlet, only one:
> He sang of battles, and the breath
>   Of stormy war, and violent death;
> And should, methinks, when all was past,
>   Have rightfully been laid at last

Where rocks were rudely heaped, and rent
   As by a spirit turbulent;
Where sights were rough, and sounds were wild,
   And everything unreconciled;
In some complaining, dim retreat,
   For fear and melancholy meet;
But this is calm; there cannot be
   A more entire tranquillity.
Does then the Bard sleep here indeed?
   Or is it but a groundless creed?
What matters it? – I blame them not
   Whose Fancy in this lonely spot
Was moved; and in such way expressed
   Their notion of its perfect rest.
A convent, even a hermit's cell,
   Would break the silence of this Dell:
It is not quiet, it is not ease;
   But something deeper far than these:
The separation that is here
   Is of the grave; and of austere
Yet happy feelings of the dead:
   And, therefore, was it rightly said
That Ossian, last of all his race!
   Lies buried in this lonely place.

Whether pro- or anti-Macpherson, such travellers provided a ready market for landlords who created 'attractions' to draw travellers to particular sites. Nowhere was this more the case than the Hermitage at Dunkeld. Landlords had long spent vast sums creating pleasure grounds which reflected the latest landscape tastes. One such remodelling of nature had been carried out in 1758 on the banks of the Riven Braan on the Duke of Atholl's estate at Dunkeld, to produce a tree garden planted with exotic species and a hermitage or hut from which to view the Falls. This was redesigned in 1783 to create what could be described as the equivalent of a modern theme park. The hermitage was remodelled as Ossian's Hall, complete with a huge portrait of the poet which swung back to reveal the Falls. Mirrors reflected the scene on to the walls and the ceiling. A new feature called Ossian's Cave was built further up the cascades. This was an imaginative structure built around a group of large boulders, and was presented as the type of place that Ossian would have inhabited. A poem by Ossian was transcribed on one of the boulders.

Visitors who already came to Dunkeld to see the waterfalls[13] were drawn in growing numbers to witness these new novelties. Although not all were favourably disposed at what M'Nayr (1797) termed the 'tinselled frippery' of Ossian's Hall, many were content with the Ossianic allusion. Cririe (1803) lyricized:

The Hall of Ossian too, reflecting still
His broad cascade, and pools of foam, with spray
He sprinkles, thund'ring down the rugged steep,
Bounded by broken precipices high.

William Wordsworth, in a poem written around 1814 entitled 'Effusion in the pleasure-ground on the Banks of the Bran, near Dunkeld', expressed also reservations about the theatricality of the presentation: 'What! Ossian here – a painted thrall/Mute fixture on a stuccoed wall.' Nevertheless he also expressed wonder at the elemental power of the scene and the inspiration that it would have given to an ancient bard.

Conclusion

These reminiscences by travellers coming in search of Ossian point again to the importance of the late eighteenth-century in the making of Scottish tourism. Economic integration and improvements in accessibility contributed to increasing flow from England and further afield. They were guided primarily by the writings of their predecessors, which advised them not just what to see but also how to go about seeing it. Naturally the contents of the travellers' tales varied. For those like Samuel Johnson the main reason for travel was the desire for acquaintance with the traditional society of the Highlands and Islands, that was the object of the expedition. For others such as Gilpin it was the search for the picturesque. As time went by further assistance became available in the shape of printed maps and companions which codified information about topography and accommodation and gave advice pertinent to the latest trends in landscape appreciation.

The last section of this chapter then examined an issue that ran longitudinally through this period and drew many travellers to Scotland, namely the quest for tangible evidence of the existence of Ossian. During the sixty years that this craze lasted, it permitted almost any accessible point in the Highlands and Islands to attract literary tourists by claiming some link to this mythic Celtic past. Whatever damage Macpherson's activities may have done to the long-term study of the roots of Gaelic culture,[14] there is no doubt that the publication of the volumes of Ossian's poetry, in the original English and in translation, spread new representations of Scotland, its people and traditional culture throughout much of western Europe. As Paul Scott (1994, 366) noted: 'The idea became established that Scotland was a special place, close to ancient virtues long lost elsewhere, with a history that merited a pilgrimage, even if the pilgrims had only the vaguest ideas about it.' It also supplied a ready market for new Scottish themes when they became available.

In time the pursuit of Ossian dwindled, partly through resentment that this was not genuine ancient bardic poetry,[15] but rather more because it was superseded by other preoccupations. These would again change the way that Scotland was represented to the outside world.

Notes

1. A detailed account of their subsequent treatment and the broader develop-ment of the crofting community lies outside the scope of this book. For more details, see Hunter, 1976, 1991; Gold and Gold, 1982, 1991; Craig, 1990.
2. Those looking for progress and improvement or fine architecture, however, did not find that much to detain them. Travelling in 1776, Gilpin dismissed Scottish pleasure grounds as fifty years behind England. He saw nothing which was elegant, and felt that both architecture and contents of houses presented 'very little ... to detain a traveller', although he admitted that things might have improved by the time of publication (1789).
3. The term 'guidebook' was not coined until the early nineteenth century, although the terms 'guide' or 'companion' were in use in the eighteenth century. The *Oxford English Dictionary* states that the earliest use of the term was by Byron in *Don Juan* (1823).
4. It also remains the only account still commonly read. Bray (1986) and, in particular, Delaney (1993) supply good examples of contemporary interest in Johnson's travels.
5. Boswell's *Journal* extends up to 21 November 1773, including activities and meetings in and around Edinburgh, but the journey to the Western Isles was complete by 9 November.
6. It is not possible within the scope of this text to undertake a detailed discussion of the relationships between the Picturesque and the Sublime, or indeed their subsequent relationships to Romanticism. For more informa-tion on these aspects, see Andrews (1989), Ousby (1990) and Daniels (1992).
7. There is dispute over whether or not this was in direct response to Burns' petition as asserted, among others, by Drabble (1979, 74). The Duke also commissioned building paths carefully designed to direct the visitor up and around the Falls, concealing and revealing the Falls by turn, and building a number of viewing houses where the visitor could rest and contemplate the scene.
8. The reverse contains a similar set of strips which cover the route north from Dalnacardoch through to Aviemore.
9. Macpherson had published some poetry while a student and had begun collecting Gaelic poetry in his spare time. He wrote an epic poem 'The Highlander' in 1758, but this did not attract much attention (Stafford, 1988, 80).
10. The Highland Society of London did publish a three-volume Gaelic version of Ossian's poems in 1805, nine years after Macpherson's death, but this has since been shown to be a Gaelic translation of his English poems.
11. The poems were presented in print as epic literature passed down in an oral tradition, with some fragments later being put into manuscript form. Stories about the main characters – the warrior Fingal, his son Ossian, and his son Oscur – were part of contemporary highland culture. However, as Stafford

(1988) suggests, Macpherson saw himself as a restorer of literature as much as a translator (in much the way an archaeologist reconstructs a vase or fresco). He believed that a literal translation would belittle the poetry, lose the spirit of the original and be despised. Macpherson believed the poems had been corrupted over the centuries (and of course were in fragments). He wanted to restore them to their former glory as true epic poetry on a par with Homer and Virgil.

12. Brochs are circular enclosures surrounded by double-thickness walls of anything up to 10 metres in height.

13. One of whom was Gilpin. In contrast to his powerful condemnation of the Falls of Bruar (see above), the waterfalls at Dunkeld met his wholehearted approval. Gilpin (1789, 115) referred to an 'astonishing scene' in which the waterfall was 'picturesquely beautiful in the highest degree. The composition is perfect. This grand view, which I scruple not to call the most interesting thing of the kind I ever saw, is exhibited through the window of a summer-house; which I suppose, gives name to the scene: but it bears no resemblance to the idea of a Hermitage.'

14. Macpherson himself clearly corrupted ancient folk traditions for his own ends. Such was the popularity of this work that interest in authentic folk ballads declined while Ossian was all the rage (Chapman, 1978). Colgan (1987) notes that a genuine collector, the Reverend Archibald MacArthur, stopped gathering Gaelic poems because they were of a type that Macpherson had denounced (i.e. they were genuine). Sadly the legitimate article did not match the Ossianic ideal and so was rejected. For more on the activity of creating an ancient past beyond effective historical continuity, either by semi-fiction or forgery, see Hobsbawm (1983).

15. Paul Scott (1994, 365) commented on the irony that Macpherson is perhaps the only person in the history of literature to be condemned because his work was his own and not a translation.

CHAPTER FOUR

Sir Walter Scott and the propagation of the highland myth

'By giving what is commonplace an exalted meaning,
what is ordinary a mysterious aspect,
what is familiar the impressiveness of the unfamiliar,
to the finite an appearance of infinity:
thus I romanticise it.'

Novalis (Friedrich Von Hardenberg), 1798

On 26 September 1835 in front of a packed audience in the Teatro San Carlo in Naples, Gaetano Donizetti staged the first performance of his three-act opera *Lucia di Lammermoor*. Set in Scotland and based on the novel *The Bride of Lammermoor* by Sir Walter Scott, it was to receive enormous critical acclaim. Nevertheless, as we will see, Donizetti was certainly not the only composer making use of Scottish themes generally or the works of Scott in particular. Indeed it was not even the first time that this particular book had been adapted for the opera house; there were three previous Italian versions as well as a Danish rendition ('Bruden fra Lammermoor', 1832) by Bredal using a poem by Hans Christian Andersen as spoken dialogue (Ashworth, 1982). In early nineteenth-century Italian opera, as Michael Barclay (1994) noted: 'It was difficult to find anyone who didn't use Scottish themes'.

This enormous upsurge of interest in Scottish themes within the arts was substantially due to Scott as writer, poet and pageant-master. Coming hard on the heels of the impact of Ossianic poetry and growing appreciation of the songs and poetry of Robert Burns, Scott created a strong interest in all things Scottish. In the process, Scott and his followers were to reinvent not just the traditions of rural Scotland, but also new ways of looking at its land and people. The implications for understanding the subsequent development of Scottish tourism are profound.

This chapter therefore sets an agenda for much of what follows. Its core concerns Scott's role in propagating the highland myth through his writings and activities in connection with George IV's visit to Edinburgh in 1822. Scott not only reinvented Scottish traditions, he also succeeded in bringing new ways of looking at Scotland, its landscape and people to an international audience. As a prelude it is important to set the scene by considering two preliminaries: development in communications during the early nineteenth century and the continuing interest in literary tourism generated by Robert Burns.

Accessibility

The nineteenth century witnessed profound changes in the travelling public. A rising tide of prosperity progressively widened the flow of tourists to Scotland. Professional middle-class travellers joined the aristocratic and academic ladies and gentlemen of the eighteenth century. Enhanced accessibility played an important part, with improvements in roads, canals and steamer services making the Western Highlands accessible for the first time. Stage-coach services allowed visitors to reach the Eastern and Central Highlands more easily. By 1800 the Highlands had around 800 miles of roads, although much of them were built to meet military needs rather than civilian requirements and were in poor condition (Haldane, 1962). The Government instigated a £1.5 million road building programme between 1803 and 1825 with Thomas Telford as engineer. The programme helped to modernize the Highlands, create jobs and check emigration. These 'Parliamentary roads' were mainly situated in the west, Inner Hebrides and north of Scotland, where they provided road access to the north coast. Nevertheless, there were gaps. In the north there were roads, for example, from Bonar Bridge to Tongue and from Bonar Bridge to Wick and Thurso, but no road as yet along the coast itself.

Canal building also played its part. Construction of major Scottish canals in the Central Lowlands began in 1768 with parliamentary approval for the first work on the Forth and Clyde Canal and its cut, the Borrowstowness Canal. Work outside the Lowlands came later. Royal assent for the Crinan Canal in Argyllshire was received in 1793 and for the more ambitious Caledonian Canal in 1803, although they were not completed until 1801 and 1822 respectively. The latter was too late to achieve the expected international trade, being too shallow for Baltic and North American ships and suffering from operational problems due to flooding.[1]

These developments, along with harbour improvements, made possible the expansion of the canal and coastal steamship network.[2] The seventh edition (1830) of *Duncan's Itinerary* (Duncan, 1805 et seq.) noted that the steamboat had made the Western Isles very accessible. It commented:

> The whole of these passage boats are filled up with great elegance; a library of books in the cabin supplies food for the mind; and the stewards can furnish the hungry tourist with the more substantial refreshment of a comfortable meal. He may thus, at a small expense, visit all the Western coast from Liverpool to Tobermoray, – or the Eastern coast from London to Inverness, without entering a stage

coach or walking a mile. And thus, when tired of the 'Land o' Cakes', he may transport himself with ease and comfort to 'Merry England, or the Emerald Isle'.

For seven shillings and sixpence the traveller could purchase *The Steam Boat Companion* (Anon., 1830) with its descriptions of the 'romantic and picturesque scenery, curious incidents of local history, antiquities, mineralogical and geological phenomena not hitherto noticed' to be seen from steamboats in the Forth of Clyde, Loch Lomond and the Western Isles. When John Bowman and John Dovaston spent a month touring Scotland in 1825 they used steam packets almost as present-day travellers might use coach services (Bowman, 1986). On one day trip, for instance, they took the Marion Steam Packet from Broomielaw (Glasgow) to Dumbarton, toured Loch Lomond and caught the St Catherine, another steam packet, from Arrochar (Loch Long) back to Glasgow.

This network would be consolidated yet further in the second half of the nineteenth century, especially in the Clyde estuary (see Chapter 5), as flows of tourists and commuters steadily built up. There were also steamship services supplying connections to Scotland from both London and Liverpool.

Romanticism and the Pastoral

These new tourists were also being lured to Scotland by new enthusiasms and interests. Two of the most significant developments came from Romanticism and from the Pastoral Vision, as mediated by Robert Burns.

The Romantic movement that swept western Europe in the 1790s and early years of the nineteenth century effectively redefined landscape tastes. Romanticism is difficult to categorize succinctly because it was a movement that was more concerned with general attitudes than with specific stylistic features, seeing beauty in the organization of natural forces rather than in an intellectual order. Placing greater emphasis on the imagination, feelings and emotion, Romanticism valued wilder landscapes, mountains and moorland with extreme weather (storms, mist, raging torrents, even natural disasters), against the cultivated and ordered landscapes so beloved of the Age of Improvement. Romanticism also valued the fantastic and the exotic (Cunningham and Reich, 1985, 354). This element fuelled an antiquarianism and scholarly interest in medievalism, viewing the landscape in terms of heroic figures involved in epic events and displaying flawless chivalry despite the barbarity of the times in which they lived. Romanticism also praised the co-existence of society and nature (Newby, 1981, 130), valuing the simple life of the rural peasant against the industrialized and urbanized society emerging in Britain.

This movement in aesthetic appreciation would partly absorb and partly redirect the tourist gaze (Urry, 1990). Romanticism built on elements of eighteenth-century taste such as the sublime, Ossian and the Celtic Revival. Romanticism in literature, especially through the work of Sir Walter Scott, and in art through the work of Turner and others conveyed a new appreciation of Scottish landscapes. Tourists were lured into new areas, such as the Trossachs and Skye in search of two types of sensation. One was to experience wild landscapes and a sense of union with the natural world for themselves. The other was to witness the scenes that had inspired the great writers and artists of their times. Cultural tourists added to their itineraries the special places linked to the lives and times of Scott, along with the scenes that he had made famous and the events, fact or fiction, that he had described.

Before moving on to Scott, however, it is important to consider the role of Robert Burns and the Pastoral Vision. The Pastoral was a complex movement that cannot be discussed in detail here,[3] but can broadly be said to represent the view of life and nature as seen from the standpoint of the common man rather than the lofty position of the aristocrat. It was not an entirely new movement since it can be traced back to Spenser, Milton and Andrew Marvell (Drabble, 1979, 46–101), but is associated most with the work of three eighteenth-century 'ploughman poets': Stephen Duck, John Clare and Robert Burns.

With a family background in gardening and agriculture, Burns's view of landscape was not Romantic, regardless of the frequency with which he used the word. It was more akin to the tenant farmer, having 'the eye of one who knows hard labour, can appreciate prosperity and productivity' (Drabble, 1979, 66). Burns was moved by the quality transferred to the landscape by the independence of its farmers and labourers; unproductive, wild hills failed to move him in the same way. On a tour in 1787, for example, his journal began: 'Left Edinburgh – Lammermuir Hills miserably dreary, but at times very picturesque' (quoted in Mackay, 1992, 305). He would make pronouncements on the aesthetics of landscape when required, as seen in the case of the Falls of Bruar (see Chapter 3). Nevertheless the poems that evoked Burns's landscapes most powerfully were not set pieces of this sort, but those that celebrated 'the nameless fields of corn rigs, barley and rye' (Drabble, 1979, 69).

As a result literary tourists came less in search of the landscapes described by Burns than those linked to the events of his life. His death in 1796, at the early age of 37, meant that the scenes associated with the poet were visited and grieved over. The Wordsworths found their thoughts on visiting Dumfries 'heart-depressing'. Even his widow and children were objects of interest. In 1825 Bowman and Dovaston visited Dumfries:

> We had in the course of the afternoon, made several calls at the house
> of Mrs. Burns, the widow of the poet, who was from home; and as
> Dovaston was very anxious to see her, we made a fourth attempt
> which proved successful ... She received us very kindly; and on
> Dovaston's apologizing for the intrusion (as he understood so many
> called), she said they did, but she knew not how to refuse them ... She
> seemed but slightly affected by the conversation; but it must be
> considered that time and the many circumstances connected with her
> husband's fame, have so long familiarized her mind to his death, that
> the idea must now be softened into a pleasing melancholy. (Bowman,
> 1986, 23)

The enduring popularity of his work, aided by the foundation of Burns
Societies throughout the world, attracted increasing numbers of visitors
to Scotland as the nineteenth century progressed. Americans were already
coming to see his birthplace in Alloway in 1817 and, a decade later, one
observer was distressed to find that souvenir hunters had so chipped away
at the gravestone of Burns's father that the inscription was illegible
(Lockwood, 1981, 78). Almost any scene connected with his birth, life or
death became a shrine for literary tourists for whom, by 1851, 'the one
who does not visit them is considered deficient in taste'. The house in
Glasgow Vennel, Irvine where Burns lodged in 1781–2, his birthplace in
Alloway, the premises of the debating society that he helped found in
Tarbolton, and his home in Mauchline were, and indeed are, places of
pilgrimage (see Chapter 7). Many other monuments erected both by
enthusiasts and by local authorities with an eye to attracting visitors
ensured a flow of visitors to Scotland that continues unabated to the
present day.[4] Yet regardless of the sizeable flow of visitors that the Burns
pilgrimage developed, in the nineteenth century it was dwarfed by that
generated by his compatriot, Sir Walter Scott.

The writings of Sir Walter Scott

There can hardly be a book on Scottish culture that does not mention
Sir Walter Scott. His influence, however interpreted, is never doubted.
Through his writing of poetry and the historical novels he generated a
passion for Scottish scenery and history which was felt well beyond
Scotland itself. His work influenced artists throughout Britain and Europe.
He inspired works in other media (painting, opera, theatre). He drew
tourists in their thousands to those parts of Scotland which were described
in his works. Indeed countless others who may never have read Scott's
novels effectively came to look at Scotland through his eyes. Scotland was
the 'Country of Scott' just as today we can talk of Hardy's Wessex and
more recently Peter Mayle's Provence. Scotland was 'where the spirits of

history, summoned up by his (Scott's) enchantments haunt visibly its mouldering temples and ruined castles' (Ritchie, 1835, n.p.).

His importance does not stop there. Scott was also an historian and antiquarian whose views of the past shaped the way that the Scots saw themselves and their country. Perhaps most significantly his love of the past and his role in Edinburgh society placed him in a unique position to influence the representation of Scottish culture – particularly in his role as master of ceremonies for George IV's visit to Edinburgh in 1822. This role as pageant-master would result in the reinvention not just of courtly protocol but also Scottish tradition in general.

Scott was born in August 1771 in Edinburgh and died at his country seat, Abbotsford, at the age of 61. After considerable ill health as a child, which gave him time for a great breadth of reading, he studied law and eventually became Sheriff-Depute of Selkirkshire and Clerk of the Court of Session in Edinburgh. Despite his legal duties he pursued antiquarian interests, collected ballads and wrote long narrative poems which were published between 1805 and 1817. It was not until 1814, at the age of 43, that he produced the first of the famous Waverley novels. In his remaining 18 years, his success and output was prodigious. Much would be driven by debt. The excessive cost of his ambitious plans for remodelling Abbotsford, his new home, in 1822 was followed by the financial collapse of his publishing venture with James Ballantyne in 1826.[5]

Twenty-nine novels appeared between 1814 and his death in 1832, along with further narrative poetry, historical, antiquarian, dramatic and shorter works. The sales of his poetry and novels were unequalled in his lifetime. In this endeavour Scott was backed by successful marketing orchestrated by his Edinburgh publishers, Archibald Constable (Hewitt, 1988, 65–6). Works were handled by booksellers with proven track records in moving books. They advertised heavily, announcing new titles several months before their appearance. They sought to have his books reviewed extensively, commissioned illustrations and encouraged translations into other media, such as stage and opera.

The results in Britain alone were sales of novels that were counted in their millions throughout the nineteenth century (Hook, 1972, 9), with release of titles in cheap paperbound editions[6] as well as hardback (Figure 4.1). Scott was published in America within weeks of his novels appearing in Britain and he was translated into most European languages. Theatres in London vied with one another to be the first to get a new Scott novel on the stage (Bolton, 1992) and many of his novels and poems, as noted above, were turned into operas.

The subject matter was invariably historical. The novels ranged from *Waverley*, which looked back to the '45, to others with medieval settings. The best remembered works were those that were wholly or partly set in

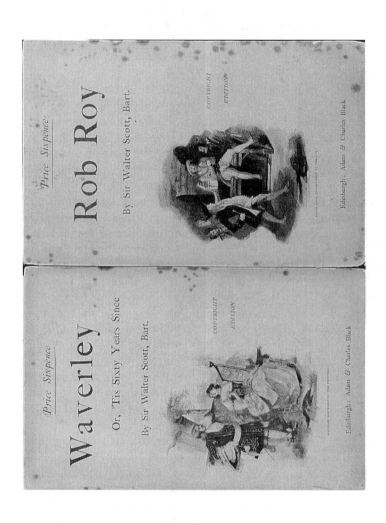

4.1 Paper-covered editions of Scott's novels. Typical cheaper editions were intended for widespread circulation among the growing middle-classes in Victorian Britain

Scotland, although some of his later work strayed as far as the Holy Land, India or Constantinople. The subject matter was often larger than life, even melodramatic: tales of love, loss, noble sentiment, tragedy, and war; something which suited the Romantic taste of nineteenth-century audiences.

Broadly his work had two main aims. The first was 'to illustrate the customs and manners which anciently prevailed', a comment made by way of a preface to *The Lay of the Last Minstrel*, but which could equally apply to other works (Scott, 1904: 1971, 1). In his introduction to the 1829 edition of *Waverley*, Scott explained that he hoped he could achieve as much for Scotland as the author Maria Edgeworth had done for Ireland through her writing – making the Irish familiar to her English readers and thus doing 'more towards completing the Union than perhaps all the legislative enactments by which it has been followed up' (Scott, 1829: 1972, 523). Scott felt he was well-placed to do this considering

> his intimate acquaintance with the subject which I could lay claim to possess, as having travelled through most parts of Scotland, both Highland and Lowland; having been familiar with the elder as well as more modern race; and having had from my infancy free and unrestrained communication with all ranks of my countrymen, from the Scottish peer to the Scottish ploughman. (ibid., 524)

He built up a formidable historical knowledge and acquired a familiarity with myths about the past for, even if not literally true, he believed that the stories he was told while travelling and in chance meetings imparted the flavour of the past (ibid., 7). Moreover he saw old poetry, plays and romances as valid historical sources (Anderson, 1981, 8).

The second aim was to present landscapes not simply as beautiful scenes but as the backdrop to characters and events. Scott loved beautiful scenery. He was particularly attracted to places where stirring events had taken place (Watson, 1970, 127) since they allowed him to convey the poignancy which landscape could evoke. Sometimes historical occurrences were placed in their authentic locations, but fictitious events were also put in suitable settings. Favoured landscapes were often pressed into service as settings for his stories. Marmion's journey from England to Edinburgh, for example, was dictated by Scott's wish to include places he wanted to describe (Watson, 1970, 132). A tale of love and betrayal, *Marmion* (1808) was set in 1513. The character is fictitious but the topographical detail is exact and locations are recognizable to the literary tourist. He confessed to having adopted much the same policy with *Waverley* (1814): 'his movements up and down the country with the Highland cateran Bean Lean, are managed without much skill. It suited best, however, the road I wanted to travel, and permitted me to introduce some descriptions of scenery and manners ...' (Scott, 1829:1972, 525).

The strength of Scott's writing came from personal experience of the scenes he described but they gained in the readers' eyes by being associated with characters and events. They wanted to recite the poems in the places where the action took place. The geography of Scott's writings was always closer to reality than the history.

The landscapes which first caught the public imagination were those of the Scottish Borders, an area which Scott knew intimately. This was the setting for his first narrative poem *The Lay of the Last Minstrel*, in which memorable lines are used to describe the essence of Scottish landscape:

> O Caledonia! stern and wild,
> Meet nurse for a poetic child!
> Land of brown heath and shaggy wood,
> Land of mountain and the flood,
> Land of my sires! what mortal hand
> Can e'er untie the filial band,
> That knits me to thy rugged strand!
> Still as I view each well-known scene,
> Think what is now, and what hath been,
> (lines 17–25 6th Canto, 123)

His third narrative poem, *The Lady of the Lake*, was the first to be set in the Highlands and contained powerful descriptions of the Trossachs. Anderson (1981) recounted the pains that Scott took with *The Lady of the Lake* to ensure the action was plausible. Concerned that his knowledge of highland scenery was insufficient, Scott revisited the area in order to fit the topography with the action, checking that it was possible to ride from Loch Vennachar to Stirling as one of the poem's characters must do. Scott also wrote that he wished to set the story at 'no very distant period', incorporating stories he had collected in the area. One of the poem's highlights comes when a hunter, supposedly King James V travelling incognito, stumbles across the virtually hidden Loch Katrine while chasing a stag. His first view of the lake contains the following description:

> Where, gleaming with the setting sun,
> One burnished sheet of living gold,
> Loch Katrine lay beneath him rolled;
> In all her length far winding lay,
> With promontory, creek, and bay,
> And islands that, empurpled bright,
> Floated amid the livelier light,
> And mountains, that like giants stand,
> To sentinel enchanted land.
> High on the south, huge Benvenue
> Down to the lake in masses threw
> Crags, knolls, and mounds, confusedly hurl'd,
> The fragments of an earlier world;
> A wildering forest feather'd o'er

His ruin'd sides and summit hoar,
While on the north, through middle air,
Ben-an heaved high his forehead bare.
(lines 261–77, 1st Canto, 147)

Into this romantic setting is placed a society of Scott's choosing. The noble clan chiefs, the code of behaviour, the fiery cross and the summoning of the clans were all part of Scott's desire to people the landscape and recreate the manners of old. Nevertheless, as in all his works, numerous notes accompany the text explaining customs and recounting stories to convince readers of the veracity of the customs described.

By virtue of the poem's considerable critical success[7] Scott is often credited with starting the passion for the Trossachs. The reality is that they had already started to attract visitors in the early nineteenth century – one of whom was Scott himself.[8] What the publication of *The Lady of the Lake* undoubtedly did achieve was to generate rapidly increasing numbers of visitors, many of whom arrived with a copy of the poem. It also made Loch Katrine a favourite with painters, engravers and finally photographers who invariably included it in any collection of pictures of scenic Scotland (see Chapter 5).

Scott also drew visitors into more remote country through his poems, Loch Coruisk on Skye being a case in point. Scott wrote in his notes to *The Lord of the Isles* that: 'It is as exquisite a savage scene as Loch Katrine is a scene of Romantic beauty' (Robertson, 1904, 475). The poem contained landscape descriptions of contemporary appeal; a desolate, empty wildness, untouched by human activity. In a copious footnote to this poem Scott remarked that the scenery here was extraordinary and 'unparalleled in any part of Scotland, at least any which I have happened to visit':

For rarely human eye has known
A scene so stern as that dread lake,
    With its dark ledge of barren stone.
Seems that primeval earthquake's sway
Hath rent a strange and shatter'd way
    Through the rude bosom of the hill,
And that each naked precipice,
Sable ravine, and dark abyss,
    Tells of the outrage still.

Such descriptions of Loch Coruisk and the Cuillins quickly attracted the more intrepid visitors. Artists, among them Turner, made their way to Skye in such numbers that it soon became a 'frequently painted scene' (Halliwell, 1990).

At the same time Scott was not without his critics. As early as 1810 a satirical poem by John Taylor poked fun at Scott's judicious use of landscape in his epic poetry:

> Another very shrewd device
> May various readers well entice:
> Our Bard, who seems a wary wight,
> And knows that scenes of youth delight,
> A local int'rest to diffuse,
> Has wisely made his rambling Muse
> Of many a spot minutely tell
> On which remembrance loves to dwell,
> Since high and low with pleasure view
> Whate'er will early days renew.
> Hence places in his work appear
> As in a Map or Gazetteer,
> And hence in fondness folk declare
> They such a time were there and there,
> And, with the zeal of patriot pride,
> Proclaim the record far and wide.

None the less such voices remained in a small minority for many years. Indeed, Scott's impact on the construction of landscape tastes would soon be reinforced by his novels.

Waverley, Scott's first novel, was published anonymously in 1814; he did not publicly admit his authorship until 1827. It established the historical novel as a new literary genre.[9] In his postscript, Scott indicated that Scotland had undergone a more profound transformation over the last half century than any other European nation. He commented on the loss of old traditions of which

> I have witnessed the almost total extinction. I have embodied in imaginary scenes, and ascribed to fictitious characters, a part of the incidents which I then received from those who were actors in them. Indeed the most romantic parts of this narrative are precisely those which have a foundation in fact. (Scott, 1829: 1972, 492–3)

Two other novels with a Jacobite theme then followed, *Rob Roy* (1818) set against the background of the 1715 uprising, and *Redgauntlet* (1824) set in 1765 describing an abortive attempt to reinstate the Stuarts but with an older Prince Charles Edward Stuart arriving in Scotland to find his cause lost once and for all. All three Jacobite novels have 'outsiders' as heroes. *Waverley* and *Rob Roy* centre upon Englishmen who, for varying reasons, travel north to Scotland and so see Scottish life through fresh eyes. Gaelic is translated for them and customs and traditions deciphered. This is the perfect device for Scott to achieve his aim of explaining Scotland to the English, or foreign readers. They get an insight into Scottish history, traditions and culture through these heroes. For its part *Redgauntlet* has an English hero living in Scotland who turns out to be of Scottish Jacobite descent.

All three novels contain strong landscape elements. *Waverley* and *Rob Roy* have the contrast of Highlands against Lowlands at their heart, and

Redgauntlet is set in the Borders. In his introduction to *Rob Roy* Scott (1962, 385) stated: 'It is the contrast betwixt the civilized and cultivated mode of life on the one side of the Highland line, and the wild and lawless adventures which were habitually undertaken and achieved by one who dwelt on the opposite side of that ideal boundary, which creates the interest attached to his name.' *Rob Roy* blends 'the wild virtues, and the subtle policy, and unrestrained licence of an American Indian' (ibid.).

The use of scenery is as important in Scott's novels as in his poetry. In *Waverley* Scott blends picturesque scenery, romance and Gaelic culture. Inspired by the scenery of Loch Ard, near Aberfoyle, Scott constructed a scene[10] in which the hero Fergus Mac-Ivor climbs up a waterfall to meet the beautiful Flora, with whom he has fallen in love:

> I have given you the trouble of walking to this spot, Captain Waverley, both because I thought the scenery would interest you, and because a Highland song would suffer still more from my imperfect transla-tion, were I to introduce it without its own wild and appropriate accompaniments. To speak in the poetical language of my country, the seat of the Celtic muse is in the mist of the secret and solitary hill, and her voice in the murmur of the mountain stream. He who woos her must love the barren rock more than the fertile valley, and the solitude of the desert better than the festivity of the hall.

She then sang a highland air to Waverley, an old battle song which urged the clans to awake 'for honour, for freedom, for vengeance' (Scott, 1829: 1972, 175).

Scott wished to extend his work on Scottish scenery further by publishing the two-volume *Provincial Antiquities and Picturesque Scenery of Scotland* in 1819 and 1826. He had persuaded Turner to be financially involved and to undertake the illustrations, which he did on a visit to Scotland in 1818.[11] Sales, however, were poor and the project was a financial disaster, providing an additional source of pressure on Scott's resources.

Pageant and protocol

Scott's influence on the representation of Scotland, as noted above, was not restricted to his writings. He was responsible for helping to develop and focus a growing movement among the Scottish establishment for the revival of highland customs. Societies for the preservation of the highland way of life had been established in the late eighteenth century by the nobility and other members of the establishment. One of the best known was the Gaelic Society of London. When started in 1777 it required all its members to be fluent in Gaelic (Withers, 1992). That criterion was relaxed in the following year and it became the Highland Society, for those of highland descent. The aim was now to preserve highland virtues and traditions, including Gaelic, and to work for the repeal of the Proscription Acts. It was one of their members, the Duke of Montrose, who introduced the Bill that successfully repealed the Act. The irony, as Jarvie (1989, 1991) points out, was that these were the same people involved in the extinction of the real highland way of life.

Scott was to draw on this groundswell of interest. Perhaps the best illustration of his role is seen in connection with the visit of George IV to Edinburgh in August 1822. With the Union of the Crowns in 1603 the Scottish King James VI left for England, after which time the monarch became an absentee. George IV's visit was the first time that the monarch had come to Scotland since 1633.[12] The staging of a royal visit at this time was intended to achieve a diverse set of political goals. The establishment wished to defeat the radicals, countering their protests against worsening economic conditions with a huge orchestrated upswell of loyalty to the government in the person of the monarch. The monarchy too, needed to improve its poor standing in the light of the royal divorce and the recent death of Queen Caroline. Lords Castlereagh and Liverpool wanted a royal engagement which would preclude the King from attending the Congress of Nations at Vienna. Landowners wanted to enhance their position since they were beginning to attract criticism over their land policies. The visit gave them an opportunity to present themselves in a paternal role as clan chiefs.

For his part Scott saw the royal visit as an opportunity to restore Scottish pride and identity, to revive old customs and finally to heal the rift between Jacobites and Hanoverians by presenting George as both the heir of the Stuarts[13] and the Chief of Chiefs. Moreover this was the opportunity to restore the Honours of Scotland (the royal regalia) to the Scottish king. Scott had been instrumental in the rediscovery of the regalia in 1818. They had been locked in a chest in a sealed room of Edinburgh Castle since the Treaty of Union in 1707. Indeed they had been locked away so long that all sense of the symbolism and protocol that surrounded them had disappeared (Burnett and Tabraham, 1993). Given the added complication of the absence of a royal presence in Edinburgh since 1603, 'tradition' needed to be invented from scratch. The Lord Provost asked Scott for help, given his detailed knowledge of the past. A committee was established including Scott, the Lord Provost, David Stewart Garth, James Skene and Alexander Keith of Raveston, heir to the rank of Knight Marischal of Scotland. The moment was not lost on Scott, who was effectively being given an opportunity to bring his novels to life; to take his knowledge of the 'lost' past and revive whatever he wished of it. It was an opportunity that few novelists before or since have enjoyed.

Scott treated the visit as a huge pageant in which the streets of Edinburgh would be transformed. Triumphal arches, galleries and stands were constructed, decorations were put up. Ground was levelled where necessary as, for example, outside the County Rooms so that judges and others could view the royal procession. The area around Holyroodhouse was illuminated by gas lighting and an immense bonfire was lit on Arthur's Seat. Edinburgh was renovated and repainted, streets repaired, shop fronts redecorated and many public works commissioned (Finley, 1981). The interiors of key public buildings were transformed, the population dressed in an appropriate manner, and their actions stage managed. In order to achieve these objectives Scott employed friends to advise on various aspects of the project, notably William Murray, the actor-manager of the Theatre Royal, who advised upon pageantry and interior design, the actress Harriet Siddons who advised on style and fashion, and David Stewart Garth who organized the highland element. Leading artists of the day, including Turner and David Wilkie, were given special viewpoints so they could record the scene.

Scott wrote the words for the regalia pageantry, as well as a pamphlet entitled 'Hints addressed to the Inhabitants of Edinburgh, and Others, in Prospect of His Majesty's Visit'. This gave information about the visit, advice on what to wear and about etiquette and behaviour generally. It is clear from this pamphlet that Scott wished to put on a dignified and orderly display, historically correct in detail but that '... this is not an ordinary show – it is not all on one side. It is not enough that we should see the King; but the King must also see us'.

This was Scotland displayed, a visual representation of national unity literally cast in highland clothing. Scott had persuaded the King to wear highland dress as part of the ceremonial, although he only wore it the once. This was at the reception for Scottish noblemen and gentlemen, or levee. The emphasis on tartan was not Scott's influence alone,[14] but he assumes prime responsibility for conflating highland identity and Scottish identity in this manner. This offended many lowland Scots both at the time and subsequently. There were complaints about the disproportionate preponderance of kilts. The writer Thomas Carlyle left Edinburgh altogether during the royal visit rather than endure 'such efflorescence of the flunkeyisms' (quoted by Morley, 1980, 431). As Lockhart (1906, 421) argued:

> With all respect for the generous qualities which the Highland clans have often exhibited, it was difficult to forget that they had always constituted a small, and almost always unimportant part of the Scottish population; and when one reflected how miserably their numbers had of late years been reduced in consequence of the selfish and hard-hearted policy of their landlords, it almost seemed as if

there was a cruel mockery in giving so much prominence to their pretensions. But there could be no question that they were picturesque – and their enthusiasm was too sincere not to be catching.'

Nevertheless such voices were muted at the time, with the allure of monarchy working to validate the proceedings (Colley, 1992, 235). Having a free hand Scott took liberties with social history. He recast the King's relationship to Scotland and its people:

> King George IV comes hither as the descendant of a long line of Scottish Kings. The blood of the heroic Robert Bruce – the blood of the noble, the enlightened, the generous James I is in his veins. Whatever Honour Worth and Genius can confer upon Ancestry, his Scottish Ancestry possesses. Still more he is our kinsman.

Scott went on to say that not only could the old Scottish families claim a relationship, but that 'in this small country, blood has been so much mingled, that it is not to be doubted by far the greater part of our burgesses and yeomans are entitled to entertain similar pretensions. In short, we are THE CLAN, and our King is THE CHIEF.' As a result he called for political differences to be buried. Part of the new ground for consensus would come from the adoption of the reinvented highland tradition and its symbols.[15]

Followers of Scott

Taken together, Scott's writings and his recasting of Scottish tradition as a romanticized version of highland tradition are pivotal in any analysis of the representation of Scotland in the ensuing years. That influence, of course, was not mediated solely through Scott's work but also involved the efforts of others who seized upon his ideas and developed them further.

Artists came to Scotland to paint the scenes popularized by Scott. As we have seen, Turner went to Skye in search of landscapes and illustrated the royal visit. The young Edwin Landseer visited Scott at Abbotsford in 1824 and painted many highland landscapes, mostly for his own amusement. As time went by artists came to depict the scenes before them as if filtered by Scott's views, with dramatic landscapes peopled by characters who appear to have been drawn directly from a Scott novel.

Playwrights, as we have noted, were particularly keen to adapt Scott's works for the theatre. Bolton (1992) lists over 4,500 productions of derivative dramas between 1810–1900 (they were only rarely adapted after 1900). Productions often appeared on the London stage within weeks of a book's publication, with companies competing with one another as to whose play would open first. The most popular works were

Rob Roy, followed by *Guy Mannering* and *The Bride of Lammermoor*. Their high quotient of action and exaggerated feeling and sensibility translated well to the Victorian stage, with its predilection for melodrama. Their strong integral scenic ingredients gave set designers a chance to display their skills and to offer the audience a spectacle that they came to expect. Theatre promoters, for their part, made special reference to scenic spectacle as a particular attraction of their productions. Dramatization of Scott's novels had the effect of reinforcing the popular view of Scottish scenery as highland scenery in an age when pictorial representations were few and colour reproductions were expensive. Many English visitors saw the plays and their associated sets before they ventured north.

The eagerness with which opera houses adapted Scott's work has already been recognized. Besides *Lucia di Lammermoor*, Donizetti wrote other operas with Scottish themes (e.g. *Maria Stuarda*); Gioacchino Rossini wrote *La Donna del Lago*, *Ivanhoe* and *Robert Bruce*; Bizet *La Joie Fille de Perth*; Mayerberg *Emma of Roxbrough*; Frederico Ricci *The Prisoner of Edinburgh*; and Giuseppe Verdi *Araldo* (set by Loch Lomond). The reasons for this interest were twofold. One, which had little to do with Scott, was censorship in the Italian states. Political and moral censorship hung heavily over the arts until around 1860. Subjects regarded as likely to give problems in this respect were best transferred into the setting of a remote region, for which purpose Scotland was ideal. Rossini's *William Tell* with its nationalistic theme, for example, was called *William Wallace*, after the Scottish patriot, when performed in Italy. The other reason was very much linked to Scott. The strong dramatic themes, striking costumes and arresting landscapes appealed to a wide range of European composers. Scottish settings were taken even if only on the title. Bellini's *I Puritani* was named after Scott's *Covenanters* even though the opera is set in Plymouth which, arguably, Bellini thought was in Scotland.

The cumulative effect of all this artistic endeavour was to popularize the scenes and history of Scotland to a degree that went well beyond anything seen before, including Ossian. Visitors flooded to the scenes described by Scott. The Borders became Scott territory with, for example, people viewing the Mare's Tail Falls through the lens of Scott's descriptions in *Marmion*. Queen Victoria was a devotee. The first novel that she ever read being *The Bride of Lammermoor* and she steeped herself in Scott before making her first visit to the Highlands in 1842. When she read Albert the first three cantos of *The Lay of the Last Minstrel* on a rainy Sunday in Taymouth Castle, her diary (11 September 1842) states that it 'delighted us both'. The previous day she had been rowed down Loch Tay while the boatmen sang Gaelic boat songs. She subsequently found a passage in *The Lady of the Lake* that fitted the scene exactly:

See the proud pipers on the bow,
And mark the gaudy streamers flow
From their loud chanters down, and sweep
The furrow'd bosom of the deep,
As, rushing through the lake amain,
They plied the ancient Highland strain.

This is a description of the progress of Roderick Dhu, the highland chief, down Loch Katrine to his home. As Queen she could easily imagine herself in the place of Roderick, recreating the scene in the poem. Later, once they had bought Balmoral, the same passage would come to mind when rowing on Loch Muick.

American visitors were particularly smitten with Scott. On leaving Edinburgh they headed directly for 'Scott-land' as Baynard Taylor described it. Ralph Waldo Emerson asked in 1856: 'What did Walter Scott write without stint?' The answer was 'a rhymed travellers' guide to Scotland' (Lockwood, 1981, 71). Even by the 1890s when Scott's appeal was waning, many would arrive clutching their volumes of his writings, which they read and debated as they travelled. The Trossachs and Loch Katrine served as a magnet for tours. Large four-horse wagonettes, able to carry twelve passengers, ran day trips to the loch, with drivers who specialized in reciting or reading long passages of The Lady of the Lake. At Loch Lomond there were so many Americans among the literary tourists that the hotel at Inversnaid routinely flew the American flag.

Tourists also came in great numbers to see Scott's country house, Abbotsford. Scott bought Abbotsford, then known as Cartley Farm, in 1812. Having bought more land in 1820 he then helped to design a new house which would embody much of his sense of history. In 1822 the old house was demolished to create a modern Gothic structure encapsulating the 'most attractive features of medieval architecture' although he regretted that 'a modern Gothic structure may excite magnificent or melancholy ideas, it cannot excite awe as halls that have echoed to the footfall of remote generations' (quoted by Pope-Hennessy, 1932). Scott incorporated masonry, carving and stonework collected from abbeys and old houses, medallions from the old Cross of Edinburgh,[16] stones from Old Penrith Roman Camp, and part of the Mercat Cross of Edinburgh incorporated into a fountain. After his death in 1832 tourists came to view the house and its effects, paying particular attention to those rooms which were as Scott had left them. The study and library excited the most interest. Over 500 Americans signed the visitors' book in 1845. After Abbotsford the regular pilgrimage was to visit Melrose Abbey and Scott's grave at Dryburgh Abbey.

Tartanry

Scott's work in resurrecting and embellishing those Jacobite symbols suppressed after the '45 was also carried forward by others. Most issues involving the multiplication of all things highland – tartans, bagpipes, the kilt, customs and the like – lie beyond the scope of this book, but two topics, which have important implications for the attraction of tourists merit further discussion.

The first was the foundation of highland games and gatherings. As noted above, Scott was not the sole influence in the recreation and re-definition of highland traditions. In 1815 Alastair Ranaldson Macdonell of Glengarry (a friend of Scott and the model for his character Fergus Mac-Ivor) founded the Society of True Highlanders, to promote the 'Dress, Language, Music and characteristics of our illustrious and ancient race in the Highlands and Isles of Scotland, with their genuine descendants wherever they may be'. They organized highland feasts (modelled on *Waverley*), stag hunts, highland balls and highland games (Bray, 1986, 204). This organization did not outlive the death of its founder in 1828, but other highland societies were founded to continue similar activities. Highland gatherings and games soon became one of their major functions, reviving the idea of the clan and chiefs gathering after harvest to discuss politics and business. These meetings also featured sports, dancing and music. One of the many societies forming at this time serves to illustrate the process. The Lonach Highland and Friendly Society was founded in 1823 with four aims: the preservation of highland garb; the support of loyal, peaceable, upright and manly conduct; the promotion of social and friendly feelings among the inhabitants of the district; and the setting up of a voluntary fund for the distribution of social relief. In the 1830s the society started holding highland games, which by this time had come to be seen as embodying much of the tradition they sought to preserve. The mid-nineteenth century saw a proliferation of highland gatherings and highland games from these early beginnings, with new games created at Pitlochry (1852), Dunbeath (1856) and Alva (1858), with gatherings founded in Glenisla (1852) and Argyllshire (1871) (Jarvie, 1991). These public spectacles, as we shall see later, became an important part of the tourist calendar in the Highlands.

The role that these events played in the romanticization of the High-lands was reinforced by royal patronage. Victoria and Albert established a close link with the Braemar Highland Gathering when they moved to Balmoral in 1848. These games, which had started in 1832, became the Braemar Royal Highland Gathering. They were held at Balmoral in 1859 and again in 1887, 1890, 1898 and 1899. The tradition was created that

the monarch or other member of the royal family acted as highland chieftain to the gathering (ibid., 1991).

This notion of the role of the chieftain leads on to the second important
aspect of the invention of the Highlands, namely, the Bonnie Prince
Charlie cult. This again preceded Scott, but undoubtedly took direction
from his work. The story of a defeated noble hero had great appeal in
nineteenth-century Europe, with the Romantic period conjuring up many
images of martyrs for social revolution and for political and national
independence (Bialostocki, 1983). As the '45 lapsed into memory and the
immediacy of the threat of insurrection receded, popular interest in the
Young Pretender grew outside remnant Jacobite circles.

One of the first to express interest had been Dr Johnson. He met Flora
Macdonald on his Hebridean tour in 1773 and had slept in the same bed
as Prince Charles Edward Stuart. Johnson praised Flora MacDonald as 'a
name that will be mentioned in history, and if courage and fidelity be virtues,
mentioned with honour' (Chapman, 1924, 60). Ballads and Jacobite songs
were written in the late eighteenth or early nineteenth centuries to sound
like authentic expressions of the uprisings (Cheape, 1991).[17]

For his part Scott declared in 1806 that: 'I became a valiant Jacobite at
the age of ten years old; and, even since reason and reading came to my
assistance, I have never quite got rid of the impression which the gallantry
of Prince Charles made on my imagination' (quoted by Sutherland, 1985,
vii). He added that he wanted to preserve these stories. Even as late as
1831 he contemplated writing a life of Charles Stuart.

The fact that an establishment figure like Scott expressed such beliefs
demonstrated that this was now a safe subject for antiquarian and romantic
interest. His first novel, *Waverley*, both codified and embellished the growing mythology that enveloped Bonnie Prince Charlie, presenting a heroic
portrait of a romantic prince surrounded by faithful and noble followers:

> A young man, wearing his own fair hair, distinguished by the dignity
> of his mien and noble expression of his well-formed and regular
> features, advanced out of a circle of military gentlemen and Highland
> Chiefs, by whom he was surrounded. In his easy and graceful manners
> Waverley afterwards thought he could have discovered his high birth
> and rank, although the star on his breast, and the embroidered garter
> at his knee, had not appeared as its indications ... Unaccustomed to
> the address and manners of a polished court, in which Charles was
> eminently skilful, his words and kindness penetrated the heart of our
> hero, and easily outweighed all prudential motives ... and Waverley
> kneeling to Charles Edward, devoted his heart and sword to the
> vindication of his rights!

Other novels repeated this theme. *Lochiel: or the Field of Culloden* (Scott,
1820), similarly presented Charles as a heroic figure clothed in Stuart
tartan: graceful, athletic, with manly looks and frank manner all 'incon-

testable proofs of his Highland origin' (ibid., 158). By this stage Charles's own lack of highland origins was lost in the mists of time.

Queen Victoria followed Scott's line that the monarchy was heir to the Stuarts and shared the sense of pathos and heroic failure attached to the character of Prince Charles Edward Stuart. On a trip to Fort William in 1874 she would record in her journal:

> Yes and I feel a sort of reverence in going over these scenes in this beautiful country, which I am proud to call my own, where there was such devoted loyalty to the family of my ancestors – for Stuart blood is in my veins, and I am now their representative, and the people are as devoted and loyal to me as they were to that unhappy race. (Victoria, 1968, 173)

In an age that favoured monumentality it was not surprising that memorials to the events of the uprisings began to appear. The first was the Glenfinnan Monument. Built in 1815 it commemorates the raising of the prince's standard in August 1745. It was erected by Alexander MacDonald of Glenaladale and consisted of a column with an internal staircase and viewing platform above. A statue of a highlander was added in 1834. It would be the first of many cairns, monuments and statues to be constructed. These and the buildings associated with the Young Pretender's brief sojourn in Scotland would in future become points of interest on highland and Hebridean tours.

Queen Victoria and Balmoral

The word 'Victorian' is often used in connection with matters of fashion and taste, but few aspects of taste received more of a contribution from Victoria herself than the romanticization of highland Scotland. Victoria and Albert helped create the passion for all things highland; indeed, as Harvie (1988, 29) laconically remarked, they 'composed' the Highlands as the first British heritage trail. Strongly influenced by Scott, they had learned 'to praise the beauty of the heather, to prefer the purple hillsides to the Swiss Alps, to find "solitude, romance and wild loveliness" in what they considered to be "the proudest, finest scenery in the world"' (Drabble, 1979, 175). Through Scott's interpretations of history Victoria had also come to see herself as part of the land's history: succeeding to the position achieved by George IV as the focus of both Stuart and Hanoverian loyalties. In due course her love for the Highlands would be popularized by publication of two volumes of her personal journals (Victoria, 1968: see Chapter 5).

Of more immediate impact was the royal couple's acquisition of Balmoral. This came after several successful royal visits to Scotland. The first was for two weeks in August 1842 when Victoria became only the third monarch to have visited since the Act of Union. Throughout their itinerary the couple were swept into a pageant of tradition reminiscent of 1822. Her reaction to the welcome that she received at Taymouth Castle would have been relished by Scott:

> the firing of the guns, the cheering of the great crowd, the pic-
> turesqueness of the dresses, the beauty of the surrounding country,
> with its rich background of wooded hills, altogether formed one of
> the finest scenes imaginable. It seemed as if a great chieftain in older
> feudal times was receiving his sovereign. It was princely and romantic.
> (7 September 1842)

That evening the grounds of the castle were illuminated, bonfires were lit on the hilltops, there were fireworks, the highlanders danced reels, pipes swirled, in the torchlight 'it had a wild and very gay effect'. Further visits in 1844 and 1847 demonstrated the royal couple's growing interest and attachment to Scotland.

In August 1848 Prince Albert bought the lease to the estate of Balmoral in the Dee Valley, Aberdeenshire, followed by the freehold (fee simple) in 1852. There would later be additional purchases of surrounding land, until the estate comprised 50,000 acres with sporting rights on a further 11,750 acres. The reasons for the purchase were an amalgam of different motives. The strongest was the royal couple's captivation with the High-lands and the wish to spend time there on a regular basis. There was also a sense of freedom in being away from the London court, with the possibility for Albert of being able to go hunting. Balmoral itself was favoured because the climate was said to be drier and healthier than other parts of the Highlands. In addition Victoria and Albert developed a sentimental attachment to the look of the land. Albert longed for the mountains and pine forests of his youth; for the valleys, lakes and swift-flowing streams of Thuringia. Deeside, and Balmoral in particular, had enough of these characteristics to be a passable substitute (Plumb and Weldon, 1977, 272).

Victoria and Albert first visited Balmoral in September 1848 within months of their purchase. Thereafter the royal family stayed annually, usually for six weeks in the autumn. After her widowhood Victoria came for longer periods until she was spending four months of the year at Balmoral. Although this was never equalled, successive monarchs kept up the practice of spending part of the late summer or autumn in Scotland.

It quickly transpired that the original house on the Balmoral estate was too small for the royal household and their guests on these extended visits. Prince Albert collaborated with the Scottish architect William Smith to create a new house which blended traditional Scottish baronial with a suggestion of German romanticism. The new house was started in 1852 and the old subsequently demolished. Figure 4.2 shows the new house shortly after completion. Painted by James Cassie RSA, it shows a distant view of the house, with the limp royal standard on the flag-pole showing that the royal family are in occupation. The house nestles in green surroundings with a minimum of created parkland, flanked by bare peaks and hills purple with heather. An angler in the right foreground indicates the sporting connections that the estate offered its new owners. At the same time the Dee is also a barrier that maintains the owners' privacy – the view of the house across the river is roughly that which the many curious sightseers would enjoy from the nearest public thoroughfare.

Victoria and Albert stayed in the new house for the first time in 1856. She wrote in her journal during that year that:

> Every year my heart becomes more fixed in this dear paradise, and so much more so now, that all has become by dearest Albert's own creation, own work, own building, own laying out, as at Osborne, and his great taste, and the impress of his dear hand, have been stamped everywhere.

Albert's creativity extended from the grounds and to the interior of the house. He decorated the Queens's rooms with Royal Stewart tartan on the walls, green Hunting Stewart tartan for the carpets and Dress Stewart for the curtains and upholstery. He also dressed the royal household in Balmoral tartan which he designed. This was based on the red Royal Stewart tartan but with the red replaced by grey to reflect the rugged Grampian peaks (Cheape, 1991).

This idyll came abruptly to an end in 1861. Victoria's mother died and shortly afterwards, at the age of 42, Albert died of typhoid. Immediately the scenes which had been all joy became sources of melancholy and grief. The Scottish landscape was henceforth seen in terms of happier times and remembrance. This was augmented by the sudden death of her servant John Brown in 1883. The preface to the second volume of her highland journal (1884) reflects this change. She described it as a record of her widowed life 'to show how her sad and suffering heart was soothed and cheered by excursions and incidents it recounts, as well as by the simple mountaineers, from whom she learnt many a lesson of resignation and faith, in the pure air and quiet of the beautiful Highlands'. For instance, she was to revisit Taymouth Castle incognito in 1866. She avoided going into the grounds but instead went up to a hill overlooking the house where she gazed down 'not without deep emotion' on the scene of her 'princely' reception twenty-four years before on her first happy visit to Scotland with Albert.

4.2 'Balmoral – HM The Queen's Highland Home' (James Cassie, RSA, 1858).

Conclusion

The purchase of Balmoral was to prove an important catalyst in many respects. It helped fashion a taste among the wealthy and the nobility for the ownership of highland estates and the enjoyment of field sports. It had a significant impact on British taste more generally in the nineteenth century. Some of that influence came through direct commissions. In the area of art, royal patronage favoured certain artists to produce highland vistas and particular scenes associated with Balmoral. For example, Sir Edwin Landseer was commissioned to paint a number of landscapes featuring the royal family. These included 'Queen Victoria Sketching at Loch Laggan' and 'Queen Victoria Meeting the Prince Consort on his Return from Deer Stalking in the Year 1850'. Many others would come to the Highlands looking to paint scenery that clearly had the royal imprimatur. The purchase of Balmoral also seized the imagination of tour promoters who sought to take advantage of new developments in transport to open up the Highlands, and other parts of Scotland, for the first time to a mass tourist market. Discussion of these points, however, necessarily awaits the next chapter.

Scott's phenomenal success during the early- and mid-nineteenth century was not destined to last. For fully half a century his was regarded as the voice that articulated the character of the scenery and society of the Highlands. He harnessed themes of nobility and chivalry and anchored them to a wellspring of sentiment that many in Victorian Britain found irresistible. Large numbers of visitors came to Scotland, especially to the Highlands, to witness the scenes of his novels and to view the countryside through his eyes.

Scott's works are now read and studied far less than Burns, although his decline was less spectacular than Ossian. Yet if Scott's direct impact as a writer and arbiter of tradition has abated, his continuing influence on the depiction of Scotland and the Scottish people was profound. By 1860 it became generally accepted that Scottish scenery was highland scenery (Holloway and Errington, 1978); a view that remained until the present. It was Scott who conflated the highland identity with Scottish identity, peopled the landscape with characters from a mythical past and ensured that visitors would feel that they needed to visit the Highlands to see the 'authentic' Scotland. In a very real sense it was Scott who wrote the script for the promotion of Scottish tourism in the years to come. This point provides an important underpinning to the discussion as we now turn to consider the key role played by the railways in opening up Scotland for the first time to a mass tourist market.

Notes

1. It was closed for three years after the severe flooding of 1834.
2. In passing, it is worth noting that the Clyde saw the launch of the world's first steam-powered ship, in the shape of the 28-ton *Comet*. She entered service on 12 January 1812 but had a short period of operating life, being wrecked in 1820.
3. The problem is that the Pastoral is a concept that is only employed with implicit or explicit reference to an antithetic set of values. 'If it champions the rural ethos, it does so as a corrective to urbanism; if it invokes nostalgia for a vanished culture it is as the antidote to a fascination with modernity' (Smiles, 1986, 11).
4. There are upwards of 180 monuments to Burns worldwide. This far outstrips Shakespeare or any other poet. Apart from royalty or megalomaniac dictators, only Christopher Columbus surpasses Burns in this respect (Mackay, 1992, 688). With regard to the continuing role of literary tourism, it is worth noting that Ayrshire addresses the international audience coming to Scotland in search of the sites connected with Burns's life by producing a Burns Trail that leads visitors on a tour through what is now marketed as 'Burns Country' (see also Chapter 6). Achievable within a day's motoring, the trail takes in Burns's residences and most of the key monuments, museums and interpretive centres in a route that leads from Irvine, through Kilmarnock, Mauchline, Tarbolton, Ayr, Alloway to finish in Kirkoswald.
5. Scott was left liable for debts that Hewitt (1988, 66) estimates as exceeding £120,000.
6. The paper editions of Scott's novels shown in Figure 4.1 were part of a series which totalled 25 paperback novels, priced at only sixpence per issue. It was intended to 'bring these renowned romances in a complete and authorised form within the reach of the entire reading public'. Each novel was published on the first of the month, and cloth cases could be purchased for binding in groups of five, making a five-volume set in all. The preliminary chapters contained romantic or melodramatic 'vignettes drawn by artists of acknowledged reputation' by way of illustration. The end sections were filled out with advertisements for such products as colt skin boots, Frazers sulphur tablets for purifying the blood, Epps's Cocoa, artificial legs and arms, and Black's General Atlas of the World. Such editions ensured that Scott's works continued to reach an ever wider public throughout much of the nineteenth century.
7. It sold 20,000 copies in its first year alone (Lockhart, 1906, 211).
8. The Wordsworths, for example, visited the area twice on their 1803 tour. They noted that a road and two huts had been provided by Lady Perth for the benefit of visitors to Loch Katrine.
9. The book's sub-title was 'or,'tis sixty years since'.
10. Indeed it was so famous that it was the ideal illustration for the book's front cover (see Figure 4.1).
11. Turner also illustrated a collection of Scott's poems in 1833–4.
12. Charles I had visited Scotland in 1633 for a coronation ceremony. Charles II was crowned at Scone in 1651, shortly before his defeat at Worcester and exile in France.
13. The death of Prince Charles Edward Stuart in 1788, followed by that of his

brother Henry in 1807, meant that there were no longer any legitimate heirs of James II.

14. For example, he was guided during the preparations for the royal visit by his friend, Col. David Stewart of Garth. Stewart had founded the Celtic Society of Edinburgh in 1820 to promote use of highland dress and had produced a monograph (Stewart, 1822) claiming that tartan displayed 'the distinctive patterns of the different clans, tribes, families and districts'.

15. There is dispute over how much this was a re-invention. For more on this issue see Bold (1978), Trevor-Roper (1983), McCrone (1992) and Withers (1992). Trevor-Roper (1983) is particularly interesting with regard to the evolution of tartan dress.

16. These came via Deanhaugh House and were given to Sir Walter in 1822.

17. Considerable effort was made to expurgate the originals (Prebble, 1989). A collection of songs was published in 1821 with a version of *Charlie is my Darling* that gave no clue to the fact that the original was sung by a strumpet beckoning the Prince from a window.

CHAPTER FIVE

The coming of the railways

'The scenery's grand, the air, oh! it's charming,
Deeside being famed for excellent farming;
The mountains stupendous, and sweet heathery plains –
Travelling's pleasant, there's well arranged trains.'

Samuel Martin, Hatter, 1866[1]

Railways were not new in the mid-nineteenth century, but their influence on the organization and patterning of everyday life grew as their networks consolidated. Dr Dionysius Lardner (1850) may have harboured strangely misguided ideas about the effects of rail acceleration on the human body, but he was remarkably perceptive when he recognized that 'distances practically diminish in the exact ratio of the speed of personal locomotion'. Journeys that previously were virtually impossible now became practical propositions provided that the destination was near a railway line or a rail head. The impact on tourism in Great Britain and elsewhere was profound.

In this chapter we consider the changes that occurred in Scottish tourism and its promotion during the nineteenth-century heyday of the railway. While accepting that this extended to the First World War or even beyond in some cases, we limit our purview here to the end of Victoria's reign in 1901. In little more than 60 years the tourist map of Scotland would be changed beyond recognition as new destinations became available to an increasingly wide segment of the population. Yet before considering this matter further it is worth commencing by recognizing the continuing significance of media representations of Scotland. As new narrative forms and media appeared so did new areas of scenic and landscape interest.

Changing media

Scotland continued to fuel the literary imagination of the British public throughout the nineteenth century. The influence of Scott remained and was endorsed by the educational establishment and leaders of society including, as we have seen, the royal family. As the century wore on the general tenor of Scott's work would be supplemented by other popular writers who invoked Scottish life and landscape. These included Robert

Louis Stevenson, the group of writers that became known as the 'kailyard' school and, perhaps surprisingly for a reigning monarch, Victoria herself.

There is no doubt that Queen Victoria added considerably to public interest in Scotland by publishing her personal journals describing her life at Balmoral (Victoria, 1968). As we saw in Chapter 4 these contained descriptions of the landscape and her observations concerning highland life and character. The decision to publish this essentially private journal was taken at the instigation of Sir Arthur Phelps (Clerk to the Privy Council). Victoria had shown him extracts on one of his visits to Balmoral, saying that she wanted to produce a book privately for family and intimate friends. Phelps argued that her subjects would like to know how her 'rare moments of leisure were passed in her Highland Home' and that a private publication would only reach the press in a garbled version. Phelps also persuaded the Queen to add to the publication her account of the early visits to Scotland prior to the purchase of Balmoral.

The result was a complete account of the Queen's impressions of the Highlands, published in two volumes: the first covering the period from her first visit in 1842 up to Albert's death in 1861; the second from 1862 up to the sudden illness and death of her favourite servant, John Brown, in 1882. The first volume was the more influential. In spite of a limited vocabulary, the Queen's enthusiasm for the scenery, views and lifestyle of Balmoral clearly emerged. Her writings described expeditions undertaken in all weathers on foot or horseback, with lengthy pauses for spartan picnics and to watch Albert shoot (Drabble, 1985, 1028–9). Avidly consumed by the upper classes, these memoirs helped to create a template about how the wild places of highland Scotland should be consumed. Moreover, with the extension of the railway into Scotland these locations were becoming accessible to her subjects by the time that the first volume was published.

Another for whom the landscape was an important feature was the Edinburgh-born author Robert Louis Stevenson, about whom it has been said that: 'Even his sense of history was topographical' (Hart, 1978, 291). In his books of travel writing, the physical landscape is a prime linking theme in the text. His guidebook and companion to Edinburgh with its elegant pen and ink sketches (e.g. Figure 5.1) provided a powerful evocation of a city that has literally colonized the three main hills of its site (Stevenson, 1889). This trend is even stronger in his novels in which he often sought to weave a story around known sites that had impressed him as suitable places for different types of action.

Kidnapped is a case in point (Stevenson, 1886), a novel with a romantic Jacobite theme. Stevenson follows Scott in providing his novels with topographical description detailed enough to be followed on the ground. The author, for example, painstakingly maps out the cross-country route

The Castle.

5.1   Castle Hill, Edinburgh.

taken by the book's two heroes as they make their way from Loch Linnhe to Edinburgh. That route partly paralleled one made earlier by Bonnie Prince Charlie. Moreover the decision to have the kidnap take place at Queensferry was based on an idea conceived well before he began writing *Kidnapped*. In an earlier essay, Stevenson had observed that:

> 'Some places speak distinctly. Certain dank gardens cry aloud for murder; certain old houses demand to be haunted; certain coasts are set apart for shipwreck ... I have lived at both the Hawes and Burford in a perpetual flutter, on the heels, as it seemed, of some adventure that should justify the place; but though the feeling had me to bed at night and called me again at morning in one unbroken round of pleasure and suspense, nothing befell me in either worth remark. The man or the hour had not yet come; but some day, I think, a boat shall put off from the Queen's Ferry, fraught with a dear cargo ...' (quoted by Daiches and Flower, 1979, 205)

That half-hatched idea would come to fruition with the writing of *Kidnapped*; indeed to some extent it can be said to have dictated what that story should be.

The third literary element which influenced the representation of Scotland in this period was the 'kailyard' school. Literally meaning 'cabbage patch', it takes its name from the words of a popular eighteenth-century song, 'Beside the Bonnie Briar Bush' in which a couplet runs: 'There grows a bonnie briar bush in our kailyard/And white are the blossoms on't in our kailyard' (Hill, 1976, 62). They were best illustrated by the works of writers such as Samuel R. Crockett, *Ian Maclaren* (Rev. Dr. John Watson), and particularly J.M. Barrie with novels such as *A Window in Thrums* (1889). Kailyard literature was essentially anecdotal, often consisting of short stories characterized by sentimentality, whimsicality, caricature, humour and respectability. Domestic concerns feature prominently, as do such settings as the school house, the manse and the doctor's surgery (Shepherd, 1988).

Kailyard novels were based on real places loosely disguised. Thrums, for example, is modelled on the town of Kirriemuir in eastern Scotland, a community set in a landscape transitional between highland and lowland, with mixed farming surrounded by upland moor (Knowles, 1983, 135). Ian Maclaren's *Drumtochty* was based on Logiealmond in Perthshire, the highland parish where he was a Free Church minister. The stories were more evocations of community life than being explicitly about landscape, but these books created an interest in rural small-town Scotland that proved particularly popular in North America.

One reason for their American success was the presence there of Scottish emigrants. The tide of emigration that took place in the first half of the nineteenth century was due primarily to the Highland Clearances, but also reflected the strong trading and migratory links that existed between Glasgow and North America (Aspinwall, 1984). As transatlantic marine communications improved (see next section), visitors came back to Scotland on nostalgic visits. The sentimentality of kailyard writings was readily assimilated into this mode of tourism and people commonly came to look for the places that had inspired the writers of kailyard novels. This interest would continue to draw visitors through into the twentieth century and, indeed, continues to contribute themes for light entertainment until the present day.

Victoria, Stevenson and the kailyard school each added new elements to the representation of Scotland but literary tourism, like other forms of tourism led by élite cultural appreciation of landscape, was already on the wane. The rise of popular culture had begun, with its first major expressions in the visual media. Images of place and landscape were diffused more widely than hitherto. A key development here was the introduction of photography dating from January 1839 when both Daguerre's and William Fox Talbot's inventions were announced (Gernsheim and Gernsheim, 1986, xxvii). Photography was enthusiastically greeted as a pastime and an abiding interest. Households in Victorian Britain had an insatiable demand for landscape photography in this pre-cinematic and televisual age. Quite naturally part of the attraction was to see exotic and distant locations, such as the American West and British colonial possessions. Yet the public also wanted to see scenes from their own country, with many photographers aiming to help their contemporaries 'discover their own land' (Rouillé, 1986, 58).

Various forms of photographic presentation of landscape were offered to the public, including illustrated journals, souvenir views[2] and lantern slides (e.g. Smith, 1983), but the most vivid medium was stereoscopic photography. This was developed in the 1850s, with the new cameras able to use exposures brief enough to take pictures of everyday scenes. The stereoscopic craze started in 1852 and remained a main source of domestic interest until cinema and the new broadcasting media of the twentieth century finally provided the family with alternative sources of entertainment (Langford, 1980). There was an intrinsic appeal in placing a card into a slot in a hand-held or stand-mounted viewer and seeing a view apparently come to three-dimensional life. Demand led to magazines devoted to the subject, such as the *Stereoscopic Magazine*, founded by Lovell Reeve in London in 1858. Each issue had three stereoscopic cards which built up into collectable sets. More important perhaps was the contribution of the London Stereoscopic Company. Founded in 1854 the company coined the slogan, 'No home complete without a stereoscope'. By 1858 it could boast a list of 100,000 different photographs covering architecture, scenery, domestic life, customs and costumes of other nations from around the world.

Its staff photographers and amateurs were to contribute a substantial inventory of Scottish views to their listings, with Highland and Island scenery, Edinburgh and the building of the Tay and Forth Bridges as popular subjects. Figure 5.2 shows two examples of such stereoscopic pictures. Both were views popular with photographers at the time. The upper pair show Loch Katrine in Perthshire, with its strong associations with the writings of Scott. The lower pair show the Loch of Parks in Aberdeenshire, a composition believed to be one of a set taken in July 1856 by Scotland's most famous nineteenth-century photographer, George Washington Wilson of Aberdeen. Though also a portraitist (he was appointed photographer to Her Majesty in Scotland), Wilson's international reputation was due to his landscapes and especially his instantaneous stereoscopic views. His collection of picturesque and historic views of Scotland ran into many thousands of separate images which were sold in the British and international markets. By propagating these images and opening up new areas, Wilson and his company are considered by many (e.g. Keay and Keay, 1994, 983) to have played a key role in the development of Scottish tourism.

The age of steam

These developments brought landscapes of Scotland to the drawing rooms of Victorian Britain. That they and, increasingly people living overseas, were now able to go and see those landscapes for themselves was mediated by dramatic improvements in accessibility. The changes brought by greater availability and reliability of coastal steamer services continued in the second half of the nineteenth century, but were dwarfed in significance by the growth of transcontinental steamship services. Glasgow was the main centre. Passenger lines established after the Napoleonic Wars were augmented by new routes in the 1830s. Tod and McGregor, the Clyde shipbuilders, launched *The City of Glasgow* in 1850 to work the direct route to New York. Developments in marine engine technology in the 1860s and improvements in vessel design boosted the Atlantic trade. Trips that took fourteen days in 1850 took just over five by the end of the century. Fares fell in relative terms and marine safety vastly improved.

These were essential conditions for the growth of the transatlantic tourist trade, since there were a large number of prosperous Scottish expatriates who could be encouraged to 'return home' either for major events such as exhibitions and festivals (see Chapter 9) or simply to visit family haunts. As early as 1872 the Anchor Line was offering cheap package tours to American tourists. Their 3000 agents in America offered Scottish tours which in turn led on to a week in Ireland, London and Paris.

5.2 Stereoscopic photographs.

The price was $475 per person. The newly affluent Americans could overlay pleasure with duty if they wished by: 'visiting the social democratic shrine of Burns, attending a temperance or evangelical congress and inspecting the moral grandeur of Glasgow's municipal government. To many it was a return to the land of their imagination if not of their ancestors' (Aspinwall, 1984, 6).

Domestically the key development was the spread of the railways which had an impact on all aspects of social and economic life. The railways changed the basis of time–distance relations and made possible flows of travellers in numbers beyond anything previously witnessed. In the process they challenged traditional social structures in the host communities and exposed rural areas to currents of modernity and change. Moreover the type of visitor changed dramatically. Hitherto visitors to Scotland came primarily from the upper echelons of society, having the time and means to overcome the problems posed by travel in difficult terrain and conditions. The coming of the railways opened up Scotland to a wider cross-section of the public, as indicated by the cartoon in Figure 5.3.

Naturally, the impact of these changes for any given place depended on its location in relation to the developing rail network. An impression of the growth of that network is conveyed by Figure 5.4, which provides comparative analysis of the Scottish rail networks in 1852 and 1914. In 1852 the system had moved past the stage of disconnected point-to-point lines and was joined to the national network by the arrival of lines at Edinburgh and Glasgow in 1850. Not surprisingly Glasgow and the industrial areas of lowland Scotland were attractive to railway investment and lines proliferated there. To the north and west matters were rather different. Here the network remained partial and disjointed, reflecting the fact that lines were expensive to construct and traffic was likely to be light. The railway had reached Aberdeen in 1850 but there was not yet any connection to Inverness.[3]

By 1914 the network had reached its zenith even though a large number of communities never achieved easy access to the network. At this stage the railways were in the hands of five principal companies: the Great North of Scotland, North British, Caledonian, Glasgow and South Western, and the Highland. The map reveals that many of the gaps had been closed when compared with 1852 but that the network established by the private companies left a legacy of problems. Expensive bridges such as those across the Tay[4] at Dundee (1878) and the Forth Rail Bridge at the Queensferry Narrows (1890) had now been built, allowing more direct communication than in 1852. In the far north and west, railway building had gradually opened up new areas, but development was significantly later than in the rest of the United Kingdom. The line to Oban, for example, only opened in 1880. Main lines in the Highlands operated at

GROWING POPULARITY OF THE HIGHLANDS

Mrs. Smith (of Brixton). " Lor', Mr. Brown, I 'ardly
knoo yer ! Only think of our meetin' *'ere*, this year, instead
of dear old Margit ! An' I suppose that's the costume you
go *salmon-stalking* in ? "

5.3   'Growing popularity of the Highlands'. This *Punch* cartoon shows a couple,
        dressed for a highland holiday, meeting by chance at Inverness station. It
        denotes the shift down the social scale occasioned by railway travel, which
        widened the scope of humour for *Punch* artists, who could add the ignorant
        middle classes to the ignorant upper classes as targets for satire. Note the
        idea of tartan and highland dress.

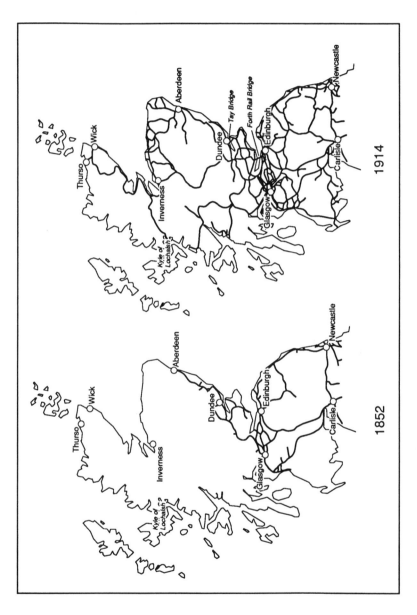

5.4 Comparison of the Scottish railway networks, 1852 and 1914.

the speed of branch lines elsewhere. The Wick–Inverness line had forty intermediate stations, later known locally as the 'Thirty-Nine Stops' (Nicolson, 1975, 118).

There were also the problems caused by the obstructive attitudes of landowners. The spa town of Strathpeffer was *avoided* by an awkward two and a half-mile detour due to the opposition of local landowners led by Sir William Mackenzie, who would not countenance intrusion of his privacy. As a result the Kyle railway had to bypass the only town with a sizeable population on the entire route (Weir, 1971, n.p.). These difficulties were compounded by conflicts stemming from the competing interests of the various private companies. At times this could work to the advantage of the travelling public. The rail races to the north in the late 1880s, which gripped the public imagination, brought savings of nearly three hours in the journey time between London and Edinburgh or Glasgow.[5]

More often the results of inter-company rivalries were adverse, such as when they prevented rational links being built. The 'Waverley Route' from Edinburgh to Carlisle was forced to avoid Langholm and thread its way through the scantily populated hills of the Border country for this reason. Another example was the proposed link down the Great Glen from Inverness to Fort William to take advantage of the favourable topography. Such a development would have meant that travellers could have reached Inverness from the west coast lines via Glasgow and Fort William. Worried at losing some of the stalking, shooting and Strathpeffer traffic destined for north of Inverness to a rival company, the Great North of Scotland Railway successfully managed to campaign for the construction of its own line over the inherently difficult terrain between Aviemore and Inverness. As a consequence the wholly preferable Great Glen route was never approved (Turnock, 1982, 130, 151). At other times landlords clamoured for halts to be built or detours taken to give access to their shooting lodges.

The expensive nature of line construction and associated problems of finance itself led to repeated problems. The Highland Railway ran out of money when building its line to the west coast from Inverness once it had reached Strome Ferry in 1870. The extension to Kyle of Lochalsh had to wait almost thirty years before completion (1897) and then relied on the Government subsidizing the extension; an almost unheard of occurrence in nineteenth-century Britain.

The pursuit of tourists

From the outset tourism was an important element in the economics of Scottish railways outside of the industrial areas, in which respect they assiduously cultivated links with steamer services.[6] Indeed certain towns owed their development to the combination of rail and steamer services. The development of Oban, for example, began in 1814 when the publication of Scott's *Lord of the Isles* had an immediate impact on tourism. The four-day Iona and Staffa tour became established, based on four-oar boats and fishing smacks of eight tons or less (Bone, 1938, 28). Nevertheless Oban still had a population of only around 1500 when the steamers arrived in 1852. These boosted Oban's prosperity and led to construction of the North Esplanade and hotels like the Great Western (1861), yet it was the arrival of the railway in 1880 and the integration of steamer schedules with rail timetables that galvanized the local economy. By the end of the century Oban had a rapidly growing tourist trade and a population of more than 5000. There were 15 large hotels in addition to lodging houses and temperance hotels where people might stay who were 'desirous of securing the comforts of a hotel, without incurring the expense or the obligation of taking intoxicating liquors' (Anon., 1862: 1971, 103).

Much the same story was experienced in the resorts on the Clyde estuary. The coming of the railway fed a steamer network that was 'unsurpassed in British coastal waters for size and quality of service' (Adams, 1978, 117). The result was rapid expansion of seaside resorts such as Rothesay, Ayr and Dunoon as holiday centres and as focal points for touring. The close associations between rail and steamers were also expressed in several branch lines, built to link up with steamer services on lochs, whose traffic was almost entirely composed of tourists. These lines included the Fort William–Fort Augustus branch for the steamer service on Loch Ness and the Dumbarton–Balloch Pier branch which linked up with steamer services on Loch Lomond.[7]

It was not only small towns that benefited from tourist-led growth. Inverness, the largest town in the Highlands, was turned into the major intersection for lines serving the north-east and the west coasts. In the process it became a convenient touring centre for the Highlands and both coasts. Even Edinburgh, ever keen to attract the cultural and literary tourist, was careful to name its chief railway station 'Waverley' in honour of the hero of Scott's most famous book.

The degree to which the railways became active participants in the process of encouraging the growth of tourism varied over time and between different companies. Most companies became involved in running special trains and excursions as early as the 1850s,[8] but the promotion of longer-distance tourism developed rather later. For the most part early promotional work was aimed at tourists already arriving in Scotland who might be encouraged to travel by train to see the scenery or visit resorts to which particular lines gave access. As noted in Chapter 2, this activity was initially piecemeal and unsystematic. By the 1850s line-side track guides and handbooks aimed at railway passengers were appearing but these were mainly written by private authors. A good example was the indefatigable George Anderson of Inverness who, with his son Peter, wrote seven guides for highland scenery and railway lines, many of which ran to multiple editions (Anderson, 1900). Their aim was to provide guides that would be complete 'even in their most remote and sequestered byways' which could be read on the road or in 'the closet or the fireside' (Anderson and Anderson, 1834). An opening portion from their *Handbook to the Inverness and Nairn Railway* (Anderson and Anderson, 1856, n.p.) provides a good indication of the texture and colour of their prose:

> the river Spey, which has ever virtually been the boundary separating the *Celtic mountaineer* from the *Lowland Scot*. The snorting of the 'iron horse' is now being heard on our lone moors and pastoral solitudes; and when the communication by rail is opened up from one end of the kingdom to the other, and men can move rapidly from place to place as members of a thus truly united brotherhood, greatly increased numbers will travel northward, to enjoy our pure bracing air and magnificent scenery. A 'Highland welcome' shall greet them all, and the interchanges of kindly relations and enlightened social intercourse will leave no room for regret at the disappearance of the semi-barbarous state of things which has kept the 'North Countrie' so long in a state of comparative isolation.

In other words, for the Andersons the coming of the railway was two-edged: a welcome source of tourist trade and an equally welcome modernizing influence for the region. The thirty-eight page handbook contained a guide to the sights visible from the train window, with copious footnotes on points of specific interest, fares and timetables. As good Invernessians the authors commend possible extensions of the line, pointing to the good returns likely for prospective shareholders.

With the passage of time the 15-mile long Inverness and Nairn Railway was consolidated into the Highland Railway, a line which now stretched from Perth in the south to Wick and Thurso in the north. By this stage publicity was on a different basis. Mutual self-interest with competitors had been established and publicity contained details of connections and attractions on rivals' lines (albeit those that would require also travelling over Highland Railway routes). The handbook itself became the precursor of the *Handbook to the Highland Railway and West Coast* published in 1890 – a 220-page book with 48-page advertising supplement which retailed for one shilling (Anderson, 1890). Now sponsored by the railway company, the author argues that the line 'certainly very far surpasses in interest and variety that on any like stretch of railway communication in the kingdom' (ibid., 3). There are pen-and-ink sketches of the major sightseeing attractions which would have been similar to those identified in the 1850s, but the text has new features. The new country houses and estates of the gentry are identified as features of interest. There is commentary on the richness of game on the moors and the plentifulness of trout in the streams. Nairn is now billed as 'the Brighton of the North', visited 'in the bathing season ... by thousands of people from all parts of Britain' (ibid., 88). It had recently built an eighteen-hole golf course which was set to become 'one of the most popular courses in Scotland'.

The range of these activities and the boosterism that the text conveys is indicative of the changes in Scottish tourism and the railways' role in those changes. Tourism had now emerged as a major organized activity. Promotional literature such as this guidebook was advertised in the press and would be on sale at certain booksellers in London. Catering for this market meant providing tours and other devices to simplify the task of working out travel arrangements. Hence among the information supplied for the tourist's perusal was a listing of 36 circular tours for which tickets of one-month duration were available. There were advertisements for 89 of the larger hotels in the region, especially those in which the Highland Railway had a stake, as well as general advertisements for whisky, clothing stores, chemists, insurance companies, other railway companies and steamers. Each recognized the patronage of the tourists brought by the railways as an important source of revenue.

Other booklets produced by the Highland served different functions in its promotional policy. One of 144 pages outlined *Holiday Resorts on the Highland Railway* (HR, 1899). Devised in pocket-book format, its cover conveyed symbols of the new leisure pursuits of the upper classes – fishing rods, two salmon, a knapsack, golf clubs and two shotguns. Inside the resorts were listed in alphabetical order with photographs of the more significant ones and suitably glowing descriptions throughout. The opening entry described Aberfeldy (Perthshire) as 'a veritable earthly paradise' for anyone convalescing from illness with its 'scenery of unrivalled grandeur', its air 'both salubrious and bracing' as well as being 'soft and balmy, fragrant with the scent of the birch, alder and hazel; while on either side it comes laden with pure ozone from the mountains'. The entries continued in this vein through to Wick (Caithness-shire) from which 'several most interesting excursions can be made' and which is possessed of a nine-hole golf course 'of a most sporting character'. A special section dealt with 'sporting hotels on or near the Highland Railway' listing the local fishing, principally for salmon and trout, and places for shooting a remarkable range of species that included grouse, wildfowling, rabbits, pigeons, rooks and seals. Many of the illustrations of scenery or buildings were labelled 'amateur snapshot', indicating the possibilities open to keen photographers. Noticeably, there were details about how the reader could reach the Highland Railway's territory from London.

The Highland was not the only line to be engaged in promotional activity. The North British Railway and West Highland Railway produced their *Official Tourist Guide to Scotland* (Melven, 1896), priced sixpence. Its author stated that 'in the selection of facts to be stated, the greatest discrimination has been used'. Intended as a pocket companion, it provided details of touring agendas carefully constructed to maximize travel over North British metals but was willing to give brief mention to rivals and the attractions that they offered. The Highland Railway's 'veritable earthly paradise' of Aberfeldy was here something rather less. It was described as 'a deep wooded dell' that had connections with Burns, a monument to the foundation of the Black Watch regiment and possessed the 'large Breadalbane mills ... famous for their manufactures of homespun'. Comments on the town's air quality, so important in the Highland Railway's version, went unreported.

Official guides also went beyond the provision of lineside commentaries and listings of attractions, hotels and circular tours. The West Highland Railway produced an elegant guide to the sights along its line accompanied by 230 drawings entitled *Mountain, Moor and Loch* (WHR, 1894). It was intended more for home reading in preparation for touring or as a souvenir than as a travelling companion and lacks the advertising so often a feature of the genre. It was a publication with an interesting history. Although no authors are cited, it was first produced under the supervision of Sir Arthur Phelps and dedicated to Queen Victoria (Phelps, 1869). Originally its contents were paintings rendered in unnatural colours so that, when reproduced in sepia tones, its illustrations would look more realistic than photographs. They were intended to illustrate the Queen's publication of *Our Life in the Highlands* (Victoria, 1968).[9] In this rendition the illustrations were replicated to illustrate scenes on the West Highland Railway's route alongside newer specially-commissioned pen-and-ink sketches. The reprinting of a thoughtful essay on Scottish scenery by the Queen's chaplain, the Reverend Norman Macleod, sits uncomfortably with the text supplied by the later anonymous copy-writer who indulged in unremitting tartanry to accompany his lineside commentaries.[10]

Significantly, too, the lines from London were producing books and brochures on Scotland for sales to their customers in England. Passengers at London's Euston Station could obtain copies of the *West Coast Tourist Guide* issued jointly by the London and North-Western Railway and the Caledonian Railway (LNWR & CR, 1886 et seq.). Along the road at King's Cross, the prospective tourist could buy the Great Northern and North Eastern Railway's *Tourist Programme* (GN & NER, 1895). Laid out as a travelogue it dealt with the scenery in a standard manner, but also pointed the reader to the merits of the newly-opened Forth Rail Bridge. Given that these railways themselves operated trains across the bridge, the author was happy to dwell on this additional element of sightseeing interest which was described as 'the latest triumph of engineering, which justly takes rank as the greatest structural work ever carried out by human agency' (ibid., 41).

Collectively these and many other brochures, pamphlets and travelogues represented just a small part of an emerging promotional industry intended to boost tourist traffic to Scotland from other parts of Great Britain. They also signified a defining moment in Scottish tourism. Promotion had become a routine activity, but promotional materials were now anonymous publications emanating from the publicity departments of railway companies or from specialist firms of travel-book publishers. Increasingly these would fill the place once occupied by volumes of Scott or Ossian.

Organized travel

While the railways opened up the prospects for movements of large numbers of people for the first time, it was a private entrepreneur, Thomas Cook, who demonstrated how they could be organized into parties for escorted tours or excursions. Cook had organized the first railway excursion, carrying over 500 people from Leicester to Loughborough to attend a temperance rally on 5 July 1841. Having negotiated a return fare of only one shilling per person, he demonstrated the economics involved when large numbers of people are encouraged to travel together as a party. The application of these same principles would lead to Cook being credited with the creation of popular tourism in Scotland, although equally Scottish tourism made the fortune of Thomas Cook (Brandon, 1991, 38).

The first Scottish tours began in 1846.[11] Cook had travelled the area extensively beforehand to work out the best route and pricing. The offer was for an 800-mile round trip from Leicester, with a charge of one guinea.[12] His invitation (quoted in Cook, 1866, 18) to join the party was couched in language that could have been written by Scott. The trip was not just to see the wonders of Scotland, those were seemingly taken for granted, but also to cement national unity:

> No laboured description of natural beauties – no far-fetched historical notices, are required to invest a Trip to Scotland with popularity. The Piper who has played in our streets, the tales we learnt in childhood, the historical associations of 'Nature's Poet' … the cheap literature of the Messrs. Chambers and others, the intermixture of Caledonians and Saxons, by commercial and matrimonial ties – in a word, the close affinity of Englishmen and Scotchmen, governed by the same laws, under the same throne, speaking the same language, sympathising with each other in religion and politics – all these circumstances, and hundreds more which might be recorded, have familiarized us with Scotland, Scottish history, Scottish scenery, until we feel that we are

one with her sons and daughters; and it cannot excite surprise that
the bare announcement of this trip should have created an intensity
of interest perfectly unparalleled in the history of Pleasure Trips.

In the event 500 people bought tickets. The handbook that was issued
gave details of the route: Leicester to Fleetwood by train, Fleetwood to
Ardrossan by steamer, and Ardrossan to Glasgow and Edinburgh by train.
Contemporary reports of the difficulties experienced on the journey by
Cook's 'tourists' testify to the problems of organizing travel at this time.
These included the absence of toilet and refreshment facilities on trains,
over-booking, a lack of cabins on the Fleetwood steamer and a severe
storm en route (Brandon, 1991, 39–40).

Two further trips took place in 1847, with a west coast trip as before
and a new east coast route using the railway, but there were no Scottish
tours in 1848 due to withdrawal of cooperation by the railway companies,
who wanted to organize the tours themselves. The tours recommenced
in 1849. Nevertheless in the short term the unreliable nature of the early
railways' timekeeping, the hazards of using steamers and continuing
problems of cooperation from the various railway companies all gave
problems. Cook invested time and effort to perfecting the Scottish tours.
From 1846 to 1860 (with the exception of the Great Exhibition year of
1851) he spent two months annually 'conducting parties to and through
Scotland and extending the area of my plans as fast as the opening of railways, and other facilities of travelling, would enable me to do so' (Cook,
1866, 106). By the next time that lack of cooperation with the railways
occurred in 1862–5,[13] it was possible to find alternative strategies to keep
the tours running.

In 1866 Cook boasted that he could provide transport over 2000 miles
of railway, steamboat and coach roads in pursuit of his aim: 'to settle,
cheapen, define, provide tickets for all sorts of conveyances, and to cause
the Tourist Ticket to be a passport to respectful treatment everywhere'
(ibid., 122). During the first twenty years, 40,000 visitors went to Scotland
on Cook's special trains; by no means enormous numbers in themselves
but a major increase on anything seen previously. Of these, 4000 had been
on Cook's conducted tours of the Western islands and 10,000 on the Loch
Lomond steamers. By combining train, coaches and steamer, Cook
managed to convey travellers to all the key tourist destinations over a
period of two weeks.

The company was assisted in this achievement by the greater reliability
of railway timetables and the consolidation of lines into networks in which
inter-company cooperation steadily improved, but it also reflected the
complementarity of transport media. The railways dominated transport
opportunities for long-distance travel in Scotland just as they did in
England. Complementarity between media, particularly with the steamer

network, was rather better north of the border. Indeed Thomas Cook and Son's great achievement was to exploit the possible interlinkages between rail, road and steamer transport long before the motor age itself; a point to which we return in the next chapter.

Thomas Cook's company distinguished between two types of traveller in its arrangements and charging policies. 'Excursionists' were those who went on escorted tours. They received the benefit of very cheap rates but had only a fixed number of days, limited use of trains and little flexibility in what they chose to do. By contrast, 'Tourists', who were charged higher rates, went unescorted. They had a choice of trains and could renew their tickets at no further expense if they wished to extend their tour by remaining in a particular district for a longer time. Excursionists were sometimes the object of scorn, but their presence symbolized a major step on the road towards mass participation in tourism. As a highland steamship captain remarked:

> I have seen a great change in the character of our traffic. For a long time, we had few except the wealthy, many of whom came thousands of miles ... to see the wonders of Fingal's Cave, and the interesting island of Iona. But now I see large numbers of the middle and humbler classes of society coming out this way, and they will constitute the sources of future success to the proprietors of these boats. (quoted by Cook, 1866, 27)

The itineraries made a feature of locations popularized by Scott. Cook's Tours drew very heavily on Scott in their promotional literature, with the expectation that visitors were also well versed in Scott's work. A tour that Cook arranged in the 1850s took a school party of 32 young ladies through the Trossachs: 'but what was most pleasing, was to see their eagerness in quoting lines from "The Lady of the Lake", assisting each other to mark the spots celebrated in History, and their pencils continually jotting down' (Cook, 1866, 120). Gradually the range of itineraries changed as new attractions appeared. Thomas Cook's were centrally involved in arranging travel to the Great Exhibitions in London, Paris, Glasgow and Edinburgh and short tours for people attending those exhibitions (see Chapter 9). Cook tried to put Balmoral on his tourist map as early as 1854. Initially he had no success, but a viewing stop soon became a regular part of the itinerary. By 1859 during one of Cook's escorted tours, the party pulled up opposite Balmoral Castle at 7.30 am. At this point the national anthem was sung and one tourist, using opera glasses, claimed to see Prince Albert at a window in a night cap (Brandon, 1991).

Despite the widening range of attractions and the decline in Scott's literary influence, the modes of representing Scotland in Thomas Cook's publicity material remained much the same. The company's brochure *Cook's Tours in Scotland* in 1901 still described Scotland as the 'land of

the mountain and the flood', a line from Scott's *Lay of the Last Minstrel*
– although how many visitors would still have known the phrase's
authorship is open to doubt. Its cover (Figure 5.5) was the first to have
used photographs rather than engravings, but whatever impression of
modernity this strategy may have lent the brochure, the landscape imagery
contained there remained much as before. Two of the three pictures
identified scenes closely associated with Scott. The first depicts the Scott
Memorial in Edinburgh, with an almost deserted Princes Street and the
hazy outline of the castle in the background. The middle picture was a
picturesque view of a loch and a mountainside framed with trees.
Representing the essence of highland Scotland, the photograph shows
Loch Katrine, which was still part of one of Cook's most popular tours.
The final picture was of the isle of Staffa, although now with more
resonances of Mendelssohn than Ossian.

Hobbyists

At the same time as allowing large numbers to travel in guided tours, the
railways brought greater opportunity for the independent traveller to
roam freely in the remoter parts of Scotland. They were assisted in this
activity by a growing array of guidebooks and pocket companions. The
Edinburgh firm of A. and C. Black and the London-based firm of Ward
and Lock produced 'picturesque guides' to Scottish towns and landscapes
(e.g. Anon., 1859; Anon., 1880). A further guidebook, *The Tourist's
Handy Guide to Scotland* (Anon., 1872), was published in Prince's Street
(Edinburgh) and mapped out an uncompromising boosterist approach in
its advocacy. Its author noted that any tourist would 'on their coming to
Scotland, regard Edinburgh as the first place to be visited, at once on its
own account, as a centre for places near it, and as the best starting-point
for any extensive tour' (ibid., iii). Edinburgh was the focus for extensive
perambulation and admiration. It was also the centre from which one
departed for picturesque tours to Oban and Staffa, to Aberdeen and
Braemar, and to the Borders. Glasgow, Edinburgh's larger rival, was quite
another matter. The itinerary for a visit to Glasgow is rent with damnation
by feint praise:

> all of the central and southern portions of the city, out even to
> the environs, have only close views full of smoke and turmoil. The
> thoroughfares, in general, are well-aligned and well-built; they
> include in the western parts, many splendid streets, terraces and
> crescents, with intermixtures of open ornamental areas; and, but for
> the predominance of murkiness and uproar, would compare advan-
> tageously with those of the most admired modern cities in the world.
> Yet they materially suffer in the effect, on one side from crowds of

5.5   *Cook's Tours in Scotland.*

factories with a forest of chimney-stalks, on another side from a profuse display of showy, excessive, unaesthetic decoration. The city on the whole is greatly more attractive to mercantile and commercial gentlemen than to tourists; but, nevertheless contains not a few objects of high interest to all intelligent strangers.

There was also greater possibility for tourists to pursue hobbies or interests. The upper classes added new leisure and sporting pursuits to the old pleasures of literary tourism or simply travelling for its own sake. These new interests included deer stalking, shooting of managed game birds (particularly red grouse), fishing, mountaineering, playing golf and photography. By their very nature these were pursuits for those with the time and means to indulge in them. The numbers actually involved in such activities were small even compared with the relatively modest numbers found on organized tours. Shooting parties for grouse could run up to several dozen, but the capacity of a deer forest running into thousands of acres might only be a handful of sportsmen. Photographers, anglers, walkers and others tended to seek solitude rather than congregate at specific points.

However, their influence in a localized sense could be considerable. Deer stalking reshaped the landscape and regional economy of large areas of the Highlands and Islands. Expansion of hobbyist tourism also produced distinctive patterns of seasonal migration to Scotland. Hunting parties in particular laid a heavy burden on the Scottish railways. In late Victorian times it was possible for sportsmen or other visitors to engage private saloon carriages for their families and servants; there was no extra charge other than the obligation to take at least eight tickets (of which four would need to be first class), or alternatively twelve third-class tickets (Nock, 1950, 31). Saloons, horse boxes, regular through coaches, sleeping cars, carriage trucks would be mixed indiscriminately. On the problems of handling such mixed trains at Perth and Waverley, prior to the latter's rebuilding, Professor Foxwell (1889: quoted Nock, 1950, 32) noted:

> On the platforms of the Waverley Station at Edinburgh may be witnessed every evening in summer a scene of confusion so chaotic that a sober description of it is incredible to those who have not themselves survived it. Trains of caravan length come in portentously late from Perth, so that each is mistaken for its successor; those have to be broken up and remade on insufficient sidings, while bewildered crowds of tourists sway up and down amongst equally bewildered porters on the narrow village platform reserved for those important expresses ...

Hobbyist tourism came in many varieties. Some built on activities that already existed in Scotland. Golf, for example, had emerged in Scotland by the fifteenth century at the latest, with St Andrew's as its major centre.

The game developed primarily on 'links' courses built on sand dunes near the sea, using the natural contours of the land to create hazards and elements of difficulty. As Table 5.1 shows, there were already 22 clubs catering for golfers in 1850 (compared with only two in England). The advent of the railway and other transport media was the catalyst for the proliferation seen in the years 1880–1902 (Lewis, 1993, 266). This remarkable expansion was not solely the product of tourism; there was also a strong domestic upsurge throughout Great Britain in the popularity of the game (as witnessed by the English figures). Nevertheless golf was regarded as part of the package that visitors looked for when coming to Scotland. Each town, as with the example of Nairn (see above), strove to have its own course and to promote the special challenges that it posed to the discerning golfer.

Table 5.1   Golf clubs in Scotland and England

	Scotland	England
1850	22	2
1870	50	9
1880	84	21
1888	164	31
1893	301	356
1902	606	751

Source: Lewis (1993, 266)

Other forms of hobbyist tourism involved activities that had little previous existence before the nineteenth century. One notable example was mountaineering. The challenge posed by peaks in the Cuillins of Skye and the far north-west started to attract climbers in the 1880s. The efforts of climbers such as W.W. Naismith, in the Ben Nevis range, and Norman Collie and John Mackenzie in the Cuillins opened up most of the standard rock climbs. The accounts of their climbs and recommendations about possible routes were avidly devoured by other climbers and by hill walkers looking for different experiences. As the highest peak in Great Britain, Ben Nevis proved particularly attractive. In 1883 a pony track was constructed up to an observatory near the summit, which greatly assisted the climb. When the railway reached Fort William in 1894, the summit became a prime goal for increasing numbers of tourists (Weir, n.d.).

While the mass tourist market centred on the well-known scenic spots and resorts, golf, mountaineering and other activities helped to reshape patterns of tourism for the upper classes. Each, as noted above, produced different seasonal migrations of devotees to Scotland and equally made different demands upon the land and on the local economy. To illustrate the nature and implications of that point more fully, it is instructive to examine two fields of hobbyist tourism which acted upon the landscape in very different ways: photography and the field sport of deer stalking.

Photography

Scotland became extremely popular with landscape photographers from 1850 onwards. More than any other European country it 'seems to have been able to inspire loyalty among photographers for whom the prospect of packing their equipment and heading for the Highlands at the first sign of favourable weather was to take on a peculiarly addictive quality' (McKenzie, 1992, 20). The notion of undertaking a 'photographic tour', alone or with a few companions, became popular with enthusiastic photographers in Britain among whom landscape photography was particularly popular.[14] Photographic tours, however, were concerned with more than just recording scenery. As McKenzie (1992, 20) explained:

> a 'Photographic Tour' involves a special relationship between the condition of being mobile and the activity of translating perceptions into pictures. From the point of view of a photographer, this can take on a quality of genuine exploration, an unfolding of personal experience chronicled through the progressive revelation of a land and its culture.

Not surprisingly those engaged in photographic tours were affluent. They needed to have the resources to indulge their passion, which could involve absences of up to several months and the hiring of assistants where necessary. Although the railways were willing to assist with the transfer of heavy baggage, plate cameras with their associated impedimenta were unwieldy and far from easily portable, despite the bland assurances of writers of photographic manuals (e.g. Otté, 1858). Indeed part of the challenge of the enterprise lay in the task of transporting the equipment to the chosen site and getting it to work once there.

The rewards were varied. Some found photography to be a powerful new medium to enhance their own awareness and appreciation of landscape. Others saw themselves using photography to compile antiquarian records, charting for posterity the buildings and way of life of traditional Scotland before they yielded to change. In 1890 the Scottish Photographic Society was formed with the specific aim of taking photographs to provide a record of places (Walsh, 1992, 71). There were also several different markets available to those with commercial motives, including the stereoscopic or souvenir view markets mentioned earlier.

For all, however, there was the sense of being pioneers; a feeling that persisted, despite the fact that many went to sites to replicate photographs that they had seen elsewhere. This stemmed from the way that photographic tourists were organized. They did not come to Scotland in the manner of Cook's tourists, but as individuals who communicated through clubs and interest groups and who, above all, saw the work of other photographers. The revelation of particular views or angles in the photographs of one person led others to visit the site and try to recapture that vision. Standardized views resulted, just as had been the case with tourists seeking to find the appropriate points from which to view picturesque landscape or to relive the setting of a novelist's fictional narrative.

New 'clusters of interest' appeared, one of the most important of which was the Border country, particularly its abbeys. William Fox Talbot had himself undertaken a series of photographs of the ruined Melrose Abbey in his *Sun Pictures in Scotland* (1845). Given that the Abbey had associations with Scott's atmospheric poem *The Lay of the Last Minstrel*, Melrose became possibly the country's most frequently photographed monument (McKenzie, 1992, 21). Other 'clusters' included the Trossachs and the Clyde estuary (including Loch Lomond and the west coast).

Deer stalking

Although the attraction of photography may have been analogous to the thrill of hunting without the bloodshed (McKenzie, 1992, 23), there was one important difference. Photographic tourism may have directed visitors to particular clusters of points, but it imposed little real pressure on the land. Deer stalking was a quite different proposition, with great implications for the use and ownership of land. At the outset it should be stressed that deer stalking was not a traditional activity. In the sixteenth century red deer were hunted by royalty and the landed gentry using stag hounds and horses. With the union of the Scottish crowns and the departure of James VI to London, the custodial rights of proprietors over the deer parks had gradually evolved into ownership. During the eighteenth century interest in this occasional pursuit waned. The last traditional hunt was organized by Lord Atholl in 1800, by which time only seven deer forests remained in Scotland (Orr, 1982).

When a revival took place in the 1830s it was in a form that had never been part of the culture of the area. Deer stalking involved shooting animals that had been followed on foot rather than hunted with hounds. It stressed the values of sportsmanship in a contest between animal and hunter in the open, not driving stags into confined spaces. Rather than an occasional recreational pastime of killing deer to supply venison as well as sport, the desire to stalk was related particularly to obtaining hunting trophies (the head and antlers rather than the meat).

Deer stalking was now organized as a commercial activity. The right to hunt became a commodity which could be sold or leased for profit, with the first letting taking place in 1800 (O'Dell and Walton, 1962, 332). Game animals, previously regarded as wild nature, were now viewed as an asset to be carefully managed. As deer stalking became commercially more attractive, so landlords reorganized their estates to increase the amount and suitability of terrain available to sportsmen. Many highland estates that had been cleared to make way for sheep readily switched to deer forests. Subdivision of estates into manageable sporting units was also common. The Duke of Atholl divided his estate into seven such sections in 1833, a development which also involved investment in building six lodges and constructing access roads and paths.

The popularity of deer stalking was spread by various writers' reflections on the sporting life on Scottish estates. One of the earliest and most influential was William Scrope's *The Art of Deer Stalking* (1838), the first book to deal with the subject in anything approaching its modern form. A keen angler (Scrope, 1843) as well as stalker, Scrope had rented a deer forest from the Duke of Atholl in 1822. This book dealt with his experience, describing in the most eulogistic terms the quality of stalking on the Atholl and Glen Bruar estates. Its influence on the subsequent behaviour of the upper classes was profound, partly because it propagated the appeal of deer stalking, but also because it created a genre. Henceforth many others would go deer stalking, or participate in other types of field sport, and feel impelled to experience the landscape in the same manner, similarly recording their memoirs as streams of reflection on sport, nature and life (e.g. Crealock, 1892; Grimble, 1896; Thornton, 1896). Such books were a staple of the English country house library.

Deer-Stalking in the Highlands of Scotland by Lieutenant-General Henry Hope Crealock (1892) provides a representative example. Reflecting on his experience of stalking on twenty different Highland and Island estates, he outlined his belief that no 'truer sport' could be found anywhere than deer stalking on the open hillside of the mountains of Scotland (ibid., 1). He noted without disparagement that the first action of those acquiring money was to purchase a deer forest since 'thrice happy is the man who is thus enabled to share the results of his good fortune with so many who cannot afford such pleasures themselves'. The book comprises many vignettes of hunting in the open, the thrill of the stealthy chase, camaraderie, the vagaries and glories of the weather, grudging mutterings about the antics of servants and ghillies and wonder at the scenery. Stalking allows the participant to enjoy: 'the health and enjoyment produced by strong exercise in an invigorating climate, rendered all the more fascinating from the wild and varied beauties of the scenery and freedom associated with it'. It was a pastime for individuals with discernment and taste. At the same time Crealock was uncompromising in his view that deer stalking was a civilizing force. He claimed that the remote localities where it was practised gained both from the culture brought by sportsmen and the money that they contributed to the local economy. Many were the locals, he added, who had been rescued from 'semi-barbarity' in this way.[15]

With greater participation came more organization. From 1835 onwards, for example, Hugh Snowie (an Inverness gunmaker) acted as agent for the estate owners and became the 'pivot of the developing moor-letting business' (O'Dell and Walton, 1962, 332). Each year he visited London during May and June to supply information about the conditions of deer forests and grouse moors. This was consolidated into an annual list in 1837, the first of which contained eight shootings to let.[16] The final seal of approval was given by Victoria and Albert. They both participated in deer stalking on their visits to Scotland in 1842 and 1844 (see Chapter 4) and it was one of their favourite pastimes while at Balmoral. The Queen's interest encouraged female as well as male members of the aristocracy to take up the sport (Orr, 1982, 29).

Enthusiasm was not limited to leasing estates during the season. English nobility with no previous highland connections clamoured for sporting estates, with at least fourteen new deer forests created in the 1840s. Another fourteen were created between 1850 and 1859 and nine more between 1860 and 1869. The expansion continued into the twentieth century. Helped by agricultural depression hitting meat and wool prices, landowners increasingly looked to deer forests as a lucrative and reliable land use (since returns were not subject to the same fluctuations as other activities). By 1912 the amount of land devoted to deer forest reached its peak of 3.58 million acres (O'Dell and Walton, 1962).

The reason for the demand was the high social prestige attached to deer stalking. English and American industrialists competed with the aristocracy in their willingness to pay very high prices for shooting rights. To participate in Scottish deer stalking was to assert one's wealth and social standing. It was also a profound expression of the class system. Some estates operated such social exclusivity that industrialists or non-aristocratic sportsmen were discouraged. Other estates offered stalking by the day, advertising their list of tariffs (e.g. hire charges for ghillies) in handbooks published by the railways and others (see above). For an activity favoured by royalty and nobility, such estates would have been viewed with undisguised disdain.

As ever in late Victorian Britain, *Punch* magazine combined humorous observation with patrician condescension in its assessment of the situation. It took great delight in portraying the English sportsman in Scotland as an ignorant buffoon, frequently outwitted by the game that he came to shoot, the landscape in which he floundered or the long-suffering ghillie whom he had hired. Figure 5.6 shows one example of this preoccupation.

Conclusion

Deer stalking was only one among many field sports that developed in the second half of the nineteenth century. Grouse moors would become increasingly popular, particularly into the twentieth century, because they provided sport for more guns, had a longer shooting season and were better suited to syndicates. There were also estates where a wide range of other birds were shot, including blackcock, ptarmigan, capercailzie, pheasants and snipe as well as wildfowl. The rivers too became a valuable commodity. Fishing rights were bought and sold. A network of angling and fishing hotels were built along the Tweed system in the south and in more remote parts of the Highlands and Islands. These different activities did not necessarily draw upon mutually exclusive groups. Many coming in search of field sports undertook tours in which they mixed together stalking, hunting, shooting and fishing, subject only to the dictates of predilection, season and personal circumstances.

The key notion to emerge here is diversification. As the nineteenth century progressed the market for tourism changed along with increasing participation. Instead of a small flow of affluent and leisured upper-class visitors coming to Scotland clutching their volumes of Ossian and reading aloud from Scott, there were now tour parties of middle-class visitors being whisked round the sights. Keeping their distance, social as well as physical, were the upper-class travellers journeying in pursuit of their many new interests in ever remoter parts of rural Scotland. Rural, and notably highland, Scotland in particular had become a playground for the rich and powerful, with the ownership or leasing of sporting estates providing the setting for fixtures on the social calendar. Yet despite the changes in tourism, there was little change in the representation of Scotland to the tourist. The notions created and codified by Scott, continued by Stevenson and others, propagated by countless guidebook writers and given the royal stamp of approval by Queen Victoria became the basis of the rhetoric used by the railway companies, Thomas Cook and other promoters of tourism.

These patterns and trends continued into the twentieth century. Just as the organized traveller would gradually be weaned away from the standard itinerary to look at new sights and localities, so the hobbyist would be encouraged to diversify further. The sportsmen, climbers and photographers would be joined by walkers, hikers, skiers, canoeists, yachtsmen, cyclists and, of course, motorists. Each group would look for

SEPTEMBER 1, 1888.]   PUNCH, OR THE LO

A LITTLE HOLIDAY IN SCOTLAND.

Energetic Friend. "NOW, JACK, STOP WHERE YOU ARE, AND YOU'LL GET A SPLENDID SHOT IN HALF-AN-HOUR OR SO!"

[*Jack is thinking that by that time it will be dark, and then what's to be done?*

5.6 'A Little Holiday in Scotland'.

different things, but many were united in seeking engagement with areas that would be portrayed by those who promoted Scotland as being far-away, traditional, authentic and offering solitude. These are themes to which we return in the next chapter.

Notes

1. An advertisement quoted in Farr (1968, 11).
2. These were the forerunners of postcards as we now know them. Sold at over 2000 establishments nationally, souvenir cards could be sent at half-rate through the post provided that there was only an address on the back. The leading purveyors were the Frith family of Derbyshire. Their coverage of the Border country in Scotland was comprehensive, but they only offered patchy coverage of the Highlands – e.g. Oban, Inverness, Perth, Callander, Braemar, Nairn and Inverness (Automobile Association, 1991).
3. The railway first reached Inverness in 1858, with an alternative route via Perth opening in 1863.
4. There were to be two bridges over the Tay, since the first collapsed in 1879. The second was opened in 1887.
5. Speeds and time savings were subsequently reduced on safety grounds.
6. The cooperation between railways and steamer services was remarkable given that there was far less railway company ownership of steamship lines than in England.
7. This could also form part of a round trip from Glasgow and the Trossachs.
8. Within a week of the opening of the first section of the Royal Deeside line in 1853, the railway company and the Aberdeen Temperance Society had chartered excursions from Aberdeen to Banchory. For the cost of one shilling-and-sixpence first class or one shilling third class, the public could leave Aberdeen at 11 am and have over seven hours in Banchory before the scheduled return to Aberdeen. In 1854 the programme for excursion trains included outings to coincide with the local Holiday in July and the newly-founded Banochry Annual Gathering and Games (see Chapter 4).
9. It was also published in an enormous format of roughly 70 centimetres by 40 centimetres between wooden covers.
10. The history of how this text, linked with the royal family, came to be freely cannibalized by the West Highland Railway is something that has defied further research.
11. Cook only organized day-excursions until 1845, when he ran his first tour to Wales.
12. Equivalent to one pound one shilling.
13. One direct consequence was a stimulus to Cook who began to run tours to the Alps.
14. Gernsheim and Gernsheim (1986, 50) argued that 'landscape photography was a field in which the British particularly excelled (as they had in watercolour views)'.
15. Crealock also mounted an impassioned plea in defence of deer stalking against those who might 'agitate' against deer forests and the system of land tenure that produced them. The expression of this argument and its

ideological overtones, however, are matters that are left to Chapter 7, with its discussion of interpretation of the highland land question.

16. The lineal descendant of Hugh Snowie's listing, *The Scottish Register* had grown to over 400 pages by the early twentieth century (e.g. WFS, 1914). It listed deer forests, grouse moors, mixed shootings as well as all manner of fishing. An accompanying form asked potential purchasers or lessees to write to the agents if they could not find what they wanted, with criteria such as how many brace of grouse they wished to bag in a day's shooting.

CHAPTER SIX

The rhetoric of the open road

> '"Glorious, stirring sight!" murmured Toad, never offering to move.
> "The poetry of motion! The *real* way to travel! The *only* way to travel!
> Here to-day – in next week to-morrow! Villages skipped, towns and
> cities jumped – always somebody else's horizon! O bliss! O poop–
> poop! O my! O my!"'
>
> Kenneth Grahame, *The Wind in the Willows*

If the nineteenth century was the era of the steam engine, then the twentieth century has most assuredly been the age of the internal combustion engine. While the railways and steamship lines have steadily declined in significance, road transport has transformed the shape and character of Scottish tourism. The motor bus, coach, the motorcycle and the car have allowed tourists to reach even the remotest areas of the Highlands and Islands. They have boosted participation in tourism to Scotland, although in the process often irrevocably changing the character of Scottish towns and cities. Road transport, and particularly the private car, also represent powerful symbols of personal mobility and freedom which progressively have become available to a wider segment of the community.

Figure 6.1 encapsulates many of these elements. It was a photograph that appeared in a guide to countryside appreciation entitled *The Countryside Companion* (Stephenson, 1946). Printed on a coarse paper that is itself indicative of the austere times in which the book was published, its primary discourse is to illustrate the joys of caravanning. A tourist caravan is parked at a remote point in a sunlit highland glen, perhaps so that its occupants can admire the solitude and the view of the distant hills. The single track road, rutted by the marks of tracks of previous vehicles, winds away into the middle distance indicating the way ahead. As it is a four-berth caravan it is likely that the car contains a family group. A woman, probably the materfamilias, is about to get back into the front passenger seat as they prepare to move on again. They come and go as they please. As the original caption noted: 'Among the Hills – amid the lonely grandeur of the Highlands a trailer caravan provides a most useful mobile home, obviating the nightly quest for accommodation.'

The secondary discourse in this photograph needs to be seen against the background of the times in which *The Countryside Companion* was published. The first faltering steps were being taken to re-establish travel

AMONG THE HILLS

Amid the lonely grandeur of the Highlands a trailer caravan provides a most useful mobile home, obviating the nightly quest for accommodation.

HUTCHINGS CARAVANS

6.1   The rhetoric of the open road.

and tourism after six years of war. The photograph evokes the joys of driving in Scotland during the golden age of motoring in the interwar period. This was frontier country: lonely, wild and grand. The roads may have been narrow and the accommodation scarce, but there were few cars on the road and few restrictions on where they could go or park. The caravan, and the car which towed it, were powerful symbols of freedom and choice.

Underpinning this discourse was a rhetoric that was the meeting point of two separate ideologies. One was mirrored in the views and writings of Tom Stephenson, the editor of *The Countryside Companion*. Stephenson was a lover of mountain and moorland and a veteran of both the National Parks movement and the Ramblers' Association.[1] In particular he loved wild, open and deserted countryside such as Sutherland and the Cuillins of Skye. Despite the intrusion of the machine into wild nature, the car, the motorcycle and, arguably, the motor coach were the means to an end. They represented a chance for people to reach places where they could stand outside the everyday world and experience peace, tranquillity and solitude of mountain and moor.

The other ideological influence is conveyed by the fact that Figure 6.1 originated as an official photograph used by Hutchings, the caravan manufacturers, in their sales catalogues. It was intended to show the versatility and reliability of the caravan in even the most difficult terrains. In doing so the manufacturers were able to attach their sales pitch to the rhetoric of 'the open road', which was propagated by motor manufacturers, petrol companies and tourist promotional agencies alike. Vehicles speeding along empty roads, sports cars with their tops down, motorcycles breasting the tops of hills, caravans stopping where their owners pleased – all expressed the same theme. The open road, the endless highway stretching onwards to the horizon offered a path towards pleasurable discovery and understanding. Travel, exploration and personal encounter with wild nature, the rhetoric suggested, were key parts of the tourist experience.

This rhetoric provides a linking theme in this chapter, which continues the account through into the twentieth century. It aims to examine trends in the promotion of Scottish tourism particularly in response to profound changes in road transport. Prior to this, however, it is important to chart some broader social and cultural changes that had a material impact on the emerging shape of tourism in Scotland.

Changing tastes and media

Scotland's appeal to the wealthy traveller underwent important changes in the twentieth century. During the previous 150 years Scotland had attracted the artistic and social élites from all over Europe. The north was a fashionable location for tourists with its association with high culture in literature and painting; the romantic and sublime having almost religious significance for many travellers. After the First World War, the élite's cultural assessment swung rapidly against Scotland. The taste for romanticism had waned. The international artistic community deserted Scotland, for it was no longer fashionable to paint bleak northern landscapes. Melancholy Victorian sentiment gave way to other concerns. The arts, particularly with the rise of modernism, gravitated towards the metropolitan cities of continental Europe: Paris and Berlin, Zurich and Barcelona, Vienna and Milan. Certainly the 'scenic and cultural strangeness that had drawn Sanby, Turner, Landseer and Millais to paint Scotland no longer attracted foreign artists of this calibre' (Holloway and Errington, 1978, 164). Tourism and fine art ceased to run together.

The north of Scotland did retain the social advantages of a region that was little frequented by the public at large, was favoured by royalty and the nobility, and had a land ownership system that offered large estates to lease or buy in order to enjoy field sports and other country pastimes. Nevertheless field sports became organized differently, often with syndicates renting or buying grounds. There were also alternative attractions for vacations in Europe. Fashion shifted in favour of summer Mediterranean sunshine and Alpine winter sports. In time, there would also be Scottish winter sports facilities,[2] but climatic and other factors meant that these did not offer a complete alternative to Alpine resorts.

Literature too was of declining significance, although the situation oscillated somewhat less. Burns, Scott and Stevenson continued to have their devotees, but only Burns sustained any sizeable flow of literary tourists.[3] As noted in the previous chapter, the kailyard writers were immensely popular in America and the places associated with the authors were attractions. Even as late as 1947 it was possible to find a writer such as S.P.B. Mais (1947) travelling round Scotland in search of the 'Crockett Country' (Galloway). By the 1950s though their works were largely forgotten. Twentieth-century writers such as Compton Mackenzie, John Buchan, A.J. Cronin, Lillian Beckwith and Iain Banks have all used identifiable regional settings for their fiction, but none has resurrected literary tourism as a leading preoccupation *unless* their works were also adapted for radio and later the cinema and television.

Television adaptations of Scottish regional literature have been common. The BBC series *Dr Finlay's Casebook* screened in the 1960s and revived in the 1990s, fitted in well with the *Weltanschauung* of a broadcasting corporation that had brought the world the Scottish country dancing and accordion music of Jimmy Shand and His Band in the *White Heather Club* and the pure dose of tartan nostalgia experienced each New

Year's Eve. *Dr Finlay's Casebook* was based on the autobiography of A.J. Cronin and his account of life in the fictional small Scottish town of Tannochbrae. Such was the popularity of the first series that visitors arriving at the railway station at Callander, where the location shots were filmed, were greeted by staff shouting 'Alight here for Tannochbrae' – well aware as to why people from all over the world were crowding the train (James, 1993, 33). Series on British television with recognizable Scottish locations have included *Take the High Road* and *Strathblair*. In 1994, after all this mock kailyard, BBC television filmed the genuine article in the shape of Neil Munro's creation of Para Handy and the crew of the coaster 'Vital Spark' (Munro, 1906) for a television series entitled *Tales of Para Handy* (BBC television, 1994). This gently evoked the towns and landscapes of the Western Isles, along with the stereotyped characters of the genre.[4]

Classic literature, as noted in Chapter 1, is a frequent basis for cinema period drama, but twentieth-century authors have also had works translated to the cinema screen. John Buchan, the first Baron Tweedsmuir, is a good example. His adventure stories contained many scenes in which 'landscapes are lovingly evoked' (Drabble, 1985, 142), with the various film versions of *The Thirty-Nine Steps* becoming cinema classics. Compton Mackenzie's *Whisky Galore!*, loosely adapted by Ealing Studios in 1949, is considered to have had a significant effect on the promulgation of Scottish images (see Figure 6.2). Filmed on the Outer Hebridean island of Barra, *Whisky Galore!* was a comedy about the consequences of the recovery of a substantial hoard of whisky after a shipwreck off a small Scottish island. As Wallace (1987, 255) commented: 'Recent paperback editions of "Whisky Galore!" and its companions confirm that Mackenzie's image has without doubt found its niche within what might be generally described as the "iconography" of popular Scottishness'.

Before leaving this point it is worth emphasizing that the modern cinema's portrayal of Scotland is not just a product of adaptation of literature. When film-makers turn to evocations of Scotland and Scottishness they unerringly return to tartanry and the Highlands. A good example is seen in the work of the film director Bill Forsyth. Films tackling petty crime or violence were set in Glasgow (*That Sinking Feeling*, 1979 and *Comfort and Joy*, 1984). A story of adolescent love was located in the new town of Cumbernauld (*Gregory's Girl*, 1980). Yet when tackling broader themes about culture in the film *Local Hero* (1982), Forsyth turned to the setting of Ferness, a fictional village on the Scottish west coast. The film depicted the culture clash between modernity, in the shape of the American oil executive Macintyre, and tradition, as represented by the local community. Macintyre was at first bemused by the local lifestyle, but later became captivated by it. The culture clash was finally resolved in favour of

6.2 *Whisky Galore!* Sammy MacCodrum's tracks in the sand give away the location of the whisky to Captain Waggett (John Gregson and Basil Radford, Ealing Studios, 1949).

tradition. Struck by the natural beauty of the area and its extraordinarily vivid displays of the Aurora Borealis, the oil company decided to build an observatory at Ferness and to carry out development elsewhere.

Travel and accessibility

Twentieth-century Scottish tourism was remade by private motor transport, particularly the car. Motor transport gave the middle classes a degree of mobility and control over their travel plans, rather than being confined to accessible channels around the rail networks or organized travel parties. For the first time they could reach and explore the far north. The élite might have deserted their summer playground for sightseeing and leisure pursuits elsewhere, but their former destinations appealed to the wider public.

The railways' role in tourism lessened over time as they struggled to cope with competition from the roads. A range of cheap return fares and excursion tickets was introduced in the 1920s and early 1930s. These materially reduced the overall cost of travelling to and within Scotland. Poster campaigns intensified, for example, with the London and North Eastern Railway's (LNER) mid-1930s 'It's Quicker by Rail' campaign (Hawkins and Hollis, 1979, 215–18). Graphic artists highlighted Gresley's newly-introduced A4 Pacific express locomotives, with their streamlined casings, speeding north to Scotland on the east coast route. Named London–Scotland express trains, such as the LNER's *Flying Scotsman*, *Queen of Scots* and *Aberdonian* and the London, Midland and Scottish Railway's (LMS) *Coronation Scot*, *Royal Scot* and *Royal Highlander*, had a strong, positive image with the travelling public.

The railway companies continued to issue handbooks, holiday guides and lists of holiday lettings as before. Holiday resorts were advertised: 'East Coast Joys: travel by LNER to the drier side of Britain'. Holiday accommodation was offered at all levels from camping coaches to luxury hotels.[5] New ventures were also undertaken to try and boost sources of revenue. A major hotel development was undertaken by the railways at Cruden Bay (Aberdeenshire) to promote the resort, with an express coach to meet mainline trains at Aberdeen. The venture was unsuccessful and the hotel was demolished in 1950, although its purpose-built links golf course remains.

Another means of increasing returns came from the railway companies' involvement in developing bus services as feeders for railway traffic. The Great North of Scotland Railway, for example, introduced one of the earliest motor bus services in Great Britain in 1904, with its Ballater–Braemar service. This ran on weekdays, with buses linking up with rail services to and from Aberdeen. In June 1907 the same company introduced a two-day 'Three Rivers Tour' based on Ballater, which used a combination of rail, motor- and horse-drawn coaches to explore the Dee, Don and Spey valleys. It was a natural role for the railways to play. Many localities in Scotland, especially in the Borders and the Highlands, had never been served by the railways and the coach tours extended their reach. Later, and more controversially, the railway companies became active investors in bus companies and other transport ventures. This helped to bring about coordination in the passage of tourists between one medium and the other and raised revenue, but the railways never held sufficient shares in road undertakings to give them a controlling voice and determine the policy of road transport in their own interests (Dyos and Aldcroft, 1974, 336).

Yet the railways were fighting a losing battle and despite this effort, decline was inexorable. Lack of investment and the search for economies of scale, as much as the desire to improve operational efficiency, led to major reorganization. Just as the regional grouping in 1923 had led to Scotland's railways being divided uncomfortably between the LMS and the LNER, so continuing under-capitalization, war damage and competition from the roads, especially for freight, contributed to the need for nationalization in 1948. In the early period of postwar recovery the position stabilized, but returns fell as mass private car ownership developed in the late 1950s and 1960s. The Beeching report of 1963 on the rationalization of British Railways was particularly savage on rural Scotland. Its most severe proposal to eliminate all lines north of Inverness was not accepted, but a large proportion of rural branch lines were axed. Hotels and resorts built in response to the spread of the railways suddenly found themselves many miles from the nearest railway station.

Another aspect of the steam age to suffer decline was marine navigation. While coastal services flourished, with modern vehicle ferries changing the character of motor touring in the Scottish islands, passenger shipping on international routes completely disappeared in the face of competition from the airlines. Glasgow Docks, once a hub of navigation on the North Atlantic route, declined rapidly from the late 1960s and have largely fallen into disuse.

It would be some years before the direct connection would be restored to Glasgow in the form of air transport. International aviation initially centred on Prestwick on the Ayrshire coast rather than Glasgow. Although Prestwick suffered from its remoteness from Scotland's main centres of population, it was chosen as the leading Scottish international airport due to its fair weather record and the fact that it was already a centre of Scottish aviation.[6] Once the new Glasgow Airport opened in 1966, Prestwick's isolated position and poor road links gradually worked against its long-term future. Although Prestwick still handles international traffic, Glasgow has now become the gateway for tourists from North America (see Chapter 9).

The impact of aviation on Scottish tourism has been considerable. It has helped to reinforce links with expatriate communities and to draw in tourists from North America and elsewhere for cultural events such as highland games, ceilidhs and clan gatherings. Improvements in direct air links have allowed Scotland to develop a tourist trade that does not rely on passengers transferring to domestic flights at English airports. Moreover, aviation has had an enhanced impact when combined with other modes of transport. Air tours had been attempted in the 1930s,[7] but this form of touring only developed fully in the 1960s with the advent of air-and-coach package tours and later with 'fly-drive' holidays. Widely canvassed in North America and western Europe, these offer tours of varying length. Package tours generally focus on the Highlands and are a familiar part of any Scottish summer, with coaches following predictable routes that are timed to reach specific points for meal breaks. 'Fly-drive' represents a marriage of flexibility through car hire with accommodation prebooked before departure. One such scheme operated in 1993–4 by the British Tourist Authority, in conjunction with Budget car rentals and the Best Western Hotels chain, offered 'themed' 3–4 day tours intended to be taken as part of a vacation. Those for Scotland included the 'Mary, Queen of Scots', linking together castles, palaces and churches associated with Mary's life and the somewhat nebulous 'Monsters, Lochs and Glens' tour in the Scottish Highlands (BTA, 1993). Other schemes use pre-paid hotel vouchers to allow greater flexibility in changing the set itinerary to suit the visitors' taste.

Road networks

The issue of road transport deserves consideration in its own right. The fact that the demise of the railways was generally no more than an inconvenience demonstrates the extent to which road transport has dominated travel patterns in the postwar period. First appearing in the 1890s, cars needed to be robust to cope with Scottish roads, but equally Scotland posed a challenge to the motorist. Recognition of the testing conditions came in 1901 when the Automobile Club of Great Britain established the Scottish 500-mile Trial, one of its earliest long-distance events. Organizers of rallying events were also soon attracted. In 1905 the Scottish Automobile Club began holding car reliability trials, which in 1932 were converted into the International Scottish Rally.

This image of cheerful pioneering through arduous conditions was part and parcel of the appeal of motoring in Scotland in the early years, although conditions varied greatly depending on the region concerned.

While trunk roads may have been of comparable standard with those in Great Britain, elsewhere many roads remained 'as Telford left (them) at the beginning of the 19th Century' with a hard surface added in the 1930s.[8] This created a contrast between regions north and south of the Great Glen: the Highlands and Islands dominated by winding single-track roads, roughly ten feet wide with passing places, which followed every undulation of the landscape (Turnock, 1970, 132). By contrast to the south the roads had been improved to two-lane highways, 18 feet wide and with gentler gradients.

Highland roads only improved slowly. In the 1930s Quigley (1936) highlighted two road developments which materially improved road transport: 'The Great North Road' (the A9 through Speyside to Inverness); and the road along the Great Glen which was finished in 1935. These provided a backbone from which lateral roads could diverge. A postwar guidebook to the north of Scotland still referred to the area north of the Great Glen as 'Unknown Scotland' in 1947, but noted:

> for although walkers, cyclists and the hardier kind of motorists have for years made adventurous excursions into the extreme north-west corner of Scotland, it is only with the completion of the huge road-building scheme that it has become possible for the tourist of the more comfort-loving habits to explore it thoroughly and with freedom from anxiety due to bad roads. Even now some of these roads are rather narrow but the surfaces are good; and for those who have not cars, buses running in connection with the trains at such places at Lairg make it easy to reach even the most outlying resorts. (Ward Lock, 1947, 17)

Developments in the 1960s saw increasing investment in road improvement, accompanied by bridge building and road building to eliminate lengthy detours and replace ferries. Such schemes included the building of the Ballachulish Bridge which meant that travellers using the A82 Glasgow–Fort William road no longer had to make a circuit of Loch Leven. Further investment in roads has come from the European Union, via the European Regional Development Fund. Further resources available to the Highlands and Islands after 1993 could mean the elimination of all single-track roads in the far north. Even so not everyone welcomed the change: 'Hikers bemoan many of the changes when what used to be a peaceful old Highland track is now part of a new motor road' (Nicolson, 1975, 124).

Further south the most significant development was the building of the motorway network in central Scotland. The completion of the M8 between Edinburgh and Glasgow in the late 1960s was followed by motorways to Perth and Stirling. Noticeably, even at the time of writing, there is still no connection to the English motorway system to the south (although upgrading of the A74 across the southern Uplands continues). Elsewhere trunk roads were improved to dual-carriageway standard, as with the A94 to Aberdeen.

This progressive improvement to the Scottish road network, combined with developments in vehicle technology and economy, has had an impact on Scottish tourism at all levels. The effective reduction in time–distance meant that formerly isolated areas became relatively more accessible and open to tourist development. This, as will be seen in the next two sections, would influence the character of both organized group tours and private motoring holidays.

Organized group tourism

The development of British motor bus and coach services began with the introduction of a motor bus service along Princes Street, Edinburgh in 1898. Although an attraction in itself it was not a financial success and the company ceased to function in 1901 (Hibbs, 1968, 42). Motor bus services continued to develop in urban areas, steadily driving horse buses from city streets but still acting as a feeder to the railways before 1914. Where there were no competing rail services, development was relatively quicker. By 1906 there were already buses running along the north coast of Scotland. Long-distance coach travel also made its first appearance. Chapman's Coaches, based in Eastbourne on the south coast of England, offered a 21-day tour north to John O'Groats before 1914 (ibid., 175). The introduction of the pneumatic tyre was important in making such travel palatable. When the Rothesay Tramways Co. offered tourists a scenic ride across the island of Bute, it was proud to offer a ride in one of their 'Luxurious Charabancs fitted with GIANT PNEUMATIC TYRES – Smooth and Comfortable as a Rolls-Royce' (ibid., 186).

After the First World War bus and coach services developed their medium- and long-distance capacity. An account of the consolidation of this network lies beyond the scope of this text,[9] but it is worth noting two important trends that had occurred by the early 1930s. First, a new network of bus and coach services had developed which would persist until the motorways allowed the creation of new long-distance services in the 1970s. Secondly, a new pattern of ownership had evolved whereby operators could be divided into two groups. On the one hand there were the larger groups, which included the municipalities, the railways and regional combines such as the Scottish Motor Traction Company, MacBrayne's, the Highland Transport Company (formed in 1930) and Alexanders' (which joined with Scottish Motor Traction in 1931). On the other hand there were many independent firms, who usually had five vehicles or less. These were particularly strong in the Highlands and Islands.

The growing presence of these operators changed the character of organized touring in Scotland. Public road transport, coaches for hire and packaged tours brought extra flexibility and economy to travel. Centres like Strathpeffer, which had all but lost their High Victorian spa trade and were steadily losing the patronage of the wealthy, adapted to the new age by becoming tour centres. Its large hotels, such as the Highland and Ben Wyvis, could cater for many coach parties at once. New touring packages mainly following tried and tested routes were actively promoted by the tour companies. The front cover of Thomas Cook and Son's brochure for 1936, for example, features an open-top coach travelling beside a loch vaguely reminiscent of Loch Lomond. Inside readers were assured that they would travel in 'leisured comfort' along the highways and byways to find:

> the real charm of close acquaintance with their manifold beauties and historic charms. Every mile reveals some new delight – now a winding lane embowered in trees ... now a tiny hamlet scarce touched by Time and progress ... now an ancient town steeped in historical or literary romance ... now a glimpse of hill and woodland, the scene, maybe, of knightly exploits long ago ... now a gem of art or architecture ... now a crystal lake in an emerald setting. (Anon., 1936a, 5)

The schedules were certainly demanding. Three tours were offered of the English Lakes combined with Scotland, one tour of the Scottish Highlands and Trossachs, one to John O'Groats and the Scottish Highlands, and one 'De Luxe Escorted Tour' by motor coach which, in fourteen days, took in the Highlands of Scotland, the Trossachs, English Lakes, Welsh Highlands and cathedral cities. Lest prospective travellers gained the impression that all life on a Cook's Motor Coach Tour was arduous, the guide provided a brief diary of a day's run from Morecambe Bay to Dumfries. Written 'by one who obviously enjoyed every moment', the diary focuses on meal breaks, sightseeing possibilities, entertainment and camaraderie. Groups of visitors 'not of our party' are to be seen admiring the lines of their coach and several such interlopers have climbed aboard to inspect the comfort of its armchair seats. Anyone concerned about timekeeping need not fret, the coach sets off 'with the precision of a main line railway station'. The coach 'glides', the views unfold, 'every prospect pleases'.

Although scarcely remembered at the present time, tours using private or hired cars were also arranged. In 'How to See Scotland' Thomas Cook and Son offered tours by private motor car for family or private parties: 'The perfection of motor touring comfort is assured by our arrangements ... for seeing Scotland by private motor car. The traveller has a minimum of trouble. He gives the order, and we plan everything in accordance with his wishes' (Anon., 1936b, 82). These tours were for chauffeur-driven cars with a courier. A number of tour suggestions were offered but the customer could adapt these or request something tailor-made if they wished. For £4.10s. per person per day for a group of four, the tourist would have a high-grade private motor car (landaulette[10] or limousine with chauffeur) and reserved accommodation with breakfast and table d'hôte luncheons en route. All sightseeing admission fees, ferry charges and tolls were covered. The cost also included a courier, all of whom would be 'gentlemen selected for their knowledge of the places of interest visited and their experience as guide-lecturers'.

Motoring holidays

Those touring by car or motorcycle were perhaps even more aware of the pleasures of the open road. Motor touring began in the early years of the present century. An American, Herbert Gunnison, boasted in 1905 that he had covered 5000 miles through England and Scotland in only 50 days' actual travelling time (Lockwood, 1981, 384). Even at that stage Americans would hire cars, purchase cars in Europe or bring their own cars over the Atlantic with them. Gunnison recorded seeing Americans picking up their cars up from the quayside in Liverpool to start their tours. For him and many other American tourists: 'To see the country and find out how people live, and explore out-of-the-way places ... one must go by auto-mobile' (Gunnison, 1905: Lockwood, 1981, 386).

Despite this early start, motoring in rural Scotland remained something not to be contemplated lightly. Even in the late 1940s poor road conditions took their toll on tyres and suspension. Filling stations were rare outside the towns and garages might find it difficult to cope with repairs. Ferries to the islands were usually unable to cope with cars, at best winching them on to available deck space. Planning routes and accommodation took place long before departure; guides, maps and handbooks were avidly sought and pored over in detail. Fortunately there were many from which to choose.

Maps and touring guides abounded. Using cartographic information supplied either by the Ordnance Survey or Bartholomew, they provided coverage of most areas of Scotland by the 1930s. Figure 6.3 shows a representative example. Produced by W. and A.K. Johnson Ltd of Edinburgh, it provides coverage at a scale of three inches to the mile of an area of the western Highlands from Loch Maree in the north to Fort William in the south. The map emphasizes the quality of the road and features of interest to be seen from the major roads of the region. The front cover encapsulates the themes identified earlier. A solitary car proceeds along a narrow wooded highland road. It is driven by a chauffeur wearing a peaked cap.

6.3   Motoring and touring map.

The couple sitting in the back admire the view, with the woman passenger leaning excitedly forward. The impression is one of discovery brought by the freedom of touring on the open road.

During the late 1920s and 1930s, many new sources of guidebooks and tourist literature appeared, some emanating from official or semi-official agencies. The first guides produced by Her Majesty's Stationery Office (HMSO) appeared in the 1930s for buildings in state hands, such as Linlithgow Palace (1934), the Abbey and Palace of Holyroodhouse (1936) and Dryburgh Abbey (1937). The establishment of the Forestry Commission's first national forest park in Argyll in 1935 led to a notable series of guides (see Edlin, 1969). These were substantive illustrated publications covering history of the area, geology, vegetation, wildlife, climbing, walking, Gaelic placenames, access and, in some cases, landscape and literature. The National Trust for Scotland for Places of Historic Interest or Natural Beauty, founded in 1931, began to produce basic visitor literature in the late 1930s, the forerunner of a large corpus of material in the postwar period (see next section).

Far more literature, however, stemmed from the efforts of private authors and publishing houses. Most were aimed at the middle-class groups that had recently taken to motoring and had a distinctly didactic strain. They sought not only to impart information about places and landscapes, but were also keen to say how they should be appreciated. One common origin was for articles initially written for weeklies or newspapers to be compiled for publication. For example, Alasdair Alpin MacGregor's evocation of the open road in *Wild Drumalbain* (1927) had started life in various publications including *The Scotsman*, *Edinburgh Evening News*, *Scots Magazine* and *Scottish Country Life*.[11] D.C. Cuthbertson's *Romantic Scotland* (1938), which appeared in articles over a period of two years in the *Scottish Field*, again celebrated travelling the highways and byways. A typical observation relating to Lanarkshire enthused about the poetry of movement:

> You will find this a winding road, worth travelling at any season, and each bend brings a sudden view of the Clyde. Enticing pools and rippling stretches, abruptly cut off again by trees and flower-decked cottages, stately homes amidst their woods and parks, and little self-contained townships, slip past in a series of entrancing pictures. (Cuthbertson, 1938, 15)

A third book of this type, H.V. Morton's *In Search of Scotland* (1929), is worth considering in more detail. The work of one of the leading travel writers of his day, Morton's book had originated in some essays written for the *Daily Express*.[12] He was clearly aware of Scotland as an imaginative creation when writing *In Search of Scotland*. As he (1929, viii) observed in his Introduction:

Sir Walter Scott, born at the psychological moment, created the modern conception of Scotland. He it was who ennobled the clans and made a kilt, hitherto an unpopular garment, aristocratic and romantic. Queen Victoria carried on the good work, and by going to live on Deeside in the autumn proved that the Highlands were not only high-minded but harmless. So the tourist's Scotland was born.

His stated approach was to avoid such preconceptions by making the journey as an exploration by car. Morton suggested that the car gave people a freedom to travel in a way that they had not done since the days of Pennant, Boswell and Carr; to move freely about the country in touch with the inhabitants. He undertook a circular tour with an itinerary similar to the early travellers: Scott country including Abbotsford, Edinburgh, Stirling, St Andrews, Perth, Braemar, Aberdeen, Inverness, Fort William, Skye, Glencoe, Loch Lomond, Glasgow, Ayr and Dumfries (Burns Country).

Much of the text was tinged with a heavily dramatized mysticism. The road itself was the path to greater understanding and awareness. The opening chapter's account of his entry to Scotland was typical of this approach. The empty road flings itself round the shoulders of hills 'running on in bleak solitude', yet he feels that every bend in the road will bring him face to face with the 'promised land' (ibid., 2). Entering Scotland at Carter Bar, he asserted: 'It is so authentically Scotland and could be nowhere else ... here is something as definite and unmistakable to a Scotsman as the white cliff of Dover to an Englishman ... There is a metal post with "Scotland" written on it. It is a superfluous post. You need not to be told that you have come to the end of England' (ibid., 6).

Morton's tour of enlightenment was no simple exposition of the appeal of the Highlands. As with his writings on Wales and elsewhere, Morton had an interest in industrial landscapes (Gruffudd, 1994). He approached the shipyards of the Clyde with picturesque sensitivity; workers in the steelworks at Motherwell, in a striking analogy, seem like devils at the mouth of Hell (see also Chapter 8). He admires the spirit of Glaswegians and the architecture of their central city. Even when dealing with the Highlands there is a measure of detachment. In lines worthy of Johnson, highlanders might be presented as 'born aristocrats' and 'Nature's last gentlemen' (Morton, 1929, 122), but there is also much social pretension surrounding highland social events. The highland gathering at Braemar was seen to bring together:

> the Clan Mayfair, the Clan Belgravia, the Clan Edinburgh, the Clan New York, the Clan Chicago, the Clan Washington ... They gather in long touring cars. They fill the hotels for miles around with bright chatter of grouse and salmon. Here and there among them is a genuine laird whose knees are voted by the beautiful girls of the Clan Chicago, 'just too cute for woids (sic)' (ibid., 132)

Despite these insights, Morton's progress was heavily filtered by literary allusion and romanticism. Every yard of the road from Braemar to Ballater is 'a coloured post card'. The Great Glen comprises primeval wildness, splendid solitudes, lonely mountain crests, and dark glooms of pine and larch. The drive along the route of the Caledonian Canal is 'almost terrible in its wild splendour' (ibid., 182). The splendour of the Trossachs is such that, due to their proximity to Scotland's main population centres, they are 'definitely unfair and should be abolished in the interests of more distant places' (ibid., 239).

The market addressed by writers such as Morton would be served in the 1930s by several series aimed at the discerning, middle-class independent tourist. While there would be no Scottish equivalent of Nikolaus Pevsner's *Buildings of England* for many years, two important series were launched in the 1930s with the same high-minded intent: the Shell County Guides and the landscape series published by Batsford.

The Shell County Guides were launched in 1934. Sponsored by the Shell-Mex petrol company on a theme with relevance to the company's products but with only limited recourse to direct advertising, the Shell Guides were architectural and landscape guides intended for the use of motorists. Produced in a spirex binding and retailing for two shillings and sixpence, they were produced under the general editorship of John Betjeman. Betjeman had a profound distaste for the comprehensive intent and cool academicism of Pevsner's project, wanting to bring a more selective approach to bear on buildings and landscapes (Lycett Green, 1994, 138–9). While superficially the guides were merely handy gazetteers of counties, they were characterized by firm direction as to places considered worth visiting. Editorial policy was to include places other than the well-known beauty spots. Handsome provincial streets, impressive mills and horrifying villas in over-rated resorts were all to receive attention. The guides were also characterized by Betjeman's fascination with typography and layout, which lent the series a distinctive and innovatory look.[13]

Full coverage of Britain was never achieved, with the only Scottish contribution in the interwar period being Stephen Bone's guide to the *West Coast of Scotland: Skye to Oban* (Bone, 1938). The text consisted of a 30-page gazetteer, interspersed with and surrounded by observations on highland life, customs and scenery, illustrative plates and engravings. There was also an extraordinary set of 17 large, unbled black and white photographs rendered by editorial decision in purple ink 'to remind one of heather' (Lycett Green, 1994, 139). The place descriptions are robust and quirky; the observations on highland life pander somewhat to the long-standing fascination with the Highlands as a source of ancient mysteries. Space is found for the Cailleach Bheur (an ancient deity), the devil, water horses, fairies, the glaistig (a supernatural female), sea serpents, second sight and urisks (a type of satyr). The author remarked with regard to witches that they 'are not common in the Highlands and never have been. The belief in them is imported from outside. The Highlands were so full of dark and appalling supernatural creatures that there seems to have been no room for witches, and very little even for the Devil' (Bone, 1938, 37).

Another important publishing venture launched in the 1930s was Batsford's *Heritage of England* and *Face of Britain* series. Despite the look of the colourful and modern dust jackets designed by the artist Brian Cook (Batsford, 1987), they were mostly conventional texts which dwelt on topography, tradition and heritage (Gruffudd, 1994). They may be characterized as companions rather than route guides; small enough to be carried on a journey and used for reference purposes, but not supplying itineraries of routes to be followed.

The Face of Scotland (Batsford and Fry, 1933) was effectively a forerunner of the *Face of Britain* series. It was illustrated with black and white photographs, a watercolour frontispiece by W. Russell Flint and line drawings by Brian Cook, who also designed the dust jacket (Figure 6.4). In stating the book's aim, the authors commented that: 'The improvement of the roads and rapid development of the light car have brought (Scotland's) remotest districts within comparatively easy reach of most southerners'. To aid the appreciation of the new visitors, its authors sought to produce a 'compact outline of Scottish topography' (Batsford and Fry, 1933, vii). Around half the book's contents were devoted to the topography of the Highlands, but comment was not purely geological and geomorphological. There were observations throughout on settlements and a final section dealt with the architectural heritage.

The most interesting feature of the text was perhaps the photography. The 115 photographs presented a country of vast open spaces, panoramas of mountain, loch and sky; a depopulated, empty country with scarcely a hint of human intervention. Occasionally a figure in the distance loaned a sense of scale, but that figure never seriously impinged on the composition. To some extent, this was a product of 1930s styles in black and white landscape and architectural photography, with their heavily-filtered cloud effects and aversion to allowing human detail to distract from the serious business of landscape. Yet it was remarkable that photographs of St Andrews, Stonehaven and Aberdeen, even Edinburgh and Glasgow displayed cities that seem almost devoid of people.

One other feature of note was the recurrent camera angle. No less than 19 of the photographs were bisected by a road. This device supplied an element of apparent motion to the picture, leading from the foreground towards the horizon. On three occasions there was a solitary car to be

6.4   *The Face of Scotland* (Brian Cook, 1933).

seen on the road, which was most probably parked there by the photographer before taking the picture. The hint of an invitation was present both from the photographs and accompanying text; that here was a deserted but accessible Scotland waiting for visitors to place themselves in the frame.

Many voices

After the disruption caused by the Second World War, there was a widespread desire to return to favourite haunts. S.P.B. Mais, for example, resumed his visits in 1945 which eventually led to the book *I Return to Scotland* (1947). As the author noted: 'We had six years leeway of enchantment to make up. We had no desire to see anything new. All we wanted was to stand where we had stood of old, meet again the friends from whom we had been too long parted, and recapture an old rapture – indeed, a whole succession of raptures' (ibid., 7). He continued that it was his hope that his return might 'inspire readers to make the journey for themselves and see how right I am' (ibid., 23). The return is seen as a healing process, restoring mind and body after war. Mais travelled around Scotland by combination of walking, public transport and car. The land reassured him in its unchanging quality. When writing about Deeside, for example, he maintained: 'Here is a land of solemn majesty, untameable by man, changeless through the ages, at once a man's solace in sorrow, inspiration in doubt, and glory in conquest' (ibid., 71).

This reassuring timelessness, however, would soon be beset by considerable change. The beginnings of motor touring, achieved in the 1920s and 1930s, had set the pattern for the subsequent development of the Scottish tourist industry in the postwar period. Growing prosperity and leisure time, the growth in car ownership in the 1960s, and the organizational changes in the holiday industry created the modern tourist industry. These developments also created a new context for tourist promotion. It was gradually accepted that modern Scottish tourism revolved around the car as the main form of transport. Increasingly tourist handbooks would be written around the needs of the motorist, with the route plans being based on assessments of the comfort and tolerance of car travellers. It was also accepted that the market had changed. The range of destinations open to the tourist, particularly in the Mediterranean, had led to a more competitive market and more aggressive marketing of locations from around the world. Scottish agencies, as noted in Chapter 2, felt that they had no option but to find a comparable response.

One readily apparent index of that response is the phenomenal rise of tourist promotional literature. The process that was begun in the interwar period has led to a proliferation of the guidebooks, maps, brochures, leaflets, and booklets that are currently produced by the wide array of public, private and commercial bodies outlined in Chapter 2. Moreover, dissemination of this literature has been greatly enhanced by the activities of the tourist boards and the network of tourist information offices, which actively distribute this material to tourists visiting Scotland. It would be superfluous to attempt comprehensive summary of this material at this point because much of it will be discussed in the three thematic chapters that follow. An interesting index of the way in which practice has changed, however, is provided by the example of material available for the battle-field site at Culloden, near Inverness (Gold and Gold, 1995).

Owned by the National Trust for Scotland (NTS), Culloden has a special place in the history of contemporary Scotland. The first gift of land on this site was made to the NTS in 1937. By the 1950s it owned most of the site, including a large part of the battlefield, monuments and Old Leanach Cottage – which predates the battle and was inhabited until 1912. The site was bisected by a road, the B9006, which ran through the centre of the battlefield itself. At this stage there were no visitor facilities nor any official guidebook. In its absence, the NTS had permission to republish the *Inverness Courier's Guide to Culloden Moor and Clara Circles* which formed part of a longer guide to Inverness.

During the 1950s the NTS became concerned that the number of visitors was increasing to 'many thousands' and that damage was being done to the site. Footpaths were being cut by visitors' feet. Vehicles stopping by the roadside to observe the site were parking on the graves. As part of a policy to manage the flow of visitors and interpret the site, Old Leanach Cottage was restored as a visitor centre. Visitor facilities were added and an official NTS guidebook was published in 1965. In 1970 a purpose-built visitor centre was opened, which was subsequently expanded in 1984. In 1985 the B9006 road was rerouted so that it passed around the edge of the site. In 1989 there were 112,100 tourists to the site.

To meet the demand for interpretive material, the shop now carries a range of purpose-written guidebooks as well as general texts from other publishers dealing with various aspects of the '45 uprising. With regard to the former, the official guide was superseded by a new version in 1990, containing site plans and bright colour photography. A leaflet in Gaelic and English published in 1992, *The Battle of Culloden* (NTS, 1992b), provides a battle plan and list of participants. Given the large number of family visits, there is also a childrens's guide to the Culloden exhibition (NTS, 1992a), comprising a large A4-sized guide with outline drawings suitable for colouring in.

This range of guidebooks, coupled with the information supplied by interpretive exhibitions in the visitors' centre and on the battlefield itself, provides the present-day tourist with a wealth of material. That material is still dominantly pedagogic in tone, but is designed to engage the attention of different types of visitor. In the next chapter, we will identify the material available in this and similar sites as the product of a 'heritage industry'. For the interim, it is worth emphasizing that despite the rapid growth of such literature, the underlying rhetoric is remarkably uniform.

Emphatic recognition of that point is provided by one of the latest ventures in publishing for the Scottish tourist market, *Scotland: The Rough Guide* (Greig et al., 1994). The 'Rough Guide' series represents the new generation of guidebooks. Aimed at the youth market and adopting a style of prose firmly suited to it, it is full of advice about such matters as pickpockets, the dangers of hitch hiking in cities, the 'abysmal' climate, possessing drugs, and value judgements about the quality of services and places worth visiting. When confronting the problem of Scotland's 'stock images', the book's preface states clearly that:

> Its landscapes are constantly reproduced on postcards and in glossy picture books; and the 'bonnie Scotland' idyll of kilts, sporrans and bagpipes is about as familiar a set of cultural symbols as it's possible to get. Whatever your view of this, the reality can't help but be an improvement, and while the authorities milk the very 'Scottishness' of Scotland for all it's worth, the real pleasures of the country need no tourist-board hype. (Greig et al., 1994, vii)

Despite these sentiments it is surprisingly difficult to confront the legacy of tartanry. The page of the 'Rough Guide' introducing part one, the 'basics', contains images of two whisky labels, some hills and the statue of Greyfriars Bobby in Edinburgh (ibid., 1). The page introducing part three, 'the contexts', has photographs of a highland cow, a pictish stone, a kilted figure throwing the hammer, and a salmon. Such images and symbols are remarkably hard to avoid. Only some artistic mirror-image pictures of North Sea oil rigs do anything to redress the balance (ibid., 431).

Conclusion

This chapter has considered trends in the promotion of Scottish tourism during the twentieth century, looking in detail at the way that private and public agencies have responded to the challenge of road transport, particularly the private car. The key to much of the analysis was the rhetoric of the open road, whereby empty Scottish roads were seen not just as convenient routes from which to admire the scenery but also as comprising a path for exploration, discovery and understanding. In promoting this message there was no sense of making a break with the past; of abandoning conventional ways of representing Scotland and creating a new rhetoric based around the modernity of a novel transport medium. Instead, writers of travel-books and others merely assimilated the traditional forms of representation. Travel in the motor age was seen as giving tourists the opportunity to go in search of dialogue between the modern world, on the one hand, and the authentic and unchanging traditions of the countryside on the other (Gruffudd, 1994).

That opportunity, long available to the upper classes, gradually filtered down the social spectrum as other groups toured Scotland by coach or private car. As they did so they effectively filled the gap left by the élite, who were forsaking Scotland for destinations elsewhere in Europe. In the course of this chapter we considered how the steady improvement in accessibility through road and, later, air transport brought Scotland steadily into the age of mass tourism. We also saw how the task of promoting Scotland was transformed into an activity involving many different agencies and voices. New promotional styles may have been introduced, but their content continued to fit the traditional mould, emphasizing tradition and tartanry, nostalgia and heritage, sentimentality and romanticism. More detailed analysis of these points will continue in the next chapter as we deal with interpretation of the highland heritage.

Notes

1. In 1952 he became the long-term secretary of the Ramblers' Association (Shoard, 1982).
2. Skiing, which was pioneered by the British in the Alps, had been attempted in Scotland as early as 1890, when W.W. Naismith experimented with cross-country or Nordic skiing. The Scottish Ski Club founded in 1907 was dominated by mountaineers who preferred cross-country skiing and saw it as an extension of the endurance skills required in mountaineering. Snow conditions, however, were rarely ideal for cross-country skiing (Keay and Keay, 1994, 881). It was not until after the Second World War that ski provision became organized on any significant scale, first with powered ski-tows on Ben Lawers (Perthshire), Glen Clunie and Glenshee. The first permanent ski lift was installed at Glencoe in 1956. The most significant development was at Aviemore in the 1960s – a purpose-built resort including hotel accommodation, conference facilities, leisure and visitor facilities, road and chair lift. Such facilities, of course, are tourist attractions in the summer as well. The success of this development led to others, the most recent being Aonach Mor near Fort William (1989).
3. It might be argued that Scott also continues to draw visitors, but this is primarily through his house at Abbotsford which now fits the requirements of stately-house tourism, particularly as it supplies a useful stopping-point for coach tours.
4. Although not of direct relevance to the present discussion, the portrayal of Glasgow as a city wallowing in industrial decline and gratuitous violence is

a staple of television series (e.g. *Taggart* and *Rab C. Nesbitt*) and is part of the legacy that modern Glasgow is attempting to counter in its promotional work (see Chapter 9).

5. The LMS was the largest hotelier in the country in the mid-1930s.
6. The airport had been established in 1935 by Scottish Aviation Ltd. It was used during the Second World War and subsequently by the American Air Force and the Royal Air Force.
7. A Thomas Cook tour in 1936, for example, used ten-seater planes, 'fitted with wireless', to transport passengers from London to Glasgow, where they would commence their Scottish tours.
8. See comments in Chapter 4 on Telford's role in creating the Parliamentary Roads.
9. For more information, see Hibbs (1968).
10. A coupé with a top of which the front and back halves can be raised and lowered independently.
11. MacGregor (1927) castigated motorists for rushing and missing sights. 'In these days of breakneck speed the average tourist is convinced that in a forenoon or so he can see in Glen Lyon everything that is worthy of his attention. And, so, he rushes past in a noisy motor-car.'
12. *In Search of Scotland* (Morton, 1929) and its sequel *In Scotland Again* (Morton, 1933) were both highly successful, each running to numerous printings and editions.
13. Strongly influenced by Betjeman's previous experience as part of the editorial team of the *Architectural Review*, perhaps the most innovative long-running arts journal of the interwar period.

CHAPTER SEVEN

Selling highland Scotland: the role of heritage

'It is not the Italians but the French who seem to have claimed Ullapool as their own. They are voracious shoppers. They snap up boxed presentation sets of single malt miniature bottles, silver-plate Nessie earrings, commemorating the yet-to-be-found monster; short-bread wrapped in Cellophane plaid; dismal videos of hairy men singing Danny Boy; and postcards of the what's-under-that-kilt variety. High road, low road, any road inbetween, few avenues are unexplored by Scottish kitsch.'

Nicholas Woodsworth, *Clear the Highlands Again!*

The place that the Highlands have occupied in the story of Scottish tourism by now needs no further emphasis. Their importance as a playground, initially for the rich and later for a wider clientèle, permeates their development from the late eighteenth century onwards. Moreover the conflation of the identity of the Highlands with that of Scotland as a whole has provided a marketing device consistently used by promoters of tourism. In this chapter we complete consideration of this theme by examining the nature and significance of the highland heritage in present-day tourism. In the process we map the continuation of tradition but draw attention to the progressive incursion of commercialism and promotional culture into the business of attracting tourists to Scotland.

Heritage and interpretation

'Heritage' and 'interpretation' constitute two further additions to the long list of contested terms thrown up by studies of social and cultural change. 'Heritage' comprises the valued legacy of previous generations; items from the past that embody tradition and which, by current evaluation, are seen as worth retaining for the benefit of present and future generations. Heritage calls for stewardship to look after these items to the best of our ability and scholarship to understand them better. Some would also argue that, as the past-in-the-present, they are an important source of national, local, even individual identity (e.g. Hewison, 1989, 15–17).

Any debate over how the legacy of past generations should be handled, of course, is itself heir to a centuries-old controversy. The tension between tradition and innovation has been recognized since the Romans copied built forms and social practices from the Greeks and then fought off the insinuation that copying was uncreative. As Lowenthal (1985, 72–3) observed:

> The benefits and drawbacks of heritage have been perennially debated ever since. The conflict sharpened during the post-Renaissance dispute between 'Ancients' and 'Moderns', the former insisting that antique excellence could never be matched, the latter arguing that observation and experiment unfettered by tradition could generate insights transcending antiquity's.

Nevertheless, reuse and further development of artefacts and styles from the past is one thing; active preservation of the past is another. In Britain the preservation movement began in the nineteenth century, although its roots can be traced back to the Middle Ages (Walsh, 1992, 71–2). The establishment of the Society for the Protection of Ancient Buildings (1877), the Monumental Brass Society (1887) and the National Trust (1895) were important indications of growing interest in heritage among the English middle classes. In Scotland the foundation of the Scottish Photographic Society in 1890 as an association for photographic record (see Chapter 5) and the National Trust for Scotland in 1931 (see Chapter 6) marked a parallel interest north of the border.

What made the period since 1950 qualitatively different is the extent of the threat to the past from planned reconstruction and the nature of the subsequent response. A long period in which an antitraditionalist ethic wrought considerable change upon Scotland's countryside and cities was succeeded by the present era in which reminders of the past are considered a valued part of most environments. Moreover that shift in opinion is newly populist. No longer are aristocrats, rich collectors and a cultivated minority of museum-goers the prime consumers of heritage; 'millions of ordinary folk now search out their roots, mobilise to protect beloved scenes, cherish their own and other people's mementoes, and dote on media versions of history' (Lowenthal, 1993, 3).

Not all commentators view the rise of concern with heritage with complete equanimity. Wright (1985), for example, warned of the conservative and antidemocratic nature of heritage interpretation and of the dangers inherent in the way that it articulates the dominant symbolism of the nation. Hewison (1987) saw the hijacking of the new consciousness of heritage by a 'heritage industry', an epithet that he believed was earned because the industry's practitioners increasingly thought of culture as a product or commodity. This commodity was offered or supplied to the consumers (or users), for whose purchasing power the various arms of the heritage industry were in competition.

The range of the commodities grouped together under the banner of 'heritage' is, of course, enormous. Historic Scotland[1] alone has over 300 historic buildings and archaeological sites. These properties vary in age from 6000-year-old dwelling remains on the island of Papa Westray and the neolithic village at Skara Brae (both in the Orkneys) to an 1898 whisky distillery at Dallas Dhu near Forres (Macniven, 1994, 225: also Historic Scotland, 1993). They also range in grandeur from Edinburgh Castle, Scotland's most popular tourist attraction, to the reconstructed turf-roofed blackhouse at Arnol on Lewis with its trickle of summer visitors. To these are added an enormous number of other properties. They include the historic buildings and archaeological sites held by other bodies (e.g. the National Trust for Scotland and private owners[2]), museums, scenery, cultural artefacts, libraries, archives, cultural gatherings, even the preserved output of television programmes and the film industry.

Successful retention of this range of phenomena makes heavy demands on scarce resources. The problem is that the scale of those resources has not matched the broadening and deepening of the scope of what is now regarded as heritage. The 1970s and 1980s witnessed a boom in new attractions with the establishment of independent museums, new galleries, heritage and clan centres, tourist 'experiences', working farm displays and the rest. There seem, however, to be few significant multiplier effects in adding new attractions. The numbers of visitors to historic buildings or archaeological sites, for example, have increased very little in the United Kingdom in recent years (Rumble, 1989, 26). This intensified competition, therefore, means that their proprietors often feel impelled to take steps to improve their financial position beyond the yield available from visitors' entry fees and takings from gift-shops or restaurants. One method is to seek commercial sponsorship, for example, as with whisky distillery spon-sorship of highland games (see Figure 7.1). Another is to increase their visibility in the marketplace by better brochures, advertising and other publicity measures. The adoption of professional approaches to marketing and promotion to direct the tourist gaze (Urry, 1990) and ensure their survival is part and parcel of this territory.

Like heritage, 'interpretation' also poses difficulty for definition.[3] Originally a term which embodied revelation and provocation, its mean-ing has recently been extended to emphasize structuring and exposition of factual information (Glen, 1994, 262). For current purposes inter-pretation is best regarded as an activity which presents, structures and reflects on information in order to help the visitor to make sense of the places or objects in question. As part of the strategic functions involved in the management of heritage, it is closely linked with communication and, increasingly now, with promotion and marketing. Goodey (1994b: quoted in Harrison, 1994, 312) suggests that interpretation has four

7.1 Crieff Highland Games leaflet.

essential elements: understanding the nature of the audience (the market); identifying the themes and stories to be told; identifying the resources to be used in interpreting these themes and stories; and considering the most appropriate and effective media to be used in the context of the three previous criteria.

Although this analysis seems logical and systematic, the fact remains that the stories told by interpretive activity depend very much on the ideology of the storyteller. Consciously or otherwise, interpretation can compartmentalize knowledge, directing the observer to identify specific elements or relationships and to neglect others. It can direct attention to items that are advantageous to the proprietors, or to commercial sponsors, or to specific interest groups. The past is inevitably viewed from different ideological positions. Moreover it is not an immutable or independent object, but something that is always revised from present positions (Crang, 1994). There is no such thing as an 'authentic' history which can be set against other 'ideological' histories.[4] Rather interpretation is inherently a realm of multiple meanings and multiple explanations of those meanings. The implications of this point are witnessed throughout the remaining sections of this chapter.

Authenticity

The notion of authenticity, highlighted in Chapter 2 as an important element in the promotion of tourism, is worth pursuing further. Earlier sections of this book have traced many waves of tourists coming to the Highlands in search of evidence of an older, traditional culture with its roots in a golden age. There is a desire to see things in their original location and condition, to experience them as people in the past would have done. Each of these points, however, is problematic. Seeing things in their original location may be difficult for reasons as diverse as the fragility of an item, uncertainty as to its original location, its security and the desire to display items to the widest audience – as when they are removed for permanent display in national, usually metropolitan, museums. Seeing things in their original condition poses even more difficulties. Is an original item, no matter how dilapidated, automatically preferable in its existing state than it would be if restored? Is a restored structure or artefact always more acceptable than a newly made replica which might give a better impression of how an object would have looked when new and presumably closer to its designer's intentions?

Authenticity may also mean that management or reconstruction of the past proceeds with some notional historical date in mind. This preserved railway station is deemed an authentic representation of how a

Caledonian Railway station would have looked around 1910, notwithstanding the fact that items of station furniture and possibly the station buildings themselves have been brought here from a fifty-mile radius. That castle has parlour maids dressed in Victorian costume despite having foundations which date back to the twelfth century, a great hall dating from the fifteenth century and a shop constructed in 1989. Finally, as we saw in Chapter 4 in particular, the image that we now have of the society that existed in the Highlands in past eras may itself have been the product of reimagining. Highland games and gatherings, now held at venues throughout Scotland, are a good example of activities presented as traditional even though many of the events are of recent origin. The social practices and customs of their antecedents, if any, are now long lost in the mists of time. Historical authenticity is at best a relative concept.

Packaging places

Packaging places represents another important dimension of interpretation. Tourist attractions are often packaged together rather than sold separately and take their meaning from that context. Hotels retailing weekend or short breaks may offer reduced price or concessionary tickets to attractions in the locality. Tourist boards also attempt conscious repackaging of existing attractions through new interpretations that bind them together in some way. The simplest method is to do so on geographical lines, packaging together items of interest that are situated within an hour's drive.

The Kincardine and Deeside Tourist Board, for example, coined the slogan 'Follow the Royal Road' to tie together a diverse collection of attractions (scenery, ancient monuments, golf courses, woodlands, fishing, pony trekking, museums and craft shops) in north-east Scotland. Although the A93 from Aberdeen travels through Deeside en route to the royal residence at Balmoral, many of the sites listed do not lie on or near this road – indeed the cartography in the relevant tourist brochure makes no attempt either to highlight the Royal Road or to suggest it as a basis for touring (KDTB, 1993).

That brochure is also worth considering in its own right, since it provides a good example of a traditional local authority product. Opening out to a 42 by 30 centimetres format, it contains no less than 17 photographs, a large map, two logos and around 1800 words of text (much of which is in a diminutive font). Unfocused in content, it relies on the general appeal of the Highlands to get its message across because no single selling proposition is identified. At best its compromise rhetoric satisfies local requirements for something to be done about publicity without favouring interests of one group against another. There is little substance in this marketing ploy other than that of keeping all sectional interests happy.

Others choose thematic packaging of tourist venues. A typical method is to conduct joint promotion of sites of interest to, say, a particular rural industry or craft. By this means, it is possible to draw together scattered and historically discontinuous items as part of a single continuous thread. One example is the fishing industry, once a thriving part of the Scottish rural economy but now greatly reduced in size and importance. The fishing villages of Scotland's north and east coasts, Orkney and Shetland, for example, are marketed by leaflets proclaiming 'Scotland's Fishing Heritage Trail', backed by the availability of a scholarly guide to the trails as a whole (MacLean, 1985). Divided into ten regional portions, the trails encourage the touring motorist to follow lightly used coastal roads to visit towns that may have little drawing power in their own right but gain a measure of wider interest when interpreted as part of a package.

Understandably trail writers were mindful of the fact that fishing continues as an economic activity and that there were possible regional development implications associated with interpretation. They tried to steer an uneasy path between heritage and the sensitivities of the remaining fishing industry; between selling the history of a bygone age and presenting fishing as an activity with an economic future. This is demonstrated by the overall guide (MacLean, 1985). On the one hand, the heritage message is communicated powerfully:

> The quays and piers are heavy with memories; the focus of the communities they serve. Wonderfully-wrought and marvellously worn by the sea, they stand like noble sculptures, monuments to the generations for whom they have provided safe harbours. And everywhere there are traces of the past – rusting winches on the boat-strand beaches, ancient barometers at the pierhead, boats built in 1900 and still in service – all the evocative detritus of the sea. (ibid., 1)

On the other hand, lest this sounded too final, the author was immediately at pains to set the record straight:

> Yet the villages of the East Coast are by no means only shrines to a past way of life. Over 60 per cent of the fish landed in the United Kingdom is landed there; fishing is still done from almost all of them, though on a reduced scale, and where the harbours are too small to handle modern boats, the fishermen travel to the major ports for work. (ibid.)

The folded-A4 regional trails also tried to retain this balance. The section dealing with Kincardine and Deeside provides a good example. Travelling northwards, the trail passes through seventeen villages or stopping points on its way from St Cyrus through Stonehaven to Aberdeen. Johnshaven now has only two working boats, but was 'the base of one of the UK's largest lobster dealers'; Inverbervie still has 'a small salmon netting station on the shore to recall its past activity as a white fish harbour' (Anon., 1987, 3). Only where alternative marine activity compensated, as with the North Sea oil business in Aberdeen, could the decline be treated in a more matter-of-fact manner without obligatory mention of the continuing vitality of some small aspect of fishing.

Interpreting the Clearances: the ideological frame

The ideological dimension is worth considering in its own right, with few examples providing better insight into the problems of interpretation than the question of the highland heritage. As we have seen in Chapter 4, highland history and tradition was reinvented in the early nineteenth century to meet a broader political and social agenda. Nevertheless, the buildings and landscapes of the Highlands still offer the potential for many different histories to be interpreted for the visitor. To give some impression of the plurality that is possible, we take two examples: the first concentrating on the view from the stately home; the second deliberately constructed to refocus the tourist's attention on the relict landscapes that testify to the human costs of the Clearances. In theory, these different approaches are joined together by a common history of landownership and tenure, possession and dispossession. From the point of view of interpretation, they demonstrate how the rhetoric of tourist promotion can be directed in completely different directions.

Dunrobin Castle

Situated at Golspie on the north-east coast, Dunrobin Castle is the seat of the Sutherland family (Figure 7.2). Although the family's connections with the area date back at least to the thirteenth century,[5] it was their contribution to the Clearances in the early nineteenth century that gives them their contentious place in highland history. The first clearance authorized by the Sutherlands created an enormous sheep farm in Strathnever at the expense of families living in the upper part of the valley, who were forcibly removed. More clearances followed, with forced evictions and considerable brutality. By 1820 the population had been cleared to the coast, with the intention that they should earn their living through a combination of agriculture and fishing. The interior was let as seven large farms. The flavour of the enterprise was conveyed in a letter sent by Patrick Seller, the assistant estate factor, to Lord Advocate Colquhoun in 1815 (quoted in Hunter, 1976, 27). His masters:

7.2 Dunrobin Castle, Golspie, Sutherland. Although it has thirteenth-century elements, the castle's château-like appearance owes most to rebuilding between 1845 and 1851 on the basis of a design by Charles Barry.

were pleased humanely to order a new arrangement of this Country. That the interior should be possessed by Cheviot Shepherds and the people brought to the coast and placed there in lotts under the size of three arable acres, sufficient for the maintenance of an industrious family, but pinched enough to cause them to turn their attention to the fishing. I presume to say that the proprietors humanely ordered this arrangement, because, it surely was a most benevolent action, to put these barbarous hordes into a position where they could better Associate together, apply to industry, educate their children, and advance in civilization.

The fact that fishing was a precarious activity and that there was gross overcrowding in coastal areas gained the Sutherland clearances the status of a cause célèbre.

Inevitably these events underpin the interpretation of the history of Dunrobin Castle and the artefacts that it displays. In tackling it, the standard guidebook *Dunrobin Castle: Seat of the Countess of Sutherland* (Anon., 1987) conforms to a general pattern of glossily-produced publications generally intended to be taken home and read rather than to guide one's route around the house, for which purpose they are normally somewhat limited. Such guides juxtapose the history of the house with a succinct and sanitized history of the landed family in question, most probably written by a staff writer in connection with the family itself.[6] Photographs of distinguished ancestors are found alongside those of the house's treasured possessions; family trees, crests and mottoes are standard fare. While purporting to be factual and informative, at a deeper and more significant level the functions of such guides is to legitimize (Morris, 1991, 144).

The interpretive guide for Dunrobin Castle followed this pattern. Its primary discourse was on the nature of the possessions on display in the rooms open to the public. It listed the more notable possessions as an indication of the owners' long tradition of good taste: carvings by Grinling Gibbons, paintings by Landseer and Sir Joshua Reynolds, Chippendale tables, Louis XV furniture and fine china. It catalogued the many family portraits, which the reader could link to the names listed on the elaborate 600-year family tree found as a centrefold in the brochure. It dwelt on the display of military banners and honours and, in particular, anything with wider resonance to the British aristocracy or to royalty: the bed where Queen Victoria slept, the robes worn by Duchess Harriet at Victoria's coronation, and the uniform worn by the fifth Duke at Edward VII's coronation.

The secondary discourse concerned the Sutherlands' place in history and the family's relationship to the Highlands. The library, it noted, contained many books on the development of the Scottish Highlands during the nineteenth century, emphasizing perhaps the learned and progressive aspect of the Sutherlands' approach. Stories told of ancient ancestors were candid if sometimes apocryphal, a colourful history of intrigue, poisonings and contested issue. More recent history, especially that of the sensitive early nineteenth century, was recounted in a guarded manner. In her foreword the current Countess of Sutherland acknow-ledged the events of the Clearances but placed these comments in the context of improvements:

> In the early nineteenth century the Marquess and his wife Elizabeth proceeded to make large-scale improvements to Sutherland's com-munications, land and townships which involved the clearance of some 5000 people from their ancestral dwellings. The Sutherland Clearances, *together with other Highland clearances* (emphasis added), were bitterly resented and remain to this day the subject of many books and plays. The House of Sutherland continued improvements in the County throughout the nineteenth century ... (Anon., 1987, 1)

Notwithstanding their notoriety it was argued that the Sutherland Clearances needed, first, to be recognized as part and parcel of a wider clearance movement involving other landlords besides the Sutherlands and, secondly, to be understood as part of a continuing, progressive-minded policy of rural improvement. Either way, if these points were accepted, the force of criticism was blunted by ameliorating circumstances and certainly deflected away from explanations that stressed the benefits of the policy for private wealth accumulation.

A rather more forceful version was told by the anonymous brochure writer. Lord Stafford, the Countess of Sutherland's husband, was por-trayed as a visionary reformer. A contemporary commentator was quoted to the effect that Stafford 'was willing to dedicate his life and fortune to making other folk do something they found desperately disagreeable for the sake of what he believed to be their future good' (Sir Iain Moncreiffe of That Ilk: ibid., 16). Moreover, using his own wealth derived from industrial activities in England, the duke sought to bring about change in the social and economic structure of the area, moving some of the inhabitants:

> to modern housing on the coast where they could earn better money working in industries which he himself had financed. Much the same sort of thing is done today by town councils who uproot people from their old, shabby but neighbourly streets and place them in ultra-modern, clinically clean but often completely inhuman high-rise flats, usually against their will.

To this remarkable defence was added the rider that clearance may have gone ahead too fast as a result of being misled by poor advisers and by the over-zealous actions of his agents. Nevertheless it was not personal gain that influenced him: 'Stafford lost a great deal of money in his "philanthropic" indulgences but it must be said of him that he created a modern communications system in Sutherland'. He may have been hated at first, but 'he came to be respected by many at his death', so much so that a huge statue, funded from public subscription, was built on a nearby hill. There was even advantage in having so many Scots being forced to emigrate since: 'It was their hardy characteristics and imaginative minds which contributed so much to the building of ... (the British) Empire' (ibid.).

The Highland Clearances Trail

Seen through the filter of the Dunrobin Castle interpretive guide, the events of the early nineteenth century and the resulting empty landscapes of Sutherland can be seen in the light of an improver's good intentions and a balance sheet not wholly unfavourable even to the evicted local community. Very different stories, however, can result from the application of different values, as is shown by the *Highland Clearances Trail* (Gibson, 1993).

Now in its fourth edition as a 38-page word-processed booklet in A4 format, the Trail represents an ever-lengthening repository of information about the Clearances.[7] Its tone is set by a cover photograph of an eviction of crofting tenants on North Uist in 1895. In essence, the Trail comprises the unauthorized version of highland history, constructing a rhetoric that deliberately runs counter to the account considered above. Here the appearance of the landscapes of highland Scotland is no accident but the direct result of clearance policy. In this version: 'Improvements by the lairds were for their profit so inevitably most of the people became surplus to the requirements of the sheep and deer forest economy' (ibid., 1). Like the Dunrobin guide, the author draws attention to the wider context, but here the message is nationalist: 'Whether in writing, in song or in the memories of the dispossessed these lessons of the Clearances relate directly to the condition of the battered little nation which Scotland is today' (ibid.).

The Trail is not an itinerary to be followed in sequence from one designated point to the next, but it is a listing of sites in six different geographical areas from Arran in the south-west to the small Shetland island of Fetlar in the north. Its coverage eschewed the great houses and castles, although Dunrobin Castle gained brief mention as a 'museum to Victorian extravagance' (ibid., 11) and the 100-foot high monument to the first duke mentioned as the subject of frequent demolition rumours. Instead the Trail focuses on the visible remains of house foundations, museums, memorials and sites of skirmishes between crofters and the forces of law and order. Each featured site or landscape tells its portion of the story. At Crochy (Strathnairn) a pile of rocks ten metres in diameter marks a spot where a village was demolished and the house stones were piled in one large heap so that the tenants could not return. The 'Destitution Road' between Gairloch and Lochbroom was built during the Potato Famine by labourers forced to give their work unpaid in return for meagre food rations. On South Uist, Barra and Vatersay in the southern Outer Hebrides, the proprietor Col. Gordon evicted 1500 destitute tenants and forced them to board emigrant ships to Canada to rid himself of them.

Presented in this manner each of these fragmentary observations cumulatively contributes to a distinctive account of highland history. Rather than being built around the tangible possessions and family trees of noble families, it employs field evidence to reconstruct the abject conditions of tenants on many highland estates during the Clearances. The heroes of one history have feet of clay in another. Yet from the point of view of tourist promotion, the existence of pluralism in interpretive texts poses no problem. Wherever one stands with regard to the issue of the highland land question, the different historical interpretation and empirical focus of the *Highland Clearances Trail* serves the valuable function of encouraging tourists to visit destinations well outside the normal ambit. In the process, the loading of visitors is spread wider across the regional economy. This is perhaps one reason why the Trail is regularly found on sale in tourist centres in highland Scotland even if its radical subject matter runs counter to the implicit tartanry of much official tourist promotional literature.

Selling folklife and culture

Conservation of rural culture has been an important theme in many of Europe's smaller nations, primarily because it is seen as one of the important roots of national identity. Norway, for example, has had open-air folk museums of rural culture for more than a century, with 'almost every self-respecting local community' having its own museum with old steadings (Våge, 1993, 99). Sweden, Finland, Ireland, Austria and Switzerland can claim similar tangible expressions of interest. By contrast Scotland has lagged well behind, in spite of having developed one of Britain's first specialist museums in this field when the Highland Folk Museum was established at Kingussie in 1935. Some of the hesitancy in developing such centres may lie in the lack of nationalist interest in folk culture,[8] but probably more important has been lack of official sponsorship and resources. All too often the task of rescuing folk customs, artefacts and music has been left to amateurs operating on shoestring budgets. Although they may benefit initially from small grants or start-up capital from official bodies, survival in a commercial world normally means compromise between, on the one hand, educational motives and the desire for cultural enrichment and, on the other hand, the commercial ethic.

To illustrate the nature and significance of this dilemma, we have selected three centres that exemplify different scales of operation and scope of ambition: the restored blackhouse at Arnol in Lewis; the reconstructed farming township at Auchindrain (Argyll); and the recently-proposed Highland Folk Park at Newtonmore in the Central Highlands. Each blends educational, cultural and commercial considerations differently as part of the message communicated to tourist visitors.

The island blackhouse

Situated in a small crofting township in the north of the Outer Hebridean island of Lewis, the blackhouse at 42 Arnol exemplifies the preservationist ethic in folklife interpretation. The blackhouse was a single-storey dwelling with double thickness drystone walls and a thatched roof. Once a common form of dwelling throughout the crofting areas of north-west Scotland, blackhouses were widely condemned during official Inquiries in the late nineteenth century due to their lack of sanitation, their use of a central peat fire without a chimney or other ventilation,[9] and for having a freely intercommunicating dwelling space and animal byre within the same building. During the twentieth century they rapidly fell into disuse although their remains are everywhere to be seen.

The preservation of the Arnol blackhouse, built in 1875, can therefore be seen as an attempt to retain an important part of highland culture before it finally succumbed to modernizing influences. The guidebook, written by the distinguished Scottish cultural historian and ethnographer Alexander Fenton, makes this orientation clear:

> Change is an inevitable part of life, to be accepted, not deplored, but it is important to understand and appreciate the main stages of cultural development. The kind of culture represented by the black-house was a very long and basic stage in the history of Highland and Island Scotland, and 42 Arnol will remain ... an enduring symbol and reflection of community organisation that in another generation will lie quite outside the memory of individuals. (Fenton, 1978, 7)

Two broad points can be made about the exhibits at Arnol. The first concerns commercial orientation. Although Historic Scotland is at pains to stress its own limited resources (e.g. Macniven, 1994, 228), the Arnol blackhouse is one of the smallest of its many sites and scarcely one that would make much impact on a balance sheet. Perhaps as a result the visible pressure of commercialization involved in this site is minimal. Although its remoteness and low visitor totals would not warrant large-scale

investment in commercially-oriented facilities, little is offered other than
the high-quality guidebook and some site-specific postcards. The educational and cultural enrichment ethics, characteristic of a traditional
museum, remain dominant.

The second point concerns the interpretive strategy which is perhaps
best illustrated by the guidebook. Impeccably scholarly in tone and
intended for home reading rather than field instruction, its 54 pages
focus initially on the building's physical structure and then move out-
wards to its immediate surroundings. There is detailed analysis of the
blackhouse's vernacular architecture and contents, replete with photographs and scale drawings. The discussion then considers what the blackhouse represented in the context of island building styles, how the basic
design was adapted to incorporate enforced changes in provision for
lighting and ventilation, and how the building design fitted the needs of
the local economy. By contrast, details of social practices appear only
indirectly, for example, mention of a secret hiding place for distilling illicit
whisky or comments on the practical use of agricultural implements. It is
left to the visitor's perusal of the building's contents and to the unforgettable sight and smell of the interior, hazy with peat smoke from the
central fire, to make contact with the biographies of those who once lived
there.

Auchindrain township

A rarity in having been left undisturbed by improvement activities, the
communal tenancy township at Auchindrain (near Inveraray, Argyll)
consists of twenty buildings made from local rubble masonry and mortar.
These were grouped together into a village which was surrounded by land
always in cultivation. Beyond this lay marginal arable land and common
grazings. The site was uninhabited when restoration work began in 1964,
the last tenant having moved out two years earlier. Since that time just
over half the buildings have been restored, with the additional construction of a visitor centre.

Auchindrain contrasts with Arnol not just in the scale of restoration
activity but also in its style of interpretation and its response to commercial
pressure. With regard to the former, interpretation of Auchindrain proceeds through the social landscape rather than through the artefactual
evidence of previous settlement. Publicity leaflets invite the visitor to 'a
living experience of the past'. The guidebook (Auchindrain Museum,
1988), for example, leads the visitor round the site blending details of the
buildings with biographical information about its former inhabitants.
Buildings are named after their last occupants and there are photographs
of people ploughing, washdays, haymaking, families standing in front of

their houses and a facsimile wedding certificate, as well as building plans and sketches of agricultural implements. Visitors are encouraged to enter the dwellings and to visualize how they once related to their surroundings.

Inevitably commercial activity is greater than at Arnol. Lacking the support of a large parent organization, the trust that runs Auchindrain Museum needs to raise funds to continue restoration and conservation work. In doing so it can take advantage of the growing expectation that museums offer catering and gift shop facilities to visitors. With the gift shop retailing locally-produced clothing and artefacts (for example, craft-work, jewellery and pottery) that have at least a place association with the museum, the visitor centre brings the cultural and commercial aspects of tourism into close alignment.

The Highland Folk Park

So far we have explained two relatively small centres at which the educational and cultural-enrichment aspects of tourism remain the principal raison d'être. Yet heritage tourism is also an important tool of economic development, bringing jobs to outlying regions where employment prospects are otherwise poor. With this in mind it is worth examining the recent proposal by the Highland Regional Council to develop a Highland Folk Park at Newtonmore in the Central Highlands. Intended to offer a 'leisure and learning' experience for 'a new millennium' (McDermott and Noble, 1994, 254), the proposal is for a scheme that goes far beyond the existing activities of the nearby open-air Highland Folk Museum at Kingussie (mentioned earlier). Developing on an 80-acre site, the centrepiece of the folk park would be a replica seventeenth-century 'highland township'. This would have 15–20 timber-framed and turf-walled buildings, plus an associated 'runrig' farming system and summer shieling settlement. At this scale, agricultural and livestock practices could be demonstrated rather than requiring visitors to visualize them.

It is too early to say at present whether this project will come to fruition.[10] Nevertheless the extent to which the commercial ethic has entered the proposers' arguments is worth highlighting. The scheme was recommended as a way of delivering a range of objectives – interpretation, education and community development – yet what was proposed was essentially a cultural theme park, a fantasy world drawn from the historic experience of the Highlands as a whole rather than being specific to one locality. Its most convincing rationale for any local authority wishing to make the long-term financial commitment necessary for the scheme's fulfilment was not cultural – given that there was already an effective folk museum in the area that provided much of what is proposed here – but economic. The scheme's advocates drew attention specifically to the relationship between tourist development on the one hand, and the region's employment base and income on the other. Proponents asserted that many jobs would be created directly (in the park itself), indirectly (in services, local crafts, hotels and catering), from economic spin-offs created by increased attraction of tourists into the area, and from hosting academic conferences and short-term courses (McDermott and Noble, 1994, 256). Problems of seasonality, the long-term commitment needed before backers are likely to see a return on their investment and the general riskiness of the theme park market mean that these arguments are difficult to sustain.

Scotland's favourite monster

This does not mean, of course, that developments at the theme-park scale cannot work in highland Scotland: indeed, as we saw in Chapter 3, the idea has been employed in the area since at least the late eighteenth century. An example that highlights the successful application of theming is the large concentration of enterprises in and around Drumnadrochit on Loch Ness.[11] One of the newer additions to the highland heritage, the hunt for the supposed living dinosaur latched on to that thread of tourist promotion that sees the region as the fount of endless legend and unsolved mystery. Since the first alleged sighting in 1933, visitors have flocked to the loch to glimpse the scene. They are treated to a finely-tuned selling machine capable of pandering to whatever strand of scientific inquiry, New Ageism or family entertainment takes their fancy.

Leaving aside boat tours and half-hearted attempts by the local tourist board to spread the load by an unfocused Loch Ness Monster Trail which incorporates everything of remote interest in a 40-mile radius (ILNNTB, n.d.), most attention focuses on the two interpretive centres in Drumnadrochit. These promote themselves to the outside world, and against one another,[12] by a mixture of science and family entertainment (see Figure 7.3). Various combinations of audiovisual presentations and three-dimensional displays are used to convey the history of dinosaurs, the nature of myth and mystery and a sense that the search for the monster has a firm scientific base. Superseded submersible vehicles, or sometimes replicas of current vessels for scientific exploration, are displayed to illustrate the continuing hunt for the monster.

Yet the scientific overtones do not mask the prominent element of family entertainment in all promotional work associated with the interpretive centres. Recent advertisements for the Official Loch Ness Monster Exhibition Centre, for instance, contain a collage of six photographs. Three illustrate aspects of the audiovisual displays. The remaining three

7.3 The Loch Ness Monster Trail.

depict respectively, the restaurant, the bar and a motel bedroom. The accompanying text devotes one sentence to the exhibition and three to visitor facilities – the various catering facilities, children's play areas, the selection of gift shops and craft demonstrations. In examining their content it is readily apparent that 'Nessie' offers great advantages to those employed in craft industries. Given that it has no known shape, almost anything that resembles a dinosaur can be passed as an acceptable souvenir. The silver-plate Nessie earrings mentioned in Woodsworth's comment at the head of this chapter are emphatically not the product of a journalist's lively imagination.

Conclusion

This discussion of one of Britain's most commodified tourist attractions brings this chapter's brief review of the interpretation and selling of the highland heritage to a close. We began by defining the meaning of heritage and identified interpretation as a process that mediates the multiple meanings of tourist discourse in a manner of the communicator's choosing. After this we discussed a series of thematic issues. The first concerned the vexed problem of authenticity. Thereafter we turned to the way in which places are packaged together for marketing purposes. The contrast was seen between traditional materials which supplied a geographical coverage but failed to direct the visitor in any coherent manner, and more focused thematic trails. We then examined the varying interpretations of history that stem from different ideological backgrounds when looking at the contested history of the Highland Clearances. Examples were taken which looked at the landscape from the standpoints, respectively, of the landed family and the dispossessed. Next the discussion turned to interpretation of traditional culture through folk museums, taking three specific examples: a state-administered ancient monument, a privately-run open-air agricultural museum, and a proposed public sector folklife theme park. These were seen not only to illustrate different scales of activity, but also to reveal varying blends of educational, cultural-enrichment, commercial and even employment motives. The final section continued the topics of theme parks and commodification with a case study of the Loch Ness interpretive centres, one of Scotland's leading tourist attractions.

Taken together, these different areas of activity indicate the varying ways in which the modern Highlands are being interpreted for the visitor and the varying ideologies brought to bear on those interpretations. The relevance of the themes located is not just confined to the rural environment of the Highlands, but can be extended to other fields of heritage. It is to the industrial sphere that we now turn.

Notes

1. The arm of the Scottish Office responsible for preserving and interpreting historic properties in state stewardship.
2. Scottish experience of stately-home tourism is chronologically similar to English experience, but is very different with regard to the meaning of such properties, especially in the sense of different systems of land ownership (see Morris, 1991).
3. There is no room here to explore the multidisciplinary literature on the philosophical and practical issues thrown up by interpretation. Among issues explored in the debate on this subject are the ideological construction of history, environmental philosophy, the commodification of place, authenticity, postmodernism, post-industrialism, nature conservation and national identity. For more information see Horne (1984), Wright (1985, 1991), Harvey (1989) and Walsh (1992).
4. A point reinforced by the manifest plurality of Scottish historical writings (see Ascherson, 1988).
5. The Earldom of Sutherland dates back roughly to 1235. This was boosted to a Duchy in 1833. At the time of the Clearances referred to in this section, however, the title was not Sutherland, but Stafford. The Countess of Sutherland acquired the title of Marchioness of Stafford when her husband acquired his family title in 1803. It reverted to Sutherland when he was subsequently made a Duke (Willis, 1991, 35).
6. No author is cited, but the probability is that the guide was written by a staff writer of the Pilgrim Press, (a firm specializing in guidebooks), acting on notes supplied by the family.
7. The 55 sites that are described in the fourth edition compare with the 40 contained in the second edition (1985).
8. Scottish nationalism is unusual among nationalist movements in that its key thrust has been economic rather than cultural.
9. The idea was that the smoke would seep its way out through the thatch. The carbon-enriched thatch would be removed periodically and spread on the land as a primitive fertilizer.
10. It must be said that highland history is littered with over-ambitious and under-capitalized schemes which failed to come to fruition.
11. In line with the definition by Boniface (1994, 101), large areas (a town, even a small region) can be considered as theme parks as long as they are unified by a specific and recognizable theme.
12. The Loch Ness Visitor Centre, which was established earlier, advises potential visitors in its advertisements that it is 'the second one coming from Inverness and the first one from Fort William'. For its part, the Official Loch Ness Monster Exhibition Centre advises its visitors to 'Avoid Disappointment: Look for Signs to the Official Exhibition'.

CHAPTER EIGHT

Selling industrial Scotland: tourism and the workplace

'If we preserve only non-industrial buildings for posterity, we cannot put the technological achievements of our ancestors into their proper perspective. Only by actually seeing them where they were built can we appreciate the scale and workmanship of these old bridges and factories. Left to itself, our imagination plays tricks with us.'
Kenneth Hudson, *A Guide to the Industrial Archaeology of Europe*

One of the most arresting sights of the 1988 Glasgow Garden Festival was a full-scale replica of a steam locomotive hanging from the arm of the huge crane at Finnieston on the north bank of the Clyde (see also Chapter 9). Built in 1932 the crane was designed for loading boilers, engines and loco-motives on to ships but was left as an isolated relic when the docks closed. The replica now hanging from its arm was no normal locomotive but one that the sculptor George Wyllie had fashioned out of straw. It aptly sum-marized the fate of Glasgow's heavy industry. As Reed (1993, 187) observed, when thinking about the symbolism of this piece:

we have become involved in an intensely serious commentary that both commemorates the city's industrial past and regrets its wasted present. Through this most memorable manifestation we come to a deeper understanding of the significance of the loss of the locomotive industry with all its attendant skills; in the giant crane put to this ephemeral and literally lightweight purpose we recognise the frustra-tion of a mighty potential power; and as the straw engine hovers forlornly over an abandoned quay waiting for a ship that will never come, we see that the Clyde that made Glasgow has itself been un-made in a most baneful fashion.

It also symbolized the importance of retaining the tangible presence of the industrial past as an aid, for the local population and visitors alike, to understanding the true spirit of place.

That expression of concern with Scotland's industrial past is a recent development. In part this is a feature shared with other western countries; a product of the widespread re-evaluation of heritage that we have already encountered in the previous chapter. Yet the pace of de-industrialization, especially in west-central Scotland, has been such that entire industries – shipbuilding, locomotive construction, coal-mining, iron and steel – and their associated landscapes are rapidly disappearing. Attention to this vanishing heritage is belatedly becoming a feature on the Scottish tourist map.

In this chapter, therefore, we consider the place that industry, both in the sense of heritage and the continuing workplace, play in modern Scottish tourism, along with the imagery projected to attract tourists. To gain some initial understanding of this matter it is initially important to understand the nature and characteristics of the industrial heritage movement in Scotland.

Industrial archaeology and heritage

Broadly speaking the chronological development of the industrial heritage movement parallels that of its rural counterpart. Until the early 1960s there were only isolated, if significant, attempts to generate awareness that the important industrial artefacts merited preservation. The establishment of the Science Museum in London's South Kensington (1899) and the opening of the first railway museum in York (1928) indicated the possibility of presenting the industrial heritage to the wider public. In Scotland Glasgow's Kelvingrove Museum and the Royal Scottish Museum in Edinburgh collected industrial artefacts to show Victorian industrial ingenuity (Johnson, 1993, 109). These initiatives were essentially concerned with artefacts, primarily from the engineering industries, which were taken and placed in museum displays. At this stage there was little concern with field interpretation in which those artefacts were understood within their normal working environments.

The first signs of changing attitudes towards the industrial past came in the late 1950s when architectural historians began to recognize the importance of past factory design in shaping the form of modern buildings (e.g. Richards, 1958). Disused iron-framed mills and warehouses were seen as structures which had influenced construction history. They could merit the same protection that historic buildings enjoyed. This was followed in the mid-1960s by the extension of archaeological study into the industrial field. Broadly defined as the 'whole life and works of industrial civilisation' (Alfrey and Putnam, 1992), industrial archaeology injected a note of urgency into matters. Deficiencies in knowledge about the character and organization of past industrial processes and life led the rapidly-deteriorating physical remains of eighteenth- and nineteenth-century industry to be regarded in a manner similar to ancient monuments – to be excavated and restored for the benefit of future generations. In the process they became features on the tourist map, generating new forms of heritage tourism and interpretive activity.

The rapid de-industrialization experienced in the 1970s and 1980s led to intensified interest in the industrial heritage. A sea change in attitudes occurred. Blighted industrial landscapes previously represented the worn-out physical fabric of a bygone era and were regarded as areas ripe for the bulldozer. Their associated social fabric was also treated with little respect, with working-class communities scattered by the urban clearance machine. Now a profound sense of loss was felt both for the technologies and for the social life that developed around them (Goodall, 1993, 93). As a result the scope of preservation steadily widened. The buildings, machinery and other remains of outmoded manufacturing, extractive industries, public utilities or communications systems became candidates for preserved status, as did workers' cottages and industrial housing.

There was also change in the style of interpretation. The conventional practice in industrial archaeology was to relate interpretation of present-day remains to the biographies of the engineers, bridge builders and architects who originally designed them. This style of interpretation led to a paradoxical end product. On the one hand it focused on the charismatic qualities of the visionary in the face of all odds yet, on the other hand, it readily embraced a conservative celebration of the society that spawned them. The result was a powerful myth of the Golden Age that hung heavily over promotional rhetoric.

The rise of the conservation movement helped to challenge this approach. The focus of attention extended beyond mere preservation of sites as islands of industrial history set in a sea of redevelopment to that of understanding their role in their true social and economic context. The reflective revaluing of the old industrial order (Robbins, 1983) has created a new agenda for the treatment of heritage. Museums and other sites are encouraged to adopt living history approaches, not just to preserve artefacts and the paraphernalia of working life, but also to show how they were used as part of the operations of factories, workshops and communication systems. Recreation of workers' living and working conditions through reconstruction, replica or audiovisual substitutes have become regular features of open-air museums. Volunteers or paid actors may play costume roles to bring scenes to life. Sites that are better endowed with resources may employ craftsmen to give displays of machine or technical skills, which sometimes lead to products on sale in the gift shop. Visitors, particularly children, are invited to participate in simple tasks and to try things for themselves. As with rural heritage sites (Chapter 7), family entertainment has progressively assumed greater weight relative to the pedagogic and culturally-enriching elements that the scholastic pursuit of industrial archaeology tended to stress. Active interpretation, visitor participation and community development have become the watchwords.

These were themselves supplemented by new interests during the course of the 1980s. Heritage no longer necessarily meant disused. A new brand of industrial tourism has seen existing firms throwing open their doors to visitors, partly to gain goodwill but often also to reap the benefit of direct sales in gift shops. As a result they have invested in visitor centres, viewing galleries and the like so that their plant can be opened to guided tours without disrupting the pattern of work.

Survey and prospect

This steady accretion of new interests and initiatives means that the industrial heritage now covers a wide array of activities, artefacts, built forms and landscapes. In the case of Scotland these include places and objects concerned with mining, quarrying, energy, manufacturing of all descriptions, public utilities, commercial buildings and communication services. At present there are 185 scheduled ancient monuments in Scotland defined as 'industrial' out of a total of 4500 such sites. Listed sites include the Dallas Dhu Distillery, the charcoal ironworks at Bonawe (Argyle), New Abbey Corn Mill, and the Forth Rail Bridge. Biggar Gasworks has become an extra-mural outpost of the Royal Museum of Scotland. Glasgow has a fine Transport Museum in the Kelvin Hall, the Paisley Museum and Art Gallery houses an interpretive museum on weaving techniques and the history of Paisley designs, and Walkerburn in the Borders has the Scottish Museum of Woollen Textiles. The model village of New Lanark (see later) enjoys special status, having been declared a World Heritage site by UNESCO. Altogether there are more than 10,000 industrial artefacts in collections (Hume, 1990; Johnson, 1993, 109).

Impressive as these numbers may sound, Scotland has fewer industrial heritage sites both in absolute and relative terms than either England or Wales. Rail preservation provides a good example. Leaving aside the summer steam specials run by Scotrail on the West Highland Line and several miniature railways, there are only two steam-powered railway lines of more than a mile currently working: the Bo'ness and Kinneil Railway, near Edinburgh; and the Strathspey Railway running from Aviemore to Boat of Garten.[1] This compares with 41 such lines in England and 11 in Wales, with their representation of a far wider range of working environments.[2] Scotland also compares poorly in terms of working and static displays of steam technology.

Other spheres of industrial heritage tell the same story. There is little of significance remaining of the Clyde shipbuilding industry aside from the small remnants still in operation. Few stretches of canal are currently navigable in the Central Lowlands, with many sections of the Forth and

Clyde Canal disrupted by road construction during the 1950s and 1960s.[3] Urban industrial sites have been vulnerable to decay, vandalism and demolition. Johnson (1993, 112), for example, noted that when a re-survey was carried out in Glasgow in 1983 of key sites included in a 1974 database (Hume, 1974), only 300 of 1100 still survived. While there are some significant exceptions, such as the conservation of Dundee's jute mills or the imaginative conversion of the Venetian-style Templeton's carpet factory in Glasgow, much of the built fabric of Victorian and Edwardian industrialism in Scotland has been irretrievably destroyed.

As elsewhere in Great Britain it has proved difficult to coordinate preservation efforts, a particularly necessary endeavour given the inter-linkage of many industrial activities. A few significant exceptions indicate what might be done. Butler and Duckworth (1993), for example, reported on the way in which an industrial interpretive trust and a rail preservation society were cooperating in a joint rail venture. The scheme would join their two main centres at Dunaskin and Minnivey in Ayrshire's Doon Valley: a development thought by some to have potential equivalent to Beamish in north-east England (e.g. Goodall, 1993). The Bo'Ness and Kinneil Railway is part of a local interpretive scheme that includes the Birkhill Fireclay Mine and a preserved worker's cottage. Nevertheless the general rule is for there to be disconnected efforts by a plethora of under-funded charitable trusts working in isolation of one another. The broader regional interpretive strategy that has emerged in many areas of traditional rural heritage is sadly absent when examining management of the indus-trial heritage.

Perhaps the greatest danger is the lack of effort to ensure that a representative sample of Scotland's industrial heritage is preserved. This has occurred despite the repeated warnings of official reports. In 1981 the Williams Committee proposed a National Museum of Industry as a means of obtaining and displaying a synoptic overview of Scottish industry (Williams, 1981). The proposal was not adopted and imbalance persists, the consequences of which are more than just academic. Nowadays much of Scotland's heavy industry and most of its engineering works either lie derelict or have been cleared. The piecemeal pattern of industrial preserva-tion means, for example, that ironworks are represented, but not iron *and* steel; that shipbuilding is poorly illustrated; and that there will be little to show for textiles, tobacco, ceramics or chemicals (Johnson, 1993, 111). With regard to coal mining, there is little in Scotland to match the colliery displays at Blaenavon or Rhondda in Wales or Beamish and Tunstall in England. Should future generations wish to reappraise the presentation of Scotland to include something more than its rural heritage, they will be left with relatively few tangible remains of industries in which nineteenth-century Scotland was a leading world force.

Having said this, it would be completely unfair to lay the blame for neglect at the doors of under-funded industrial archaeologists or museum curators. There is marked indifference at either governmental level or official tourist boards about projecting imagery of Scotland that lies outside the rhetoric of highland tradition and rurality. As seen in Chapter 1, Scotland is simply not represented to the tourist by the national tourist boards as an industrial nation. Indeed local tourist boards vary markedly in the extent to which they even mention industrial heritage in the materials that they supply to visitors. Although in the process of actively creating a new image for itself separate from its industrial past (see Chapter 9), Glasgow still directs visitors to industrial heritage in the city itself and in the nearby Inverclyde, Monklands and Renfrew areas (e.g. GGTBCB, 1992). Glasgow, however, is an exception. Rather more representative is the tourist board in an industrialized area of central Scotland that makes scarcely any reference to some of the finest industrial heritage sites in Scotland in an extensive general leaflet that otherwise concentrates on rural crafts, farming heritage, literary figures, explorers, castles, country parks, golf, walking and pony trekking. Indeed promotion of the tourist attractions of industrial Scotland rests primarily with voluntary groups or with industry itself.

Interpreting New Lanark

New Lanark, one of the most complete mill towns surviving from the Industrial Revolution and one of Europe's leading industrial heritage sites, is a case in point. It was classified by UNESCO in 1986 as a World Heritage Site, placing it on par with Stonehenge and Avebury. Nevertheless it was only saved from decay and dereliction by the work of concerned individuals acting through a charitable trust which has operated the site since 1974. By contrast officially-sponsored assistance has been relatively minor.

New Lanark was located in a steep-sided section of the upper Clyde valley at a point where the nearby Falls of Clyde would provide a consistent source of water power for its cotton mills (Figure 8.1). The settlement was founded in April 1785 as an industrial village based around its cotton-mill by an Ayrshire-born industrialist, David Dale.[4] Dale gained a contemporary reputation for enlightened treatment of child apprentices, which made the town a stopping-point for late eighteenth-century travellers. Nevertheless it is for the model community created by Dale's son-in-law Robert Owen that New Lanark has achieved lasting fame.[5]

Assuming responsibility for running the mill in 1799, by then the largest in Scotland, Owen introduced a series of changes in social and industrial

8.1   The New Lanark Heritage Trail.

practices. Without going into great detail here,[6] these involved alterations to the system of factory management and educational reforms. The latter included the construction of a prototype adult education centre, the New Institution for the Formation of Character (1816), and a School for Children (1817). By the time that Owen left in 1825 to undertake a more ambitious and ill-fated exercise in model community building at New Harmony in Indiana, the settlement had attracted wide interest from visitors from Continental Europe and beyond. Early nineteenth-century literary tourists, such as the Wordsworths in 1803, found time to call in at New Lanark while taking in the splendours of the Falls of Clyde. William Cobbett, a severe critic of Owen over some of the more ambitious elements of his model community ideas,[7] was favourably impressed by the site. He wrote:

> In going from the town of Lanark, down to the new village, you come to a spot, as you descend the hill, where you have a full view of the great falls of the Clyde, with the accompanying rocks and woods which form the banks of the river. At the same time you see the green hills, and the cattle and sheep feeding on them, at the summits of the banks on each side, and over the tops of the trees. The fine buildings of the factory are just under you; and *this*, all taken together, is by far the most beautiful sight that my eyes ever beheld. (Cobbett, 1833, 98–9)

After Owen's time the social practices at New Lanark were largely continued by his immediate successors, the Walkers, but then gradually atrophied.[8] Nevertheless a steady stream of tourists interested in social and economic reform continued to visit the site especially in summer. As an 1855 guidebook stated: 'the manufactory of New Lanark and the schools which are there established are now interesting objects of curiosity to all tourists' (quoted in Donnachie and Hewitt, 1993, 141). This curiosity continued into the twentieth century, with the name of New Lanark becoming intimately connected with the history of socialism in Great Britain.

Little of this interest, however, rubbed off on to the local economy. Economic and industrial change, particularly due to competition in the cotton industry, placed pressure on the mills, which eventually closed in 1968. Although the mill buildings were sold to a metal fabrications company, the buildings deteriorated quickly, with the roof of the school partly collapsing in 1971. Certainly when visiting in April 1969, the overall impression was that of a ghost town that seemed to have no prospect for conversion, given the awkwardness of the site and its isolation. Indeed it seemed that it was only isolation that had kept vandalism down to a minimal level: the population which had been 1562 in 1811 and 1901 in 1831 had shrunk to around 80 by the early 1970s. Whole rows of terraced housing stood empty and semi-derelict.

The story of New Lanark's restoration since 1974 by the New Lanark Conservation Trust is told elsewhere (Arnold, 1993). Broadly it consists of a continuing effort to restore and open an increasing proportion of the site and gradually to enhance the visitor facilities. Interpretation is rightly understood as a problematic subject. Paying visitors are vital for continuing viability and visitors expect to receive interpretation of the buildings and site. While it might seem that 'the physical presence' of the village, and the mechanics of factory production are strong enough stories in themselves: 'the significance of the village goes far beyond this banal immediacy. In the works and presence of Robert Owen, and in the principles he sought to apply, we have one of the roots of the way we understand our society today' (Arnold, 1993, 219–20). The root of interpretation, then, is the historical narrative of Owen and his place in the development of social and economic reform. The alternative narrative, which locates New Lanark in the social and economic history of the Scottish and world cotton industries, is secondary.

Interpretation for the 400,000 people who visit the village each year is handled by heritage trails and displays in the visitor centre rather than by external plaques on the buildings. A self-guided trail illustrates the main features, indicating their connection to Owen's biography wherever relevant. The visitor centre supplies a fuller and more structured analysis. Housed in the institute and on different levels in one of the mills, the exhibits illustrate the energy sources used, provide audiovisual presentations on the factory's work, have sections devoted to Owen's life and ideas, and working demonstrations of machinery.

The centrepiece is the 'Annie McLeod Experience'. This borrows techniques originally developed in the USA by Disney and others and pioneered in Britain at the Jorvik Viking Centre in York, the Last Labyrinth at Land's End (Cornwall) and by Cadbury's for their 'Cadbury World: The Chocolate Experience' at Bournville. Known as 'tourist experiences', they aim to combine the established educational virtues of the museum with interpretive practices based on family entertainment; a marriage of the workplace and the theme park.[9] Tourist experiences make use of theatrical techniques, animation and advanced audiovisual presentations, which are usually experienced by people sitting in moving vehicles on fixed tracks in a specially-converted building (Wylson and Wylson, 1994). The normal strategy is to move people through a sequence of scenes or tableaux, with the vehicle stopping for commentary at significant points. Bends, changes in level and dark sections are often employed to heighten the experience.

The 'Annie McLeod Experience' is a representative example of the art. It comprises a controlled interpretive experience of ten minutes' duration in the form of a 'dark-ride'. Visitors ride in two-seater modules suspended from a rail. These travel on a fixed route through 14 scenes separated by dark corridors, with special effects that include low light diffused through aromatic fog, holograms and lasers. The linking theme is the commentary provided by a semi-fictional ten-year old mill girl, Annie McLeod, who describes living and working conditions at New Lanark around 1820, as well as some material about Owen.

The style and content of the overall package of interpretive materials are not without their critics. Calder (1994), for instance, complained that the spirit of the late twentieth-century theme park has overtaken early nineteenth-century reality and that the best of the village is only revealed when one escapes from the interpretive experience. It can also be argued that the interpretive material implicitly conveys an image of New Lanark as a place apart, conceptually as well as geographically isolated. The wider context of industrial practices elsewhere and the continuing evolution of the Scottish cotton industry, indeed the later development of New Lanark itself, are inevitably downplayed. Given the international interest in Owen, however, it can be justifiably argued that interpretation of these wider dimensions of industrial heritage could better be tackled elsewhere. What is required is that other suitable sites be made available to supply that interpretation.

Industrial tours

There has always been some interest among tourists in Scotland's industrial landscapes. Late eighteenth-century visitors made a point of visiting the Carron Ironworks, especially at night when the fire from its furnaces reminded them of the gates of hell. As Sir Richard Sulivan noted on his tour in 1778, the ironworks were: 'wonderful to a stranger ... hell itself seems open to your view', with the noise like 'the yelling of all the infernal deities together' (Sulivan, 1780, 213). In the nineteenth century, viaducts, bridges, shipyards, mines, mills and workers' cottages all drew visitors interested in seeing new symbols of progress and improvement. The large audiences that attended the Great Exhibitions in Edinburgh and Glasgow later in the century and on various occasions in the twentieth century (see Chapter 9) showed that displays of modern industrial practices were powerful attractions for tourists.

In recent times this sense of the interest, even awe, that visitors feel when witnessing industrial processes has again become part of tourism. Growing recognition of the direct commercial advantages (on-site sales) and indirect benefits (goodwill, knowledge of brand names) of inviting visitors into the workplace has led many Scottish firms to invest in interpretive materials and visitor centres. These vary considerably in scale. At the level of craft industry this may comprise little more than printing a contextual leaflet and creating space for a salesroom, an increasingly common feature in the textile industry. Visitors to tweed or plaid weavers in outlying areas are encouraged by leaflets left at hotels and tourist information centres to visit workshops to see traditional methods of production. The typical pattern is a short talk outlining the history of the craft, followed by a working demonstration of the weaving process. An image is steadily built of product steeped in the Scottish heritage that, by virtue of being handmade to traditional designs, is both high-quality and distinctive. Leaving visitors to peruse the salesroom at the end of the visit supplies an opportunity to convert interest into purchases.

Larger industrial companies that encourage visits often deal with flows of visitors that dwarf those of the leading historic buildings (Barke and Harrop, 1994). This pattern was set by a number of famous English firms that pioneered techniques of interpreting the workplace for visitors.[10] More recently some Scottish companies have adopted the same policy of arranging visits replete with commentaries favourable to the company's activities and products. The remaining Clydeside shipbuilder offers a brief accompanied tour of the yard. Hydro-electric power stations offer visits to the turbine rooms deep in the hillside. Until its recent closure the nuclear electric installation at Dounreay provided a painstakingly-crafted tour assisted by a lavish interpretive centre. Its content took its cue less from local circumstances than from a national policy instituted by British Nuclear Fuels Ltd in 1986 by which they try to win the hearts and minds of the general public regarding the safety and desirability of their product.

The Baxters Experience

The market leader in this respect, however, is Baxters Soups of Fochabers, with annual visitor figures of 180,000. The Baxters tour, which centres on a programme entitled the 'Baxters Experience', was initiated in its present form in 1985. Its theme, by now perfectly familiar, is to associate an image of high product quality with the tradition and stability of the Highlands and its people. Baxters is a local family firm founded in 1914. The aim of the experience, in the words of two senior executives of the company, 'is to combine interpretation of the Baxter family heritage with that of the local area' (Baxter and Weir, 1993, 251). Publicized by press advertising and leaflets that outline the site's main features, admission to the experience is free. In return the visitor receives a carefully structured tour that leads progressively towards a promotional message.

Its construction is an interesting example of the art. Aimed at a family audience, it recognizes that the attention span of children is an important parameter of how much adults are likely to enjoy the visit. It therefore seeks to provide variety (essential for retaining the interest of children present on family visits), along with the ability to self-pace towards the end. The formal part of the tour is a conventional works' visit. Visitors see an audiovisual presentation which explains the company's activities against the backdrop of the four generations of family history. This is followed by an optional factory tour with most interpretation conducted by a guide from a specially constructed viewing gallery. It ends in the labelling department, where the products become recognizable as the finished items.

This is followed by a visit to the Old Shop, a stone-built structure belonging to the family which formerly stood in the High Street in Fochabers but was dismantled and reassembled on its new site in 1968. Simulating the products and display of the late nineteenth century, visitors are shown round by a guide in old-fashioned grocer's apron. Adjacent to this is a museum with further interpretive materials about the family, the firm and its products. There is then a gallery with the full range of products offered by the firm, a Victorian kitchen with women 'appropriately attired in mob caps with Victorian aprons' (Baxter and Weir, 1993, 256) that acts as a retail outlet, and a 120-seat restaurant. Its windows look out over the River Spey and fields in which graze long-horned highland cattle, that most imageable element of the Scottish countryside. The links between product and the land, and between tourism and retailing, are further cemented.

The whisky industry

Of all Scottish businesses it is the whisky industry that has implemented the most widespread and integrated policy of promoting industrial tourism, permeating all levels of activity from individual distillery, through regional packaging of places to a purpose-built national interpretive centre based in Edinburgh. These are worth considering in further detail.

Individual distilleries commonly advertise free tours for visitors during the summer months. Assisted by the industry's general publicity and marketing efforts, they are again marketed along the theme of traditional craftsmanship leading to a unique and high quality product. Given a visitor throughput that commonly runs into thousands during the summer months, distilleries often set aside dedicated space for introductory audiovisual presentations. These invariably stress the link between the product and the land, placing present-day products in the light of the distillery's history and stressing the natural ingredients of the drink. The presentation is followed by a tour that is structured to follow the various stages of the production process. At its completion, there are tastings of specimen malts, before leading visitors to the distillery shop at the point of exit.

At the regional level there are various attempts to improve awareness of individual distilleries and to provide a trail that visitors might follow. One example is the Malt Whisky Trail, a 70-mile signposted road tour linking eight distilleries and a cooperage in the Grampian Highlands (Figure 8.2).

The trail is supported by a custom-designed leaflet, produced by an advertising agency (Benison Design). Opening out to a 62 by 48 centimetres format, its main content is a schematic map, a poster-size representation of the distilling process, two photographs, facsimiles of the trademarks of the distillers and no more than around 400 words of text in any one of the six languages employed.[11] Brief notes tell about the six stages in producing malt whisky, with drawings of key stages in the process and implements used. The trail tells little about the delights of highland scenery, apart from those features that contribute to the taste of the whisky.

The clarity of the leaflet marks it out against many other attempts to package locations as part of the promotional process (see Chapter 7). The key element in the Malt Whisky Trail is the offer of a unique selling proposition. Produced by cooperation between the whisky and heritage industries, it employs promotional material to strip the selling message down to its simplest form. The hours of opening of each distillery and the cooperage are listed and it is stated that: 'At all the centres you will be conducted around by competent guides and given the chance to purchase products in the gift shops' (BTA, 1993). The leaflet links the rhetoric of tourist promotion to the selling of an internationally recognized product which is also one of Scotland's leading manufactured exports. The multilingual presentation was less for guiding visitors around Speyside than for circulation abroad. Promotion of place is linked to that of a valued and valuable commodity. Promotion of tourism thus takes its place in the wider marketplace.

Recently the industry has invested in a national forum with the creation of the Scotch Whisky Heritage Centre. Situated in an old school building at the top of Edinburgh's Royal Mile adjacent to the castle, it represents an attempt to take industrial tourism beyond the factory gates. The centre maintains an uneasy balance between pedagogic and commercial objectives. Its promotional rhetoric insists that the goal is that of spreading knowledge about the making and distillation of whisky for those people who cannot travel to the areas where whisky is produced. Nevertheless, since it competes for custom in an area with many alternative attractions, it has been necessary to invest in state-of-the-art interpretive techniques. The prime example of this is a tracked 'tourist experience' of similar type to that used at New Lanark.

8.2 The Malt Whisky Trail, Speyside.

The tour follows the pattern undertaken at any whisky distillery, following the product cycle from raw ingredients to bottled article. The main embellishments are audiovisual aids to represent more of the historical background to whisky-making and three-dimensional models to increase understanding of the distilling process. After visiting static exhibits and receiving an introductory talk from a guide, the visitor sits in a four-seat barrel-shaped tracked vehicle for a circuitous ride around the exhibits, moving through a set of scenes which recount the history of the product in a manner of the industry's choosing.

Whisky is portrayed as 'the spirit of Scotland', intimately intertwined with the land and the people as it has been 'for hundreds of years' (SWHC, n.d.). The exhibits tell the story of the development of the whisky industry as part of the social and economic history of the Highlands. There are images of the Jacobite uprisings and Bonnie Prince Charlie; the romance of 'the illicit distiller in his hillside bothy' and the smuggler outwitting the excisemen; the visit of George IV and the royal stamp of approval for the national drink; the progressive integration of the highland distilleries into the national economy. More recent history is that of Empire, trade, decline, recession and rejuvenation. On that upbeat note, visitors end their tour in the gift shop.

The Scotch whisky industry stands out as one that has studiously created a promotional rhetoric for its tourists. From the individual distillery, through to regional and national level, it projects an imagery steeped in the craft and folk traditions of the Scottish Highlands. While education and cultural enrichment are given weight in all the industry's interpretive activities, they lead inexorably to an overt, albeit not heavy-handed, selling message. The whisky industry has effectively crafted an integrated approach to its heritage and its continuing economic vitality by appropriating the traditional imagery of highland Scotland.

Conclusion

The early parts of this chapter were concerned with the role of industrial heritage in present-day tourism. We examined the origins and development of concern with industrial heritage, noting the significance of the rise of industrial archaeology. After considering the nature and scope of those elements of Scotland's industrial heritage that are already conserved, we commented on the long-term significance of the failure to develop a representative collection of sites or a coordinated approach to industrial heritage. An exception to this rule is to be found in the case of the restored mill town at New Lanark, one of Europe's finest and most complete early industrial settlements. We considered the variety of interpretive practices employed, ranging from standard use of heritage trails to a 'tourist experience' involving a tracked ride and advanced audiovisual techniques. We then moved from heritage *per se* to discussion of industrial tourism, stressing that heritage need not mean disused. The growing use of this form of tourism as part of the marketing process was noted, looking in detail at the food-processing and whisky industries. Both were found to be tackling the task of interpretation firmly in the language of heritage. The whisky industry, in particular, was found to have crafted an approach to interpretation which is applied at all levels of tourist activity from distillery visits, through regional trails to a national centre in Edinburgh. The commodification of highland landscape and society that has been identified at so many points in this book was again an integral part of that interpretation and the promotional message that is presented to tourists.

Notes

1. This is at the time of writing. A seven mile extension to Granton-on-Spey is projected.
2. A listing of all sites of relevance to rail preservation in Great Britain (Crombleholme and Kirtland, 1985) contained 41 sites in Scotland, many of which are comparatively minor collections. This compared with around 350 in England.
3. Although plans do exist to restore canal navigation between the Forth and Clyde.
4. The Scottish cotton industry was essentially founded in the 1780s. Although the first mill of any significance was established at Penicuik in Lothian (1778), the industry quickly came to be centred around Glasgow (see Donnachie and Hewitt, 1993).
5. For more on New Lanark's context as a model village, see Bell and Bell (1972), Hall (1989) and Greed (1993).
6. For more on Owen's contribution as social and economic reformer, see Butt (1971), Donnachie and Hewitt (1993).
7. For example, Owen's notions of a landscape dotted with hollow-square Villages of Unity and Mutual Cooperation as laid out in his *Report to the County of Lanark* (Owen, 1821), were condemned by Cobbett as 'parallel-ograms of paupers' (see Donnachie and Hewitt, 1993, 121).
8. There is, however, controversy over this point: see Donnachie and Hewitt (1993, 141–63).
9. It is worth noting that Disney regarded his parks as 'museums of living facts' (Rojek, 1993, 130).
10. These include Pilkington Brothers at St Helens with 200,000 visitors annually, Wedgwood (Stoke-on-Trent, 177,000), Boots (Nottingham, 100,000) and the Ford Motor Corporation (Dagenham, 27,000).
11. English, French, German, Italian, Spanish and Japanese.

CHAPTER NINE

Cities of culture

'for four hundred years after it was discovered the Apollo (of the Belvedere) was the most admired piece of sculpture in the world. It was Napoleon's greatest boast to have it looted from the Vatican. Now it is completely forgotten except by the guides of coach parties, who have become the only surviving transmitters of traditional culture.'

Kenneth Clark, *Civilisation*

Many of the world's largest cities have long acted as magnets for tourists. The presence of historical architecture, ecclesiastical treasures, museums, theatres, cinemas, art galleries, important seats of learning and other cultural attractions appeal to an international clientèle. Yet with the exception of capitals such as London, Paris and Edinburgh which are part of a network of international tourist centres, few large cities have traditionally regarded themselves as important tourist centres. City authorities might well have advertised their civic and social amenities to the outside world, but have invested little time or money in attempting to attract visitors (Ashworth and Tunbridge, 1990; Law, 1993, 1).

The economic stringencies of the late 1970s and early 1980s witnessed a significant change in attitudes. Structural economic decline and mounting unemployment, particularly in inner-city areas, led to a re-evaluation of the potential of tourism and ancillary service industries as alternative sources of jobs and local income (e.g. ETB, 1981). In their survey of British industrial cities, for example, Barke and Harrop (1994, 98) reported that over 80 per cent of local authorities now included tourist information in their promotions packages compared with only 28 per cent in a 1977 sample. While it is true that the relationship of urban tourism to local economic development remains problematic (Jeffrey, 1990; Law, 1991), the much publicized efforts to develop tourism in places such as Bradford, Wigan and Scunthorpe (Buckley and Witt, 1985 and 1989) reveal that tourism can thrive even in locations where it would have once been considered unlikely. Few local authorities are able to pass up the prospect of developing tourism if any realistic opportunity exists to boost revenue.

This chapter examines the way in which Edinburgh and Glasgow, Scotland's two main cities, now market themselves to tourists as cultural centres. Before looking specifically at their current policies, however, it is important to gain some perspective on the role of fairs and festivals as staged spectacle and their implications for urban tourism.

Fairs and exhibitions

Towns and cities have long played a key part in cultural transmission through their role in staging festivals, fairs, games and public rituals. A regular feature of town life in the Middle Ages, fairs provided an element of spectacle that sought not only 'to massage the senses but also to engage the mind' (Borsay, 1984, 237). On a grander scale, city festivals served overt ideological ends. The ceremonial processions and games of antiquity were revived by the princely pageants of the Renaissance, with their lavish and carefully contrived temporary transformations of the urban setting. Jarvis (1994) traced the historical development of such events into more recent times. He noted how the newly established French Revolutionary Republic used spectacular displays for political messages. These displays involved not just lavish sets but mass participation by the population in choreographed ceremonies. As Jaques-Louis David, pageant-master to the French revolution, wrote: 'National festivals are instituted for the people; it is fitting that they participate in these with a common accord and that they play the principal role there' (Ozouf, 1988, 176).

During the nineteenth century the visit of George IV to Edinburgh in 1822 demonstrated that this tradition was not dead. Nevertheless in an age captivated by the machine and the transforming power of industrialization, new sources of spectacle were at hand. Their most obvious expression took the form of Great Exhibitions and World's Fairs which allowed states and municipalities to advance their political goals obliquely by exalting the economic power and wealth of their industry and commerce.

The precedent was set by the 'Great Exhibition of the Works of the Industry of All Nations' in London's Hyde Park (1851). Over six million people visited the exhibition to witness stands containing 'all that is beautiful in nature or in art'. Many of the visitors came from considerable distance. Thomas Cook was involved in arranging rail travel and accommodation in London for an estimated 150,000 persons from the Midlands alone. Others came from further afield, including North America, western Europe and the colonies. The gathering of these materials in London was partly seen by the organizers as addressing an idealistic commitment to the advance of art and industry. Yet while the tone was educational, commercial and national interests were also well served (Kinchin and Kinchin, n.d., 11). The exhibition evoked a powerful surge of nationalism, temporarily obliterating the host of social and political problems that had surfaced in the 1840s (Billinge, 1993, 103). The royal family, in particular, would never be more popular. A popular ballad sheet of the day, for example, praised not only the exhibition, but also the Prince Consort's part in designing it (Newburg, 1976, 205). A verse proclaimed:

> Great praise is due to Albert,
>   For the good that he has done,
> May others follow in his steps
>   The work he has begun,
> Then let us all, with one accord,
>   His name give with three cheers,
> Shout huzza for the Crystal Palace,
>   And the World's great National Fair!!

London held another Great Exhibition in 1862, but no further such event until the White City Exhibition of 1908 (Girouard, 1985, 295). During the interim the mantle of Europe's festival city passed to Paris. In 1855 visitors flocked to a World's Fair in the city, which besides honouring French enterprise and the nation's place in the industrial world, also aimed to foster *rapprochement* between Britain and France and to consolidate the legitimacy of Louis Napoleon (Ley and Olds, 1992, 183). There would be a further four fairs or expositions between 1855 and 1900, drawing in tourists from all over Europe and North America.

As time progressed the required level of spectacle increased. Each suc-ceeding great exhibition faced mounting expectations on the part of both the paying public and the city authorities who looked for prestige from these events. A common response was to increase the quota of architectural wonders, with both temporary and permanent structures. The main build-ing at the 1867 Paris Exposition was 1.5 kilometres in circumference; the 1889 Paris World's Fair saw the construction of the Eiffel Tower. Attendance figures steadily rose, from 1855's five million, to 11 million in 1867, 16 million in 1878, 32 million in 1889 and 51 million in 1900. Many other cities saw the potential of exhibitions, although often suffered huge financial losses in the process (e.g. Vienna in 1873). Interest also spread to the New World, as reflected by the 27 million visitors to Chicago's 1893 World's Columbian Exposition (held to celebrate the four-hundredth anniversary of the discovery of America). Containing imposing neoclassical structures grouped into a Beaux Arts White City and imposing lagoons around which people were ferried by gondolas or silent electric launches, the design of the Chicago Exposition influenced American town planning for more than a generation (Girouard, 1985, 353).

Scotland's major cities entered this market near the end of the century, albeit on a more modest scale (see also Chapter 5). Edinburgh was first with its International Exhibition of Industry, Science and Art in 1886. Edinburgh had never developed a manufacturing sector on the same scale as Glasgow or even Dundee. Most of its industry comprised skilled craft-work carried out in workshops producing such goods as furniture, iron-work, pottery and glass (Keay and Keay, 1994, 286). The notion of holding an exhibition represented a civic initiative to try to boost its industrial base.

An exhibition hall containing five galleries and covering seven acres was built in the Meadows to accommodate this venture. Contemporary descriptions indicate that this was relatively small beer compared with the wonders displayed at exhibitions elsewhere, with one observer noting that it contained: 'fine art galleries, iron and steel exhibits, models of architecture and engineering, stills for the manufacture of the national beverage – whisky, hosiery, carving, groceries, brass work, various branches of needlework ...' (LNWR, 1886, 31). The grounds contained model, if traditionally designed, artisans' dwellings and an 'Old Edinburgh Street' reconstructed by architect Sydney Mitchell from photographs of demolished buildings. The exhibition drew in 2.5 million visitors, with Thomas Cook and Son arranging tours and accommodation from London and the English Midlands. It was deemed a great social success, but the mood of the time was swinging from industrialism back to revivalism. The much greater success of Glasgow's International Exhibition amply demonstrated the fragility of Edinburgh's industrial aspirations (McKean, 1991, 204).[1]

Stung by competition from Edinburgh and from Manchester's Royal Jubilee Exhibition (1887), Glasgow launched its first International Exhibition in May 1888.[2] Located in Kelvingrove Park in the West End, its aims were openly boosterist in the general sense of the city's prestige and the narrow sense of promoting regional industry, commerce and tourism. The exhibition drew 5.7 million visitors, who came from other parts of the United Kingdom, North America and Western Europe as well as from Scotland. Much of the North American interest came from Scottish expatriates and their descendants – an early manifestation of the encouragement of Scots to 'return home' that was discussed in Chapter 6. For this reason the organizing committee of the Glasgow exhibition arranged package deals with steamship companies and excursion rates on the railways.

When visitors arrived at the showground they were confronted with buildings and pavilions in an eclectic riot of oriental styles. The exhibits were drawn from a wider range than the Edinburgh exhibition, with more emphasis placed on industrial artefacts, working models of production processes and displays revealing the new wonders of electricity. There would be three more open-air exhibitions held in Glasgow in the next fifty years: in 1901, 1911 and 1938. Seen against the background of changing economic circumstances, they blended educational, cultural and commercial objectives in different combinations. A late expression of Victorian self-confidence, the 1901 International Exhibition gathered together industrial and design exhibits within pavilions that were again finished in oriental styles. Among special exhibits was an early display of cinematography by the Caledonian Railway, taking their audiences on a cinematic journey by train. With 11.5 million visitors, it was the largest British exhibition to that date. It was also one of the first truly international events to be held in Great Britain, with steamship lines arranging package deals that brought in an international clientèle. Conferences and professional meetings were also held in Glasgow that year to reinforce the impact of the exhibition.

The 1911 Scottish Exhibition of National History, Art and Industry switched the focus to Scottish history and to Glasgow's 'energetic bid for the cultural leadership of Scotland so casually exercised over the centuries by Edinburgh' (Kinchin and Kinchin, n.d., 96). The pavilions and other structures were now primarily in Scottish baronial style, with a higher proportion of Scottish themes.[3] It had an explicitly cultural aim in that part of the exhibition's purpose was to raise finance to found a chair of Scottish History and Literature at Glasgow University and to reassert a sense of Scottish identity and an awareness of indigenous culture (Gifford, 1988, 11). Its 9.5 million visitors were offered a variety of tours and packages. The railway companies offered round trips with accommodation; Thomas Cook ran weekend non-conducted tours taking in the exhibition and a tour of the Scott country.

The 1911 exhibition took place against the backdrop of cyclical recession, which caused problems for several of Glasgow's heavy industries. The longer-term structural problems that this presaged would be clearly revealed by the events of the Great Depression in the 1930s. The depression not only eroded the city's industrial base, it also created a crisis of confidence. As the poet Edwin Muir noted in 1935:

> Thousands of young men started out a little over twenty years ago with the ambition of making a modest petition in the world, of marrying a wife and founding a family. And thousands of them have seen that hope vanish, probably never to return for the rest of their lives. This is surely one of the most astonishing signs of our time ... (quoted in Berry and Whyte, 1987, 212)

Against this background, it was not surprising that one aim of the 1938 Empire Exhibition should be 'to stimulate Scottish work and production and to direct attention to Scotland's historical and scenic attractions'. Having outgrown the space available at Kelvingrove, the 1938 exhibition was held on a larger site at Bellahouston Park in the depressed south-west of the city. With its modernist-styled temporary pavilions and 300-foot observation tower (the 'Tower of Empire') by Thomas S. Tait, architectural spectacle was again a prominent device in attracting visitors. Altogether more than twelve million attended.

The festival city

It would be the last such event until London's Festival of Britain (1951) rewrote the agenda for fairs and festivals. In the meantime Edinburgh had established an event which would transform the nature of its summer season and leaven the diet of fine architecture and post-Scott tartanry that characterized Edinburgh's tourist sector. It also permitted the city to participate in a wider spectrum of cultural tourism than it had previously enjoyed.

Curiously the initiative for the creation of its International Festival of the Arts in 1947 did not come from the city itself. Conscious of the problems that the arts would face in the immediate aftermath of war, Rudolf Bing, the director of the Glyndeborne Opera, was anxious to investigate the possibility of staging an arts festival somewhere in the United Kingdom during the summer of 1946. At an ad hoc committee meeting in London in 1944, the basic conditions were sketched out (Bruce, 1975, 18). It should be held in a town of reasonable size, capable of absorbing anything between 50,000 and 150,000 visitors over a period of three weeks to a month. Like Salzburg it should have considerable scenic appeal and be likely to attract tourists and foreign visitors. It would need to have sufficient theatres, concert halls and open spaces for the staging of a varied programme. Above all the chosen city would need to show willingness 'to embrace the opportunity and ... to make the festival a major preoccupation' (ibid.). Various cities were considered as possibilities, with Oxford and Cambridge front-runners along with Edinburgh. In some respects Edinburgh and Scotland's lack of prominence in music and the arts at the time made it less favoured than its rivals, but eventually the greater availability of auditoria[4] and degree of commitment in Edinburgh were decisive.

The first Edinburgh International Festival of Music and Drama, which opened in August 1947, laid down the pattern for all ensuing festivals. The official programme had a strong emphasis on music and consisted of concerts, opera, recitals, exhibitions and theatre. Most of the performing companies were English; Scottish representation, particularly in drama, was conspicuously absent. Partly as a result, eight smaller theatre groups came to Edinburgh spontaneously. They hired small halls to perform their own shows and did so at their own financial risk. These included amateurs and professionals from Scotland, a professional company from London and a local puppet company (Dale, 1988, 10). From this beginning grew the annual Festival Fringe,[5] a loosely-aggregated collection of 450–550 companies who engagingly colonize any available venue for the three-week duration of the Festival.

Film was also initially absent, not being considered as part of the international festival's remit. Through the efforts of a group led by Norman Wilson and members of the Film Guild, a self-funded festival was launched. To give it a distinctive character from the two existing festivals at Venice and Cannes, the film festival initially concentrated on the works of the documentary movement. This focus was relaxed in the early 1950s, after which it contained 'as crazy a variety as Edinburgh pleases' (John Grierson, quoted in Hardy, 1992, 32).

The Edinburgh Festival is now an umbrella term for five separate festivals: the International Festival, the Fringe, the Film Festival, and the Jazz and Book Festivals (which started in 1980 and 1983 respectively). Due to its timing, the festival also embraces the Military Tattoo (first held in 1950). Recent impact studies (reported in Law, 1993, 99) indicate the importance of the annual three-week programme to the regional economy. Together the festival attracts 600,000 visitors annually, generating between £30–40 million and helping to turn the city into Great Britain's second largest tourist attraction after London. Most attending the arts festivals are predominantly middle-class, whereas the Tattoo attracts a wider cross-section of the population. Although only lasting three weeks, the festival is responsible for contributing 19 per cent of tourist income. Moreover, these are only the direct quantifiable benefits. Various other festivals held in Edinburgh during the year can trade off the reputation of the August festival.[6] It is also probable that the publicity surrounding the festival may encourage people to visit at other times of the year (Law, 1993, 100).

It is fair to argue that Edinburgh, internally, has succeeded in assimilating the events of the festival without disturbing its traditional character. Tourists in August find the mixture as before apart from the Fringe's fly-posting activities, the constant offer of handbills for shows and the ever-present difficulties with accommodation. Prince Charlie's Scottish Extravaganza still offers an evening's hospitality complete with 'a Wonderful Jacobean Ambience'. The tartan and woollen shops still ply their 'Scottish wares'. Yet while it is business as usual on the Royal Mile, the city has been able progressively to construct a new promotional identity for itself around the festival. Edinburgh Festival information literature is carried by the British Tourist Authority worldwide. More detailed literature, such as the official guide and the fringe programme (Figure 9.1) is carried by cultural associations, public libraries and tourist information bureaux throughout Great Britain. The literature contains little of the traditional imagery of Edinburgh, but much on the festival's international character. The 1993 fringe programme noted that, after the festival's small beginnings with just eight groups, that year's festival contained 571 companies from 'every corner of the globe' drawn to Edinburgh 'because of the Fringe's reputation for exposing the best'. Visitors were invited to soak up the atmosphere and absorb the Festival at their own pace, frenetic or otherwise. There was, the rhetoric continued, 'nowhere quite like it anywhere else in the world' (FFS, 1993, 1).

9.1 Programme, Edinburgh Festival Fringe (Anna Landucci, 1993).

Reimaging Glasgow

When William Cobbett toured Scotland in 1833 he expressed open admiration for the fine architecture and cultured society of Glasgow, which he regarded as 'a city of the greatest beauty' scarcely inferior to Edinburgh (Berry and Whyte, 1987, 64). Over the course of the next 150 years the fortunes of the two cities diverged considerably. Queen Victoria so disliked the city after her visit in 1849 that she is reported to have said that she never wanted to go there again (Kinchin and Kinchin, n.d., 51). Despite Edinburgh's 'Auld Reekie' nickname – gained for the extent of its air pollution – its prestige for culture and learning was contrasted to Glasgow's reputation for gritty industrialism. This was not regarded as a fatal flaw for Glasgow while its ships-and-engineering-based manufacturing economy thrived, but it became a severe liability when that economic base declined. Glasgow's economic problems from the First World War onwards and its severe housing problems were not assisted by a reputation for crime and labour militancy. The novel *No Mean City* (McArthur and Kingsley Long, 1935) encapsulated many popular preconceptions of Glaswegian life in the character of Johnnie Stark, the hard-bitten and violent criminal, from the decrepit tenements of the Gorbals. This imagery remained despite the aims and intent of a postwar urban reconstruction policy that profoundly reshaped the city and its region. The stereotypes contained in *No Mean City* symbolized the challenge that the city authorities would have in trying to improve Glasgow's image in the outside world.

That challenge has been met by what has elsewhere been called a 'reimaging' process. This involves a wider spectrum of activity than simply tourism. Part of the strategy is for planners to promote 'a critical mass of physical development spearheaded by flagship projects' which, in concept and physical design, 'dilute the backward looking symbolism of the present' (Neill, 1992, 8). In this way, industrial regeneration, infrastructural improvement and cultural development go hand-in-hand as part of a broader policy that aims to enhance the attractiveness of the city in the eyes of the outside world and at the same time shedding the legacy of negative stereotypes. What makes current strategy different from previous approaches is that the development of cultural tourism is no longer an incidental component of the equation. As Jacobs (1992, 195) remarks, culture, 'once seen as the superstructural icing on the Marxist economic cake, is now accepted as central to the process of urban transformation'.

For Glasgow the cultural dimension of the reimaging process began in 1983 with the launch of the 'Glasgow's Miles Better' campaign, complete with a Mr Happy logo in case the audience failed to spot the double-entendre. The campaign lasted from 1983 to 1989 at a cost of £1 million and sought to lay the ghost of *No Mean City* (Arlidge, 1994a, 24). Part of the city's policy sought to draw Glasgow's considerable cultural heritage to the attention of the wider public. One step in this direction came with the opening in 1983 of the Burrell art collection in Pollok Park. Another was participation in festivals that promoted the new image of Glasgow as a postmodern city of culture, fashion, the arts and cultural tourism. An early initiative was the establishment of an annual arts festival, the Mayfest, followed by two major festivals that brought Glasgow to the notice of an international audience.

Garden Festival

The first of these was the Glasgow Garden Festival of 1988. This was the third of five such festivals held in Great Britain between 1984–92.[7] The idea was first pioneered in Germany as a mechanism for restoring bomb-damaged areas and for developing new areas of parkland and public gardens. Associated housing developments were also included in many instances. In the British versions the garden festivals were conceived as part of the government's inner-city policy. Festival sites were to be areas of derelict industrial land, which would be reclaimed over a period before the festival was held. Festivals would provide a welcome boost for the local economy by attracting tourists, but were also intended to supply lasting benefit in the sense of new parkland, social amenities or housing. There was relatively less emphasis on the festival being a showcase for horticulture.

Being precisely fifty years on from its last Great Exhibition, the Glasgow Garden Festival was conceived with an eye to its predecessor. The advance publicity billed it as 'the UK's biggest single consumer event of 1988, an international occasion, which will rank alongside the great Empire Exhibition held fifty years ago' (Kinchin and Kinchin, n.d., 169). The comparisons were not entirely apt. The Great Exhibitions had often included extensive gardens, parkland and pleasure grounds, but their primary purpose was to advertise the might and potential of the manufacturing economy. The garden festivals, by contrast, were intended to offset and ameliorate the consequences of that economy's decline.

The festival was held on a site of almost 120 acres at the disused Prince's Dock on the south bank of the Clyde. Marketed under the slogan 'A Day out of this World', it fitted into the established pattern of themed family entertainment that was pioneered by the two earlier garden festivals in England. The visitor was offered a well-crafted leisure package framed around tram rides, fairground entertainment, children's activities, retailing and catering facilities as much as exhibits specifically devoted to horticulture. Compared with Glasgow's Great Exhibitions, there was comparatively little to engage the attention of the visitor about the city's industrial achievements or potential. The main expression of Glasgow's industrial heritage was perhaps conveyed by the visual arts. Three-dimensional sculptural displays, including the Finnieston crane (see Chapter 8), were a conspicuous part of the landscaping and many made symbolic reference to the Clyde and its maritime history (Murray, 1988). They were a reminder of the place-specific boosterism that used to characterize such occasions.

European City of Culture

The net impact of the British garden festivals in any long-term sense on the development of tourism has been questioned (e.g. Kerslake, 1988).[8] In the case of Glasgow, however, this matter was not fully tested due to the imminence of the year-long celebration of Glasgow's designation as European City of Culture in 1990. This was a European Community initiative which stemmed from an idea originally proposed by the Greek Minister of Culture, Melina Mercouri. She suggested that member states should make a special award each year to one city in Europe. The chosen city would hold the title of Cultural Capital of Europe for that year and be asked to mark the accolade in ways that could demonstrate particular aspects of the city's culture to the rest of Europe. The scheme was accepted and introduced in 1985 with the designation of Athens. The City of Culture would then rotate to each member state in turn.

The United Kingdom was invited to nominate one of its cities for 1990. The Minister of Arts approached local authorities for nominations, resulting in a shortlist consisting of two Scottish cities (Glasgow and Edinburgh), two from Wales (Cardiff and Swansea) and five in England (Bath, Bristol, Cambridge, Leeds and Liverpool). Glasgow's bid centred on its existing museum and art gallery provision, plus the fact that it was the base for Scottish Opera, Scottish Ballet, the Scottish National Orchestra and the Royal Academy of Music. Despite this, it was somewhat surprising that Glasgow was chosen in 1986 given that the norm among other member states was for capitals or well-established tourist-historical cities to be chosen.

In the ensuing four years, the city constructed a new concert hall and renovated and stone-cleaned much of the existing urban fabric. Its reign as Cultural Capital of Europe was marked by a year-long programme of events involving all the main arts, exhibitions, street theatre, a Gaelic *mod* (cultural festival) and sports (including the Special Olympics). During the year 6.59 million people attended events and attractions associated with the Year of Culture.

The advertising campaign produced to promote the programme was coordinated by an international agency, Saatchi and Saatchi, under the slogan 'There's a Lot Glasgowing On in 1990' and a 'flying G' logo. A special 'Highlights' brochure including selected events planned for the year was published, with two million copies distributed throughout the United Kingdom and at British Tourist Authority outlets worldwide. Quarterly information brochures were produced and distributed in the United Kingdom. Ancillary publicity media included advertising on buses and taxis, umbrellas, badges, T-shirts and posters (see Figure 9.2). Particular efforts were made to promote the year's proceedings through the British Tourist Authority's New York office, which would also promote direct flights to Glasgow Airport. A 1990 information desk was opened at the British Travel Centre in London, a focal point for visitors seeking assistance with travel outside of the capital (Anon., 1992).

The publicity material focused on awareness. Despite media reportage and other free publicity,[9] it could not be assumed that the general public would associate Glasgow with the Year of Culture; indeed some might have assumed that any such event in Scotland would have been held in Edinburgh. The poster in Figure 9.2 was intended for display at travel agents, libraries and public meeting places. Designed by a Scottish agency, Pointsize Associates, it incorporates a painting of the city by Willie Rodger. Faced with the problem of a city with a complex topography and few emblematic landmarks that would be instantly recognizable to a broader audience, the artist showed a schematic slice through Glasgow from the University tower down to the Clyde (replete with the 'Waverley' puffer in full steam). The densely packed urban texture suggested the city's tenement character. Interwoven into the composition are most of Glasgow's more imageable buildings, ranging from the medieval St Mungo's Cathedral through to the system-built tower blocks of the 1960s. The lettering of the word 'Glasgow' is reminiscent of the distinctive font devised by Charles Rennie Mackintosh, the architect whose calligraphy, to the consternation of some (e.g. Laurier, 1993), is now an unofficial symbol of Glasgow.

Opinion on whether the Year of Culture had a lasting beneficial impact on the city's potential for attracting tourists and stimulating the employment base is, as we shall see, varied. The city council's own immediate assessment of the tourist benefits of the Year of Culture was that it had succeeded in expanding the tourist base (Anon., 1992, 29). Overseas markets accounted for 38 per cent of trips to Glasgow in 1990, with 71 per cent of the non-English tourists having come to Glasgow for the first time. There was satisfaction that the cultural community had become a new partner in the process of urban regeneration. The strategy included continuation of promotion of Glasgow as a cultural tourism destination and to develop the associated 'cultural industries' (ibid., 29, 34).

9.2   Glasgow: Cultural Capital of Europe, 1990.

The return of 'Mr Happy'

Advertising was seen as a basic vehicle for this endeavour. The 1990 slogan, 'There's a Lot Glasgowing On', was replaced by the 'Glasgow's Alive' campaign. This continued to hammer away at the past; that this is 'no mean city', that there is vibrant culture, that 'Glasgow's on the move'. In doing so the city made use of an imagery that is replicated endlessly in place promotion. Cities throughout the world now sell themselves by reference to their cultural attractions, the mirror-glass post-modern buildings, newly created central plazas, tastefully converted shopping arcades of their central business districts, and the new marinas situated in their former docklands (Gold, 1994). Glasgow followed suit. A popular advertisement in its 1992–4 'Glasgow's Alive' campaign was a collage of images aimed at the business market uncompromisingly put forward under the heading 'Glasgow: No Mean City'.[10]

Another common advertisement, hinting more at the leisure and tourist market, is shown in Figure 9.3. Its primary discourse concerns the alfresco delights of Glasgow's new café society. Young people sit at pavement tables outside the Guzzini Caffe Italia in the new Italian Centre. Casually but smartly dressed, they relax with their morning cappuccinos and designer-label beverages. The accompanying text emphasizes their leisured progress among the fine old buildings ('Victorian and Georgian splendours') and the new architectural spectacle ('glass fronted edifices') of modern Glasgow. Children run where they please in the art nouveau-styled Princes Square shopping mall. Adults take in the shops and gravitate to the cafés and wine bars to relax. The day's events include concerts and sporting events. The spirit of the Year of Culture remains intact.

The secondary discourse again confronts and continues to hammer away at the negative legacy of the past. This is no grey and crowded centre of a city with severe social and economic problems. The people sitting at the tables could be in any of Europe's major cities, drinking the same drinks and wearing much the same clothes. Their youth and demeanour, their green surroundings of potted palms and trees in leaf and the cultural allusion to Michelangelo in the statuary are a world away from *No Mean City* and *Rab C. Nesbitt*. This is a youthful and forward looking Glasgow, a European city in which it is well worth spending time.

General image-building of this type, however, has more recently come under scrutiny. Developments since 1990 suggest that the boost given to the city by the Garden Festival and the Year of Culture was only temporary. These special events focused national and international attention on the city in a manner that is difficult to sustain. Recent studies are at best cautious, and at worst caustic, about whether Glasgow has managed to 'catch the imagination' and provide the basis for tourist and service

9.3 'Glasgow's Alive' advertising campaign.

industrial growth to compensate for the relentless decline of the manufacturing economy (e.g. Cosgrove and Campbell, 1988; Reed, 1993; Arlidge, 1994a).

Implicit acceptance of some of this criticism is expressed in the decision in October 1994 to abandon the more abstract and confident 'Glasgow's Alive' campaign in favour of a return to (a revamped) Mr Happy and the 'Glasgow's Miles Better' slogan. At the same time the use of cultural festivals as a focus for tourist development is being reactivated. In 1994 Glasgow successfully beat off challenges from Edinburgh and Liverpool to win the title of British City of Architecture and Design in 1999. Interestingly the programme for 1999 is being led by Pat Lally, the leader of the City Council, and Michael Kelly, a public relations specialist. Plans mooted to celebrate the event include remodelling George Square and transforming Buchanan Street into 'the British equivalent of Fifth Avenue or the Champs Elysées' (Lally, quoted in Arlidge, 1994b, 4). Yet perhaps the most intriguing proposal is for reconstruction of Tait's observation tower in Bellahouston Park as originally built for the 1938 exhibition. As the most popular exhibition attraction with tourists of a previous generation, there are few structures that could be a more poignant symbol of a city's long-term commitment to the notion of spectacle as a tool for economic and cultural improvement.

Conclusion

This brief portrait of Glasgow as paradigm or as purveyor of illusion brings to an end this survey of the marketing of Scotland's two main cities as centres for cultural tourism. In the course of this chapter we discussed the historical importance of spectacle in the life of cities, noting the cultural and political roles of fairs and pageants. The re-invention of spectacle in the shape of Great Exhibitions and World's Fairs as celebrations of industrial capitalism attracted the attention of civic authorities in both Edinburgh and Glasgow. In the case of Edinburgh it can be seen in retrospect as a brief flirtation along the city's path towards becoming a world centre for cultural and historic tourism. That position was founded on the city's long-standing reputation as a seat of culture and learning, but was developed much further with the establishment of the International Festival in 1947. This event, together with its four associated festivals, enabled Edinburgh to be developed into an international Mecca for the arts that does not trade directly on the city's traditional tourist virtues.

The relative effortlessness of Edinburgh's progress in this respect contrasts markedly with that of Glasgow. The latter's four great exhibitions represented a deep investment in and commitment to the city's self-image as a force in world manufacturing industry; an ambition that was betrayed by the relentless decline of its heavy manufacturing base. Realization of this fact led in the 1980s to a thoroughgoing attempt to 're-image' the city through marketing and promotion as a city of culture. While this involved some rediscovery and marketing of the city's half-forgotten architectural and cultural heritage, the policy was led by energetic competition for prestige cultural events. The garden festival and the programme for Glasgow's year as European City of Culture focused international tourist attention on Glasgow as never before, a focus that is being maintained by tourist agencies. It was noted that wider doubts about the efficacy of a tourist-led recovery in the local economy have led to revision of the rhetoric being conveyed by the city's promotional agencies.

Notes

1. It should be noted in passing that Edinburgh did host a Scottish National Exhibition between June and September 1908. Although of some importance for tourism in that year (as noted in Chapter 5), it did not seriously alter the projection of Edinburgh as a historical and cultural centre.

2. The national rivalry with Edinburgh still exerts a hold. Writing from an Edinburgh perspective, McKean (1991, 203) referred to Glasgow's as a 'copycat exhibition'. From a Glaswegian perspective, Kinchin and Kinchin (n.d., 19) disparagingly note that most of the important exhibitors in Edinburgh 'had been Glasgow firms'. On a different note, the rivalry between Glasgow and Manchester was due to economic and commercial considerations. Glasgow prided itself as being the Second City of the British Empire and was keen to resist the rival claims of Manchester with which it shared interests in North Atlantic trade, especially in the cotton industry.

3. A notable feature of the 1911 exhibition was an amusement area containing people from throughout the world along with their native dwellings. Alongside the Laplanders and Equatorial Africans was a highland village ('An Clachan') with Scotland's own 'aborigines' displayed as an endangered species in their blackhouses, speaking Gaelic and practising native crafts. A larger version, with similar intent, would be constructed at the 1938 Empire Exhibition.

4. Edinburgh had suffered less bombing than many towns and cities and most of its concert halls and infrastructure were still intact (Hardy, 1992, 15).

5. The name comes from a report by the playwright Robert Kemp in *The Scotsman*, who in 1948 noted that: 'Round the fringe of official Festival drama there seems to be more private enterprise than before ...' (Dale, 1988, 12). The name stuck, with the Fringe Society set up in 1959 to coordinate matters. For more on the Fringe, see Edwards (1991).

6. A good example is the Folk Music Festival, normally held in April.

7. Liverpool (1984), Stoke-on-Trent (1986), Glasgow (1988), Gateshead (1990) and Ebbw Vale (1992).

8. Although not within the scope of this text, it may be noted in passing that there are stronger grounds for doubting the efficacy of the garden festival as

a mechanism for urban regeneration. The site remained a derelict eyesore after the festival finished, with housing development taking place painfully slowly.

9. Although there were alternative views (e.g. Stewart and Birt, 1990), by and large the favourable reportage made the press effectively an extension of the promotional machine.

10. The six photographs used in the collage were: a view of Clydeside at sunset with fine buildings partly obscured by the European Union flag (the European dimension or possibly an allusion to the Year of Culture); a post-modern glass tower of vacant office space (advanced economy, available space); ornamental ironwork (heritage); a computer operator at work (technology), golfers leaving the clubhouse in autumnal sunlight (leisure appealing to the business market); and the tail fins of American Airlines aircraft (superior communications). For more on the general use of this imagery, see Gold (1994).

CHAPTER TEN

Conclusion

'Narration does indeed have a content, but it also belongs to the art of making a *coup*.'
Michel de Certeau, *The Practice of Everyday Life*

Story-telling is an important cultural activity. It helps make sense of complex realities and conveys important ideas. Story-telling can also be very reassuring, helping to identify heroes and villains and telling people which is the best side to be on. At the same time, it is also a source of power. By participating in this activity, story-tellers can construct tales that suit their own ends or justify their own positions. They can fudge inconvenient details so as to engage the audience and permit the moral of the tale to shine through. All that is essential for the story-teller is that the story is regarded as persuasive or, if not that, then at least plausible.

In the course of this text we have explored a range of stories that have been told as part of the business of attracting tourists to Scotland. We began in the mid-eighteenth century, a time when the Enlightenment was creating interest among intellectuals in the role of Europe's peripheral regions as repositories of traditional culture. The modernizing influences let loose during the aftermath of Culloden led those like Samuel Johnson to journey to the Highlands and Islands to make acquaintance with a traditional society that they believed was rapidly disappearing. Others came to view the Scottish landscape in the manner of their choosing, whether picturesque, sublime or romantic. They were accompanied in their travels by the writings of previous travellers. In due course their own memoirs and reflections would guide successors on their tours of Scotland.

This process of accretion was not simply one of gathering information, for travellers' tales also created frameworks that structured the experience, of others. Nowhere was this more clearly seen than in the quest for evidence of the existence of Ossian and the authenticity of his poetry. Stories disseminated throughout Europe about the possibility of a long-forgotten cultural hearth to rival classical Greece and Rome. Travellers came to Scotland in search of a culture that they wanted to find and were happy to interpret what they saw in that light. In time, the influence of Ossian waned as the nature of Macpherson's activities became clear, yet a market for Scotland and things Scottish had been created. It would be brilliantly exploited by Sir Walter Scott.

Relatively little need be added at this stage about the role played by Scott in the invention of modern Scotland. His poems and novels created a largely imaginary world of chivalrous deeds and noble intent taking place against a backdrop of spectacular, but readily identifiable, highland and border settings. His writings captivated readers across western Europe and North America and exerted a powerful influence over the stage and the opera house. His activities as pageant-master for George IV's visit to Scotland allowed him to conflate Scottish identity with highland identity, effectively recasting reality in the shape of his imaginative creations.

The effect of Scott's story-telling on the tourist industry was immediate and catalytic. For more than 50 years large numbers of visitors came to Scotland specifically to visit the localities made famous by Scott and to imagine highland landscapes peopled by his characters. In time literary tastes changed and the attraction of these specific sitcs diminished, but his distinctive depictions of Scotland and the Scottish people prevailed. His stories, as we observed, effectively wrote the script for the promotion of Scottish tourism through the nineteenth and twentieth centuries. The romantic Highlands, along with the architectural splendours of Edinburgh, would be the quintessence of the tourist's Scotland. The rest became largely invisible to the tourist gaze.

Yet if the outlines of the script were written, there was still much room for interpretation. As the nineteenth century progressed the market for tourism changed in various ways, most notably due to increasing participation and greater accessibility. Instead of being characterized by small numbers of aristocratic and academic travellers, Scottish tourism steadily drew increasing numbers of middle-class visitors, individually and in organized groups, to tour the sights.

Their arrival, coupled with the desire of the railways to boost their traffic, created a defining moment in two respects. First, promotion became a routine and organized activity undertaken by the railway companies' own publicity departments or by specialist travel-book publishers. Moreover unlike the great works of the literati, their publications were almost invariably anonymous. This was a far cry from the world of literary tourism, where visitors journeyed from place to place reading aloud from *Fingal* or *The Lady of the Lake*. Secondly, much greater diversification was witnessed in tourist markets. The upper classes pursued their many new hobbies and interests in ever remoter parts of rural Scotland. Aided by a system of landownership favourable to the creation of sporting estates, many followed the royal family in turning the Highlands into a playground for the social élite.

Despite the style of promotion and the nature of tourist markets changing, there was little impact on the prevailing mode of representation. The ideas promulgated by Scott and his followers clung tenaciously to

Scottish tourism. In the nineteenth century they underpinned the rhetoric used by the railways, Thomas Cook and others in their promotion of tourism. In the twentieth century the same ideas would be assimilated into promotional materials despite the advent of mass tourism and the continuing diversification of tourist markets. The rhetoric of the open road, so important in promoting tourism to motorists, was seen to be a continuation of, rather than a break with, the past. The further advent of new media and the growing incursion of professional agencies into the promotion of Scottish tourism made little practical difference. The standard representation of Scotland and Scottish lifc remained centred around sentimental and romanticized notions of the Highlands.

Yet even if representations have resisted change, the stories which feature those representations do vary considerably. The importance of this point was seen in several chapters that considered the heritage industry. These examined the current interpretive practices of Scottish heritage sites from museums to theme parks, noting the balance struck between education and cultural enrichment on the one hand, and commercial and wider economic considerations on the other. With regard to the highland heritage, we noted the differences brought by contrasting ideologies and by the varying degrees of commodification. With regard to the industrial heritage, attention was drawn to the problems of omission as well as commission. Failure to retain a representative collection of sites for industries in which Scotland was once a world leader or to ensure a coordinated approach to interpretation pose problems. ln particular there will be little tangible evidence remaining for any future reappraisal of the representation of Scotland to include anything other than its rural heritage.

The next chapter examined another aspect of contemporary storytelling, namely the attempts made by major cities to revive the notion of using spectacle to enhance their economic and cultural interests. Edinburgh and Glasgow were seen to be in the business of selling themselves as cultural capitals. In the case of Edinburgh, this involved continuation of long-standing trends notwithstanding a brief late nineteenth-century flirtation with improving the city's industrial profile. In the case of Glasgow, cultural boosterism represented a distinct departure. After holding four great exhibitions to celebrate its industrial power, it was a melancholy reflection on the city's industrial economy that the tradition would be revived after half a century to try and ameliorate some of the consequences of decline. Through marketing efforts and judicious use of urban festivals Glasgow has attempted to break with the standard rhetoric of Scottish tourist promotion. The extent of its success in doing so perhaps lies less in breaking the mould than in the fact that Glasgow's cultural heart now receives mention in many, if not all, national tourist brochures as being somewhere worth visiting. That, in itself, constitutes progress.

'When Will You Go?'

A final index of the current promotional style is revealed by the Scottish Tourist Board's (STB) most recent publicity campaign.

During August 1994, a month when the Edinburgh Festival gives Scotland its brief annual burst of publicity, the STB initiated a campaign to promote short-break autumn holidays. It was based around the enigmatic slogan 'When Will You Go?' and employed a brown leaf motif. The campaign was one of the most intensive and integrated undertaken by the STB. It lasted for two months and featured television advertising, newspaper and magazine advertising, and packs of brochures sent by mail or distributed to inquirers at travel agents.[1] A follow-up questionnaire was sent in late November to gauge audience response and provide some measure of the effectiveness of the campaign.

For present purposes, the most interesting feature was the short burst of television advertising that comprised the campaign's centrepiece. It was based on a single video made by Faulds, a prestigious Edinburgh-based agency that has a wide range of national and international accounts. The video, however, was shown in two different forms. One version, lasting 60 seconds, was screened on Scottish television. Another, slightly edited version lasting 40 seconds was shown once-nightly in prime-time slots on English and Welsh independent television channels over a period of a week.[2] Both versions were intended to create audience awareness of the promotional opportunity and encourage them to inquire further, but the English version was more immediately connected to a promotional campaign by offering a telephone number for direct inquiries.

Figure 10.1 conveys the full storyboard for the advertisement, along with the locations employed.[3] Cryptic and multi-layered in content, it was intended to yield meaning at a single showing, but was complex enough still to engage audience attention after several viewings. The advertisement attempted to convey the appeal of Scotland by means of a folk-music score – the Silencers' version of the folk ballad *The Wild Mountain Thyme*[4] – and a collage of atmospheric visual imagery delivered at almost subliminal speed. At its simplest, the advertisement could be read as a story of parting and reunion. A young woman sits on a train reading a book of poetry [scenes 4–8]. She looks up dreamily from her book to see, in her mind's eye, a solitary surfer on a wild Scottish beach [9–10]. Flashback sequences suggest that they were childhood sweethearts who were pulled apart; he remaining in the Highlands [13], she taken by her family to the city [11, 12]. She has now returned for an assignation. Seen taking a shower and gazing out the window of her hotel room [14, 16], there is the suggestion of the hotel's air of traditional refinement as well as the sexual underpinning of the forthcoming assignation. She arrives at a highland railway

1. Storm waves pound the Atlantic sea-shore (Tiree, Inner Hebrides); the opening instrumental bars of *The Wild Mountain Thyme*.

2. A mountain with cascading streams (Glencoe). Speeded up clouds (and shadows) scud across the scene.

3. A tree in full leaf with a yellow autumnal glow. A flock of birds takes flight. *Voice-over by Norman MacCaig: 'Then sleep/And then was the morning/ Smiling in the dance of everything'. Lasts until scene 7.

4. A young woman on a train crossing Forth Rail Bridge. She gazes into space perhaps stimulated by ...

5. ... the passage of poetry in the book on her lap.

6. Cuts back to young woman's face.

7. The Forth Rail Bridge. Effects indicate passage from night into misty day.

8. Back again to the woman's face, now perhaps seeing in mind's eye ...

9. ... a solitary surfer and surfboard on a beach (Tiree).

10. Close up of the surfer, in wetsuit top. He turns to camera.

11. Roof-tops of terraced houses built on hill-side (Victoria Terrace, Edinburgh). More speeded up cloud effects.

12. A family group with a small girl hand in hand with her parents. Filmed in Heriot Place, Edinburgh, with the Castle Hill in the background, the street is decked with flags and bunting. The small girl, resembling the young woman seen earlier, looks round as if she is missing something (or someone).

13. A small boy pushes his bicycle across a wooden highland bridge (Lower Glencoe). He too looks longingly behind him, then continues on his way.

*14. The woman dries her hair after a shower.

*15. A highland valley, with distant hills. A stand of trees in the middle blocks the view. Repetition of cloud effects.

16. A hotel room (the Howard Hotel, Edinburgh). The woman is dressed in a full-length bath towel with her hair in another towel. She has a tea-cup and saucer in her hands. She gazes out through the hotel window as if waiting.

17. Repetition of 15.

Figure 10.1 Storyboard for 'When Will You Go?' advertisement.

Scenes omitted in the edited version shown on English Independent Television networks in August 1994 are indicated above with an asterisk.

18. The man's face again and the release of a white dove, seemingly representing the free spirit.

19. The woman's face, holding back her hair to prevent it blowing in her eyes.

20. A highland castle near the shore (Castle Ti'Oram, Loch Moidart). Speeded up effects of the tide coming in.

21. A pool teeming with wild salmon (Kilninver).

22. The man in a thistle-covered field. He looks over his shoulder before turning reflectively to the camera.

*23. Train doors opening on arrival at a station.

24. The woman on the platform of a deserted rural railway station (Gleneagles). She carries two travel bags.

*25. Looks up to the station clock; the minute hand moves to 3.07 pm.

*26. Curtains blowing in the wind, dissolves to …

27. … a table set for a meal with fine linen, cutlery and wine glasses.

28. The window again, with the wind blowing the curtains.

29. The woman holds up two lighted candles which flicker in the breeze.

30. Close up of man driving, looking purposeful.

31. His Land Rover crosses highland bridge (Glencoe). The voice-over continues over the next three scenes: 'Only men's minds could ever have unmapped into abstraction such a territory'.

*32. The woman stands alone at the doorway of a country cabin.

33. The book again, now held by aged hands. Camera pans back to see …

34. … the book on Norman MacCaig's lap. (Edited version has scene with the camera panning from the author's profile to frontal, which covers the omission of scene 32).

35. A loch on Rannoch Moor, with an island containing a single tree.

36. The couple reunited at a cabin (near Tarbert, Loch Fyne). He stands, she sits. He places his hand fondly on her shoulder.

37. Closing shot of highland valley with an isolated cottage, possibly where the couple are staying. Superimposition (bottom right) of caption: 'When will you go?', along with the logo of the Scottish Tourist Board. The edited version adds a telephone number (Holiday Scotland) to contact for a follow-up brochure pack. 'Or see your travel agent'. End of song.

station and walks along the deserted platform [23–25]. The man drives a
Lant Rover through highland scenery to the meeting, while she waits for
him, scanning the view from the doorway of a country cabin [32]. The
couple are shown, together again, on the verandah of their cabin [36]. She
is seated, he stands with a gentle possessive hand resting on her shoulder.
The wistful background accompaniment of a verse from *The Wild
Mountain Thyme*, with its chorus of 'will ye go, lassie, go?', added to the
nostalgic theme of separation and underscores the campaign's central
slogan. Repetition of that slogan invited the viewer to identify with the
advertisement's central theme of return and reunion.

This relatively straightforward message was embellished by layers
of naturalistic symbolism and philosophical overtones. Characteristic
autumnal colours and lighting were used to create atmosphere and under-
score the central theme of the campaign [e.g. 3]. Passage of time was
indicated by sepia tones and accelerated cloud and tidal effects [2, 11, 15,
17, 20]. The man was identified with the regular cycle of the tides and the
stability of the countryside; the woman with air, wind, movement, the
flight of birds and modernity. The man released a white dove, seemingly
representing the free spirit of the woman [18]. The woman held two
lighted candles, symbolizing hope, which flickered in the breeze, but still
burned brightly [29].

Further dimensions were added by inclusion of the poetry of Norman
MacCaig, much of whose work is strongly inspired by the landscapes of
the West Highlands and the life of Edinburgh (Drabble, 1985, 600).
MacCaig supplied two voice-overs of lines from his poetry which,
respectively, started and ended the advertisement. At the start [3–7],
MacCaig intoned three lines from his poem 'The Red and the Black'
(MacCaig, 1990, 446) that seemed to have caused the woman's reveries:
'Then sleep/And then was the morning/Smiling in the dance of everything'.[5] Later, MacCaig made a personal appearance [31–34] as his voice-
over intoned two lines from 'The Celtic Cross': 'Only men's minds could
ever have unmapped/into abstraction such a territory' (MacCaig' 1990,
69). Seen against the background of the backdrop of the highland scenery,
its use here was designed to be evocative of the physical strength of the
Scottish landscape.

To cram such richness of meaning into a short advertisement employed
in a limited television campaign would be risky, of course, if it was not
possible for the advertiser to make connection with that rich imagery of
place and landscape which is so readily linked to Scotland.[6] At key points
in the advertisement striking pictures were presented from the repertoire
of landscapcs and artefacts that have been such a familiar part of this
book: the Forth Rail Bridge, Edinburgh's terraces and Castle Hill, majestic
mountain and glen, a highland castle down by the shorelinc. Whatever

sense viewers might or might not make of the multi-layered advertisement itself, these apparently emblematic images effectively anchor the storyline. They provide visual cues that many would quickly associate with Scotland and its people.

Imagination constrained

This quality of ready association is important. The makers of this advertisement have taken the selling themes of Scottish tourism and welded them into an intriguing new synthesis. Yet despite its televisual sophistication, this advertisement remains recognizably rooted in precisely the same imagery as found in more straightforward examples of current publicity materials – nostalgic, sentimental and wreathed in the Celtic mistiness of the romanticized Highlands.

Viewed dispassionately, that continuity is both benefit and constraint. Scottish tourist boards have an advantage that their counterparts in many other parts of the world would be delighted to possess, namely they have little difficulty in producing publicity materials with an easily recognized and attractive promotional message. Whenever they are needed, representations that have existed for more than a century can always be pressed into service to create an advertisement or brochure that an international audience will immediately perceive as relating to Scotland.

Nevertheless, it cannot be denied that this advantage is also a constraint. Regardless of their colourful appearance and nostalgic appeal, tartanry and glimpses of highland scenery are undeniably predictable. Although a ready and dependable market can be reached through the traditional promotional messages that they support, they are unlikely to serve as the basis for attracting the type of growth in tourist markets that policy makers currently desire. Nor are they likely to generate a selling message that will persuade visitors 'to come not only during the peak months; to visit not only the more obvious places; and to stay longer and spend more' (Reid, 1994, x). Effective promotional activity seeks to make and remake images of place and landscape to interest the widest possible, range of potential tourists. To do so requires new stories to be told about Scotland and its people: stories that are inclusive of the nation as a whole rather than continually directing tourists' attention to its highland fringe. While not breaking the mould, the promotion of Glasgow demonstrates that the standard repertoire can profitably be expanded. Other cities of Scotland could also advance their claims as centres for cultural tourism. Other areas of rural Scotland, especially Galloway, Fife, Tayside and the now neglected Borders, could easily be added to the list of regions worth visiting. So, too, could areas in which the remains of the industrial past can be harnessed towards creating greater understanding of the mainstream of Scotland's history in the nineteenth and twentieth centuries.

Finally we return to a point made at the outset, namely that tourism is one of the main ways in which a nation is represented to outsiders. It has not been part of this book's remit to discuss whether or not the representations considered here are harmful to Scottish culture and identity.[7] What is clear, however, is that conventional promotional policy propagates a conservative and incomplete picture of Scotland which in turn may limit the nation's ability to broaden its tourist base and to gain vital new sources of economic development. Ironically, then, the representations of Scotland so long employed by tourist agencies may now limit the potential of tourism rather than expand it.

Notes

1. Although the campaign would continue to be used into 1995.
2. It was shown between 8–9 pm in breaks during popular comedy and drama series on the Independent Television networks. This latter version contained six fewer scenes and had an additional closing caption. The scenes that were omitted are shown in Figure 10.1.
3. The scenes were shot over a five-day period between 27 and 31 July 1994.
4. Recorded on EMI Records. *The Wild Mountain Thyme* is a traditional Scottish air with lyrics based on 'The Braes of Balquither, by Robert Tannahill (1774–1810). It was subsequently copyrighted by Francis McPeake, a Northern Irish piper of Scottish descent.
5. This first voice-over is not used in the version shown on English, Welsh and Ulster television.
6. It can be argued that the landscape element appears relatively stronger in the edited version seen outside Scotland, because omission of key scenes make the human interest story-line somewhat harder to follow.
7. Twentieth-century Scottish writers, for example, have often felt the need to commit themselves to the possibility of a socialist transformation of society before they can imaginatively grasp its present reality. Only by giving back a future that tartanry ignores and which kailyard suppresses into static passivity can the dynamic of the present be realized (Cairns, 1982, 14).

Bibliography

The references listed in this bibliography include both the primary and secondary sources used in writing this book. Full details of publishers are not always supplied on sources that appeared before 1900, since many were privately published and bear only the names of their printers.

Adams, I.H., 1978, *The making of urban Scotland*, Croom Helm, London.

Alfrey, J. and Putnam, T., 1992, *The industrial heritage*, Routledge, London.

Anderson, G. and Anderson, P., 1834, *Guide to the highlands and islands of Scotland including Orkney and Zetland*, John Murray, London.

———— 1856, *Handbook to the Inverness and Nairn Railway, and the scenes adjoining it with the time tables, list of fares, and regulations of the line*, Courier Office, Inverness.

Anderson, I.H., 1900, *An Inverness lawyer and his sons*, Aberdeen University Press, Aberdeen.

Anderson, J., 1981, *Sir Walter Scott and history, with other papers*, Edina Press, Edinburgh.

Anderson, P., 1890, *Handbook to the Highland Railway and west coast*, ninth edition, Northern Chronicle Office, Inverness.

Andrews, M., 1989, *The search for the picturesque: landscape aesthetics and tourism, 1760–1800*, Scolar Press, Aldershot.

Anon., 1830, *The steam boat companion; or stranger's guide to the Western Highlands and Islands of Scotland, including Staffa, Iona and other places, usually visited by travellers; with a topographical description of the River Clyde and the adjoining scenery of Loch Lomond*, James Lumsden and Son, Glasgow.

———— 1859, *Black's picturesque tourist of Scotland*, A. and C. Black, Edinburgh.

———— 1862, *The railway traveller's handy book of hints, suggestions and advice before the journey, on the journey and after the journey*, Lockwood, London. (Reissued, ed. J. Simmons, 1971, as *The railway traveller's handy book*, Adams and Dart, Bath).

———— 1872, *The tourist's handy guide to Scotland*, William Paterson, Edinburgh.

———— 1880, *Ward and Lock's (late Shaw's) tourists' picturesque guide to Oban, Staffa, Iona*, Ward, Lock and Co., London.

———— 1936a, *Cook's motor tours: Great Britain and Ireland*, Thomas Cook and Son, London.

———— 1936b, *How to see Scotland*, Thomas Cook and Son, London.

———— 1986, *Scotland's fishing heritage trail: North East*, Fishing Heritage Trail, Edinburgh.

———— 1987, *Dunrobin Castle: seat of the Countess of Sutherland*, Pilgrim Press, London.

———— 1992, *The 1990 story: Glasgow Cultural Capital of Europe*, Glasgow City Council, Glasgow.

Arlidge, J., 1994a, 'Blob on the landscape', *The Independent*, 17 November, 24.

———— 1994b, 'Glasgow hopes shrivel after the hype', *Independent on Sunday*, 2 October, 4.

Arnold, J., 1993, 'The New Lanark story', in J.M. Fladmark, ed. *Heritage: conservation, interpretation, enterprise*, Donhead, Wimbledon, 215–33.

Ascherson, N., 1988, *Games with shadows*, Radius, London.

Ashworth, G.J. and Goodall, B., eds, 1990, *Marketing tourist places*, Routledge, London.

Ashworth, G.J. and Tunbridge, J.E., 1990, *The tourist-historic places*, Belhaven, London.

Ashworth, W., 1982, *Donizetti and his operas*, Cambridge University Press, Cambridge.

Aspinwall, B., 1984, *Portable Utopia: Glasgow and the United States, 1820–1920*, Aberdeen University Press, Aberdeen.

Auchindrain Museum, 1988, *Auchindrain: a historic and traditional farming community*, Inveraray: Auchindrain Museum.

Automobile Association, 1991, *Ordnance Survey illustrated atlas of Victorian and Edwardian Britain*, Automobile Association, Basingstoke.

Barclay, M., 1994, 'Music Matters', BBC Radio 3, 2 October.

Barke, M. and Harrop, K., 1994, 'Selling the industrial town: identity, image and illusion', in J.R. Gold and S.V. Ward, eds., *Place promotion: the use of publicity and public relations to sell towns and regions*, John Wiley, Chichester, 93–114.

Barnes, T.J. and Duncan, J.S., 1992, 'Introduction', in T.J. Barnes and J.S. Duncan, eds, *Writing Worlds: discourse, text and metaphor in the representation of landscape*, Routledge, London, 1–17.

Barrie, J.M., 1889, *A window in Thrums*, Hodder and Stoughton, London.

Batsford, B.C., 1987, *The Britain of Brian Cook*, Batsford, London.

Batsford, H. and Fry, C., 1933, *The face of Scotland*, Batsford, London.

Baxter, G. and Weir, F., 1993, 'Baxters and its visitor centre', in J.M. Fladmark, ed., *Heritage: conservation, interpretation, enterprise*, Donhead, Wimbledon, 251–8.

Baynes, K., Bohman, J. and McCarthy, T.M., eds., 1987, *After philosophy: end or transformation?*, MIT Press, Cambridge, Mass.

Bell, C. and Bell, R., 1972, *City Fathers: the early history of town planning in Britain*, Penguin, Harmondsworth.

Bell, D., 1977, 'Ideology', in A. Bullock and O. Stallybrass, eds, *The Fontana dictionary of modern thought*, Fontana, London, 298–9.

Berman, M., 1983, *All that is solid melts into air: the experience of modernity*, London: Souvenir Press.

Berry, S. and Whyte, H., eds, 1987, *Glasgow observed*, John Donald, Edinburgh.

Bialostocki, J., 1983, 'The image of the defeated leader in Romantic Art', in J.C. Eade, ed., *Romantic nationalism in Europe*, Australian National University, Canberra.

Billinge, M., 1993, 'Trading history, reclaiming the past: the Crystal Palace as icon', in G. Kearns and C. Philo, eds, *Selling places: the city as cultural capital, past and present*, Pergamon Press, Oxford, 103–31.

Blumenberg, H., 1987, 'An anthropological approach to the contemporary significance of rhetoric', in K. Baynes, J. Bohman and T.M. McCarthy, eds, 1987, *After philosophy: end or transformation?*, MIT Press, Cambridge, 429–58.

Bold, A., 1978, *Scottish tartans*, Pitkin Pictorials, Andover.

Bolton, H.P., 1992, *Scott dramatised*, Mansell, London.

Bone, S., 1938, *West coast of Scotland: Skye to Oban*, Shell Guide 12, Batsford, London.

Boniface, P., 1993, 'Theme park Britain: who benefits and who loses?', in J.M. Fladmark, ed., *Cultural tourism*, Donhead, Wimbledon, 101–9.

Borley, L., 1994, 'Cultural identity in a changing Europe', in J.M. Fladmark, ed., *Cultural tourism*, Donhead, Wimbledon, 3–11.

Borsay, P., 1984, 'All the town's a stage: urban ritual and ceremony, 1600–1660', in P. Clark, ed., *The transformation of the English provincial towns, 1600–1800*, Hutchinson, London, 228–58.

Boswell, J., 1785, *The journal of a tour to the Hebrides with Samuel Johnson, Ll.D.*, Charles Dilley, London.

Botfield, B., 1829, *Journal of a tour through the Highlands of Scotland during the summer of MDCCCXXIX*, London.

Bowman, J.E., 1986, *The Highlands and Islands: a nineteenth century tour*, Alan Sutton, Gloucester.

Brandon, P., 1991, *Thomas Cook: 150 years of popular tourism*, Secker and Warburg, London.

Bray, E., 1986, *The discovery of the Hebrides: voyagers to the Western Isles, 1745–1883*, Collins, London.

Brownhill, S., 1994, 'Selling the inner city: regeneration and place marketing in London's Docklands', in J.R. Gold and S.V. Ward, eds,

Place promotion: the use of publicity and public relations to sell towns and regions, John Wiley, Chichester, 133–51.

Bruce, G., 1975, *Festival in the north: the story of the Edinburgh Festival*, Robert Hale, London.

BTA (British Tourist Authority), 1993, *Britain: motoring itineraries*, British Tourist Authority, London.

———— 1994, *The lands of Britain: your vacation planner*, British Tourist Authority, London.

Buck, R.C., 1977, 'The ubiquitous tourist brochure: explorations in its intended and unintended use', *Annals of Tourism Research*, 4, 195–207.

Buckley, P.J. and Witt, S.F., 1985, 'Tourism in difficult areas: case studies of Bradford, Bristol, Glasgow and Hamm', *Tourism Management*, 6, 205–13.

———— 1989, 'Tourism in difficult areas: case studies of Calderdale, Leeds, Manchester and Scunthorpe', *Tourism Management*, 10, 138–52.

Burgess, J.A., 1982, 'Place promotion: environmental images for the executive', *Regional Studies*, 16, 1–17.

———— 1990, 'The production and consumption of environmental meanings in the mass media: a research agenda for the 1990s', *Transactions of the Institute of British Geographers, new series*, 15, 139–61.

Burgess, J.A. and Gold, J.R., 1985, 'Place, the media and popular culture', in J.A. Burgess and J.R. Gold, eds, *Geography, the media and popular culture*, Croom Helm, London, 1–32.

Burgess, J.A. and Wood, P., 1988, 'Decoding Docklands: place advertising and the decision-making strategies of the small firm', in J.D. Eyles and D.M. Smith, eds, *Qualitative methods in human geography*, Polity Press, Cambridge, 94–116.

Burkart, A.J. and Medlik, S., 1981, *Tourism: past, present and future*, Heinemann, London.

Burnett, J. and Tabraham, C.J., 1993, *The Honours of Scotland: the story of the Scottish crown jewels*, Historic Scotland, Edinburgh.

Butler, R.W., 1985, 'Evolution of tourism in the Scottish Highlands', *Annals of Tourism Research*, 12, 371–91.

Butler, S. and Duckworth, S., 1993, 'Development of an industrial heritage attraction: the Dunaskin experience', *Built Environment*, 19, 116–36.

Butt, J., ed., 1971, *Robert Owen: prince of cotton spinners*, David and Charles, Newton Abbot.

Buzard, J., 1993, *The beaten track: European tourism, literature, and the ways to 'culture', 1800–1918*, Clarendon Press, Oxford.

Cairns, C., 1982 'Myths against history: tartanry and Kailyard in 19th-century Scottish literature', in C. McArthur, ed., *Scotch reels: Scotland in cinema and television*, British Film Institute, London, 7–15.

Calder, S., 1994, 'Heroic tales of the riverbank', *The Independent*, 23 July, 36.

Cameron, J.M.R., 1974, 'Information distortion in colonial promotion: the case of the Swan River colony', *Australian Geographical Studies*, 12, 57–76.

Cavers, K., 1993, *A vision of Scotland: the nation observed by John Slezer, 1671 to 1717*, HMSO, London.

Chapman, M., 1978, *The Gaelic vision in Scottish culture*, Croom-Helm, London.

Chapman, R.W., ed., 1924, *Johnson's 'Journey to the Western Islands of Scotland' and Boswell's 'Journey of a tour to the Hebrides with Samuel Johnson, L.L.D.'*, Oxford University Press, London.

Cheape, H., 1991, *Tartan: the highland habit*, National Museums of Scotland, Edinburgh.

Clark, K., 1969, *Civilisation: a personal view*, British Broadcasting Corporation and John Murray, London.

Cobbett, W., 1833; 1984, *Cobbett's tour in Scotland*, Aberdeen University Press, Aberdeen.

Colgan, M., 1987, 'Ossian: success or failure of the Scottish Enlightenment?', in J.J. Carter and J.H. Pittock, eds, *Aberdeen and the Enlightenment*, Aberdeen: Aberdeen University Press.

Colley, L., 1992, *The Britons: forging the nation*, Yale University Press, New Haven, Conn.

Constantine, S., 1986, *Buy and build: the advertising posters of the Empire Marketing Board*, HMSO, London.

Cook, G., 1992, *The discourse of advertising*, Routledge, London.

Cook, T., 1866, *Cook's Scottish tourist directory*, Thomas Cook, London.

Corbett, E.P.J., 1971, *Classical rhetoric for the modern student*, second edition, Oxford University Press, New York.

Cordiner, C., 1780, *Antiquities and scenery of the north of Scotland in a series of letters to Thomas Pennant by the Reverend Chas. Cordiner, member of St Andrew's Chapel Banff*, London.

Cosgrove, S. and Campbell, S., 1988, 'Behind the wee smiles', *New Statesman and Society*, 1(28), 16 December, 10–12.

Craig, D., 1990, *On the crofters' trail: in search of the Clearance Highlanders*, Jonathan Cape, London.

Crang, M., 1994, 'On the heritage trail: maps and journeys to olde Englande', *Environment and Planning D: Society and Space*, 12, 341–55.

Crealock, H.H., 1892, *Deer stalking in the Highlands of Scotland*, London.

Cririe, J., 1803, *Scottish scenery or sketches in verse, descriptive of scenes chiefly in the Highlands of Scotland accompanied with notes and illustrations*, London.

Crombleholme, R. and Kirtland, T., 1985, *Steam British Isles: the complete guide to railway preservation, minor and miniature railways*, David and Charles, Newton Abbot.

Cunningham, L. and Reich, J., 1985, *Culture and values*, alternate edition, Holt, Rinehart and Winston, Fort Worth, Tex.

Curley, T.M., 1976, *Samuel Johnson and the age of travel*, University of Georgia Press, Athens.

Cuthbertson, D.C., 1938, *Romantic Scotland: the story of the shires*, Eneas Mackay, Stirling.

Daiches, D. and Flower, J., 1979, *Literary landscapes of the British Isles: a narrative atlas*, Paddington Press, London.

Dale, M., 1988, *Sore throats and overdrafts: an illustrated story of the Edinburgh Festival Fringe*, Precedent Publications, Edinburgh.

Daly, M., 1994, 'Incidental tourism shames', *Times Higher Education Supplement*, 29 July, 12.

Daniels, S.D., 1992, *Fields of vision: landscape imagery and national identity in England and the United States*, Polity Press, Cambridge.

de Certeau, M., 1984, *The practice of everyday life*, University of California Press, Berkeley, Cal.

Delaney, F., 1993, *A walk to the Western Isles: after Johnson and Boswell*, HarperCollins, London.

Donnachie, I. and Hewitt, G., 1993, *Historic New Lanark: the Dale and Owen industrial community since 1785*, Edinburgh University Press, Edinburgh.

Drabble, M., 1979, *A writer's Britain: landscape in literature*, Thames and Hudson, London.

———— 1985, *The Oxford companion to English Literature*, Oxford University Press, Oxford.

Duncan, J., 1805 et seq., *The Scotish itinerary containing the roads through Scotland on a new plan, with copious observations for the instruction and entertainment of travellers and complete index*, James and Andrew Duncan Booksellers, Glasgow.

Dyer, G., 1982, *Advertising as communication*, Methuen, London.

Dyos, H.J. and Aldcroft, D.H., 1974, *British transport: an economic survey from the seventeenth century to the twentieth*, Penguin, Harmondsworth.

Eagleton, T., 1991, *Ideology: an introduction*, Verso, London.

Eames, A., 1994, 'Summer in Scotland', *High Life*, June, 112–16.

Edlin, H.L., 1969, *National Forest Parks*, Forestry Commission Booklet 6, HSMO, London.

Edwards, O., 1991, *City of a thousand worlds: Edinburgh in festival*, Mainstream Publishing, Edinburgh.

Enos, T. and Brown, S.C., 1993, *Defining the new rhetoric*, Sage, London.

ETB (English Tourist Board), 1981, *Tourism and the inner city*, English Tourist Board, London.

Farr, A.D., 1968, *The Royal Deeside Line*, David and Charles, Newton Abbot.

Fenton, A., 1978, *The island blackhouse, and a guide to 'The Blackhouse' no. 42 Arnol*, HSMO, Edinburgh.

Ferguson, A., 1767, *An essay on the history of civil society*, Edinburgh.

FFS (Festival Fringe Society), 1993, *Edinburgh Festival Fringe programme*, Festival Fringe Society, Edinburgh.

Finley, G., 1981, *Turner and George the Fourth in Edinburgh 1822*, Tate Gallery in association with Edinburgh University Press, London.

Fiske, R., 1983, *Scotland and music*, Cambridge University Press, Cambridge.

Fletcher, R., 1988, 'Culture', in A. Bullock, ed., *The Fontana dictionary of modern thought*, second edition, Fontana, London, 195.

Foucault, M., 1970, *The order of things: an archaeology of the human sciences*, Tavistock, London.

Fox Talbot, W.H., 1845, *Sun pictures in Scotland*, London.

Geertz, C., 1973, *The interpretation of cultures: selected essays*, Basic Books, New York.

Gernsheim, H. with Gernsheim, A., 1986, *The history of photography: from the earliest use of the camera obscura in the eleventh century up to 1914*, Oxford University Press, London.

GGTBCB (Greater Glasgow Tourist Board and Conference Bureau), 1992, *Greater Glasgow, Scotland: where to stay*, Greater Glasgow Tourist Board and Conference Bureau, Glasgow.

Gibson, R., 1993, *Highland Clearances trail*, fourth edition, Highland Heritage, Dingwall.

Gifford, D., 1988, 'Introduction', in D. Gifford, ed., *The history of Scottish literature*, vol. 3, Aberdeen University Press, Aberdeen, 1–12.

Gilpin, W., 1789, *Observations relative chiefly to picturesque beauty, made in the year 1776 on serveral parts of Great Britain; particularly the High-Lands of Scotland*, vol. 1, London.

Girouard, M., 1985, *Cities and people: a social and architectural history*, Yale University Press, New Haven, Conn.

Glen, M.H., 1994, 'Telling the story in museums', in J.M. Fladmark, ed., *Cultural tourism*, Donhead, Wimbledon, 261–73.

GN & NER (Great Northern and North Eastern Railways), 1895, *Tourist programme: the east coast express route to Scotland*, Great Northern and North Eastern Railways, London.

Gold, J.R., 1974, *Communicating images of the environment*, Occasional Paper 29, Centre for Urban and Regional Studies, University of Birmingham.

———— 1980, *An introduction to behavioural geography*, Oxford University Press, Oxford.

———— 1994, 'Locating the message: place promotion as image communication', in J.R. Gold and S.V. Ward, eds, *Place promotion: the use of publicity and public relations to sell towns and regions*, John Wiley, Chichester, 19–37.

Gold, J.R. and Gold, M.M., 1982, 'Land settlement in the Scottish Highlands: a study of land reform in a developed nation', *Nordia*, 16, 129–33.

———— 1985, 'Napier at 100: the intractable problems of crofting in the Highlands and Islands of north-west Scotland,' in A. Leidlmair and K. Frantz, eds, *Environment and human life in highland and high-latitude zones*, Innsbrucker Geographische Studien 13, Innsbruck, Selbsteverlag des Institutes fur Geographie der Universitat Innsbruck, 35–41.

———— 1990, ' "A Place of Delightful Prospects": promotional imagery and the selling of suburbia', in L. Zonn, eds., *Place images in the media: portrayal, meaning and experience*, Savage, MD, Rowman and Littlefield, 159–82.

———— 1991, *Scottish crofting: a new selected bibliography*, Discussion Paper in Geography, 26, Geography Unit, Oxford Brookes University (formerly Oxford Polytechnic).

———— 1994, ' "Home at last!": building societies, home ownership and the rhetoric of suburban place promotion', in J.R. Gold and S.V. Ward, eds, *Place promotion: the use of publicity and public relations to sell towns and regions*, John Wiley, Chichester, 75–92.

———— 1995, 'Landscapes of regret: Culloden as symbol and myth', unpublished MS.

Gold, J.R. and Ward, S.V., eds, 1994, *Place promotion: the use of publicity to sell towns and regions*, John Wiley, Chichester.

Goldman, R., 1992, *Reading ads socially*, Routledge, London.

Goodall, B., 1993, 'Industrial heritage and tourism', *Built Environment*, 19, 93–104.

Goodey, B., 1994a, 'Art-full places: public art to sell public places?', in J.R. Gold and S.V. Ward, eds, *Place promotion: the use of publicity and public relations to sell towns and regions*, John Wiley, Chichester, 153–79.

———— 1994b, 'Interpretive planning', in *Manual of Heritage Management*, Butterworth Heinemann, London.

Goodwin, M., 1993, 'The city as commodity: the contested spaces of urban development', in G. Kearns and C. Philo, eds, *Selling places: the city as cultural capital, past and present*, Pergamon Press, Oxford, 145–62.

Greed, C., 1993, *Introducing town planning*, Longman, Harlow.

Greig, D., Humphreys, R., Lee, P., McLachlan, G. Parker, M., Roy, S., Smith, T. and Whatmore, M., 1994, *Scotland: the rough guide*, Rough Guides Ltd, London.

Gren, J., 1992, *Place-marketing in Europe: a manual*, Institut d'Etudes Politiques, Grenoble.

Grimble, A., 1896, *The deer forests of Scotland*, Longman, Green and Co., London.

Grossberg, L., Nelson, C. and Treicher, P., eds, 1992, *Cultural studies*, Routledge, London.

Gruffudd, P., 1994, 'Selling the countryside: representations of rural Britain', in J.R. Gold and S.V. Ward, eds, *Place promotion: the use of publicity and public relations to sell towns and regions*, John Wiley, Chichester, 247–63.

Gunnison, H.F., 1905, *Two Americans in a motor car: touring in Europe*, Brooklyn Daily Eagle, New York.

Haldane, A.R.B., 1962, *New ways through the glens*, Thomas and Nelson, London.

Hall, P., 1989, *Urban and regional planning*, Penguin, Harmondsworth.

Hall, S., 1977, 'Culture, the media and the "ideological" effect', in J. Curran, M. Gurevitch and J. Wollacott, eds, *Mass communication and society*, Edward Arnold and the Open University Press, London, 315–49.

Halliwell, M., 1990, *Highland landscapes: paintings of Scotland in the 19th century*, Garamond, London.

Hammerton, J.A., ed., n.d., *c.*1895, *Mr Punch in the Highlands*, Educational Book Co, London.

Hampson, N., 1968, *The Enlightenment: an evaluation of its assumptions, attitudes and values*, Penguin, Harmondsworth.

Hanway, M.A., 1775, *A journey to the Highlands of Scotland with occasional remarks on Dr Johnson's tour by a lady*, Fielding and Walker, London.

Hardy, F., 1992, *Slightly mad and full of dangers: the story of the Edinburgh Film Festival*, Ramsay Head, Edinburgh.

Harrison, R., 1994, 'Telling the story in museums', in J.M. Fladmark, ed., *Cultural tourism*, Donhead, Wimbledon, 311–21.

Hart, F.R., 1978, *The Scottish novel: a critical survey*, John Murray, London.

Harvey, D.W., 1989, *The condition of postmodernity: an inquiry into the origins of cultural change*, Basil Blackwell, Oxford.

Harvie, C., 1988, 'Industry, religion and the state of Scotland', in

D. Gifford, ed., *The history of Scottish literature*, vol. 3, Aberdeen University Press, Aberdeen, 23–41.

Hawkins, J. and Hollis, M., 1979, *The thirties: British art and design before the war*, Arts Council of Great Britain, London.

Heron, R., 1793, *Observations made in a journey through the western counties of Scotland; in the autumn of MDCCXCCII relating to the scenery, antiquities, customs, manners, population, agriculture, manufactures, commerce, political condition, and literature of these parts*, 2 vols, London.

Hewison, R., 1987, *The heritage industry: Britain in a climate of decline*, Methuen, London.

————— 1989, 'Heritage: an interpretation', in D. Uzzel, ed., *Heritage interpretation*, vol. 1, 'The natural and built environment', Belhaven Press, London, 15–23.

Hewitt, D., 1988, 'Walter Scott', in D. Gifford, ed., *The history of Scottish literature*, vol. 3, Aberdeen University Press, Aberdeen, 65–85.

Hibbs, J., 1968, *The history of British bus services*, David and Charles, Newton Abbot.

Hill, C.W., 1976, *Edwardian Scotland*, Scottish Academic Press, Edinburgh.

Historic Scotland, 1993, *A list of ancient monuments in Scotland*, HSMO, Edinburgh.

Hobsbawm, E., 1983, 'Introduction: inventing traditions', in E. Hobsbawm and T. Ranger, eds, *The invention of tradition*, Cambridge University Press, Cambridge, 1–14.

Hobsbawm, E. and Ranger, T., eds, 1983, *The invention of tradition*, Cambridge University Press, Cambridge.

Holcomb, B., 1990, *Purveying places: past and present*, Working Paper 17, Centre for Urban Policy Research, Rutgers University, Piscataway, NJ.

————— 1993, 'Revisioning places: de- and re-constructing the image of the industrial city', in G. Kearns and C. Philo, eds, *Selling places: the city as cultural capital, past and present*, Pergamon Press, Oxford, 133–43.

————— 1994, 'City make-overs: marketing in the post-industrial city', in J.R. Gold and S.V. Ward, eds, *Place promotion: the use of publicity and public relations to sell towns and regions*, John Wiley, Chichester 115–31.

Holloway, J. and Errington, L., 1978, *The discovery of Scotland: the appreciation of Scottish scenery through two centuries of painting*, HSMO, Edinburgh.

Holloway, J.C., 1988, *The business of tourism*, Pitman, London.

Hook, A., 1972, 'Introduction', in Sir Walter Scott, *Waverley*, Penguin Books, Harmondsworth, 9–27.

Horne, D., 1984, *The great museum: the re-presentation of history*, Pluto Press, London.

HR (Highland Railway), 1899, *Holiday resorts on the Highland Railway*, Highland Railway, Perth.

Hudson, K., ed., 1965, *The industrial past and the industrial present*, Univesity of Bath, Bath.

———— 1971, *A guide to the industrial archaeology of Europe*, Associated University Presses, Cranbury, NJ.

Hughes, G., 1992, 'Tourism and the geographical imagination', *Leisure Studies*, 11, 31–42.

Hulme, P., 1986, *Colonial encounters: Europe and the native Caribbean 1492–1797*, Methuen, London.

Hume, J.R., 1974, *Industrial Archaeology of Glasgow*, Glasgow, Blackie.

———— 1990, *Scotland's industrial past*, National Museums of Scotland/ Scottish Museums Council, Edinburgh.

Hunter, J., 1976, *The making of the crofting community*, John Donald, Edinburgh.

———— 1991, *The claim of crofting: the Scottish Highlands and Islands, 1930–1990*, Mainstream Publishing, Edinburgh.

ILNNTB (Inverness, Loch Ness and Nairn Tourist Board), n.d., *The Loch Ness Monster Trail*, Inverness, Loch Ness and Nairn Tourist Board and the Highlands and Islands Development Board, Inverness.

Jackson, P., 1989, *Maps of meaning*, Unwin Hyman, London.

Jacobs, J.M., 1992, 'Cultures of the past and urban transformation: the Spitalfields Market redevelopment in East London', in K. Anderson and F. Gale, eds, *Inventing places: studies in cultural geography*, Longman Cheshire, Melbourne, 194–211.

Jakobson, R., 1960, 'Concluding statement: linguistics and poetics', in T. Sebeok, ed., *Style in language*, MIT Press, Cambridge, 350–77.

James, B., 1993, 'Dr Finlay, I presume', *Radio Times*, 27 February, 35–6.

Jarvie, G., 1989, 'Culture, social development and Scottish highland gatherings', in D. McCrone, S. Kendrick and P. Straw, eds, *The making of Scotland: nation, culture and social change*, Edinburgh University Press in conjunction with the British Sociological Association, Edinburgh, 189–206.

———— 1991, *Highland games: the making of a myth*, Edinburgh University Press, Edinburgh.

Jarvis, R.K., 1987, 'The next best thing to being there: the environmental rhetoric of advertising', *Landscape Research*, 12(3), 14–19.

———— 1994, 'Transitory topographies: places, events, promotions and propaganda', in J.R. Gold and S.V. Ward, eds, *Place promotion: the use of publicity and public relations to sell towns and regions*, John Wiley, Chichester, 181–93.

Jeffrey, D., 1990, 'Monitoring the growth of tourism related employment at the local level: the application of a census-based non-sruvey method in Yorkshire and Humberside, 1981–1987', *Planning Outlook*, 33, 108–17.

Johnson, I., 1993, 'The identification of industrial heritage sites in Scotland: towards a national strategy', *Built Environment*, 19, 105–15.

Johnson, R., 1983, *What is cultural studies anyway?*, Stencilled Occasional Paper 74, Centre for Contemporary Cultural Studies, University of Birmingham.

―――― 1986, 'The story so far: and further transformations?', in D. Punter, ed., *Introduction to Contemporary Cultural Studies*, Longman, London, 277–313.

Johnson, S., 1775, *A journey to the Western islands of Scotland*, Cadell, London (for the version cited here, see Chapman, 1924).

Jones, H.M., 1946, 'The colonial impulse: an analysis of the promotion literature of colonisation', *Proceedings of the American Philosophical Society*, 90, 131–61.

KDTB (Kincardine and District Tourist Board), 1993, *Follow the royal road*, KDTB, Aberdeen.

Kearns, G. and Philo, C., eds, 1993, *Selling places: the city as cultural capital, past and present*, Pergamon Press, Oxford.

Keay, J. and Keay, J., 1994, *Collins encyclopedia of Scotland*, HarperCollins, London.

Kerslake, B., 1988, 'Garden festivals: good for tourism?', in H. Cameron, ed., *The Tourism Industry, 1988–9*, Tourism Society, London.

Kinchin, P. and Kinchin, J., n.d., *Glasgow's Great Exhibitions: 1888, 1901, 1911, 1938, 1988*, White Cockade Publishing, Bicester.

Kipps, H., 1994, 'Ideology, rhetoric and Boyle's New Experiments', *Science in Context*, 7, 52–64.

Knowles, T.D., 1983, *Ideology, art and commerce: aspects of literary sociology in late Victorian Scottish kailyard*, Gothenburg Studies in English 54, Arts Faculty, University of Gothenburg, Sweden.

Kotler, P., Haider, D.H. and Rein, I., 1993, *Marketing places: attracting investment, industry and tourism to cities*, Macmillan, New York.

Langford, M., 1980, *The story of photography from its beginnings to the present day*, Focal Press, London.

Lardner, D., 1850, *Railway economy: a treatise on the new art of transport with an exposition of the practical results of the railways, in the United Kingdom, on the Continent and in America*, London (reprinted 1968, David and Charles, Newton Abbot).

Larrain, J., 1983, *Marxism and ideology*, Macmillan, London.

Laurier, E., 1993, 'Tackintosh: Glasgow's supplementary gloss', in G. Kearns and C. Philo, eds, *Selling places: the city as cultural capital, past and present*, Pergamon Press, Oxford, 267–90.

Law, C.M., 1991, 'Tourism and urban revitalization', *East Midland Geographer*, 14, 49–60.

———— 1993, *Urban tourism: attracting visitors to large cities*, Mansell, London.

Leiss, W., Klein, S. and Jhally, S., 1990, *Social communication in advertising: persons, products and images of well-being*, second edition, Routledge, London.

Leneman, L., 1987, 'The effects of Ossian on Lowland Scotland', in J.J. Carter and J.H. Pittock, eds, *Aberdeen and the Enlightenment*, Aberdeen University Press, Aberdeen, 357–62.

Lettice, I., 1794, *Letters on a tour through various parts of Scotland in the year 1792*, London.

Lewis, J., 1993, 'The British Golf Museum', in J.M. Fladmark, ed., *Heritage: conservation, interpretation, enterprise*, Donhead, Wimbledon, 259–70.

Ley, D., and Olds, K., 1992, 'World's Fairs and the culture of consumption in the contemporary city', in K. Anderson and F. Gale, eds, *Inventing places: studies in cultural geography*, Longman Cheshire, Melbourne, 178–93.

LNWR (London and North Western Railway), 1886, *Facts and information for visitors to the exhibitions in London, Liverpool and Edinburgh*, London and North Western Railway, London.

LNWR & CR (London and North Western Railway and the Caledonian Railway), 1886 *et seq.*, *West Coast Tourist Guide*, London and North Western Railway, London.

Lockhart, J.G., 1906, *The life of Sir Walter Scott*, Dent, London.

Lockwood, A., 1981, *Passionate pilgrims: the American traveller in Great Britain, 1800–1914*, Cornwall Books, East Brunswick, NJ.

Lowenthal, D., 1985, *The past is a foreign country*, Cambridge University Press, Cambridge.

———— 1993, 'Landscape as heritage: national scenes and global changes', in M. Fladmark, ed., *Heritage: conservation, interpretation, enterprise*, Donhead, Wimbledon, 3–15.

Lowenthal, D. and Prince, H.C., 1965, 'English landscape tastes', *Geographical Review*, 55, 186–222.

Lycett Green, C., ed., 1994, *John Betjeman: letters*, vol. 1 '1926 to 1951', Methuen, London.

Lyon, R., 1987, 'Theme parks in the USA: growth markets and future prospects', *Travel and Tourist Analyst*, 9, 31–43.

McArthur, A. and Kingsley Long, H., 1935, *No mean city*, Longmans Green, London.

McArthur, C., 1982a, ed., *Scotch reels: Scotland in cinema and television*, British Film Institute, London.

———— 1982b, 'Scotland and cinema: the iniquity of the fathers', in C. McArthur, ed., *Scotch reels: Scotland in cinema and television*, British Film Institute, London, 40–69.

MacCaig, N., 1990, *Collected poems: new edition*, Chatto and Windus, London.

MacCannell, D., 1976, *The tourist: a new theory of the leisure class*, Macmillan, London.

———— 1992, *Empty meeting grounds: the tourist papers*, Routledge, London.

McCrone, D., 1992, *Understanding Scotland: the sociology of a stateless nation*, Routledge and Kegan Paul, London.

McDermott, W., and Noble, R., 1994, 'Interpretation in the Highlands', in J.M. Fladmark, ed., *Cultural tourism*, Donhead, Wimbledon, 248–59.

MacGregor, A.A., 1927, *Wild Drumalbain, or the road to Meggernie and Glen Coe*, W. and R. Chambers, London.

Mackay, J., 1992, *A biography of Robert Burns*, Mainstream Publishing, Edinburgh.

McKean, C., 1991, *Edinburgh: portrait of a city*, Century, London.

McKenzie, R., 1992, 'The "Photographic Tour" in nineteenth century Scotland', *Landscape Research*, 17(1), 20–7.

MacLean, C., 1985, *The fringe of gold: the fishing villages of Scotland's east coast, Orkney and Shetland*, Canongate, Edinburgh.

MacLean, M. and Carrell, C., eds., 1986, *As an Fhearann: from the land*, Mainstream Publishing, Edinburgh.

McLuhan, H.M., 1964, *Understanding media*, Sphere, London.

Macniven, D., 1994, 'Presenting historic Scotland', in J.M. Fladmark, ed., *Cultural tourism*, Donhead, Wimbledon, 225–36.

Macpherson, J., 1760, *Fragments of ancient poetry, collected in the Highlands of Scotland, and translated from the Galic or Erse language*, Edinburgh.

———— 1762, *Fingal, an ancient epic poem in six books: together with several other poems composed by Ossian, the son of Fingal*, Edinburgh.

———— 1763, *Temora: an ancient epic poem in six books: together with several other poems composed by Ossian, the son of Fingal*, Edinburgh.

———— 1765, *The works of Ossian, the song of Fingal. Translated from the Galic language by James Macpherson*, Edinburgh.

Mais, S.P.B., 1947, *I return to Scotland*, Christopher Johnson, London.

Martin, M., 1695, *A description of the Western Islands of Scotland*, London.

Mavor, W., 1798, *The British tourists; or a traveller's pocket companion through England, Wales, Scotland and Ireland comprehending the most celebrated tours in the British Islands*, London.

Melven, W., 1896, *North British Railway and West Highland Railway: official tourist guide to Scotland*, T.C. and E.C. Jack, Edinburgh.

Mitchell, W.J.T., 1986, *Iconology: image, text, ideology*, University of Chicago Press, Chicago.

M'Nayr, J., 1797, *A guide from Glasgow to some of the most remarkable scenes in the Highlands of Scotland and to the falls of the Clyde*, Glasgow.

Morley, F., 1980, *Literary Britain: a reader's guide to writers and landmarks*, Hutchinson, London.

Morris, A., 1991, 'Popping the cork: history, heritage and the stately home in the Scottish Borders', in G. Day and G. Rees, eds., *Regions, nations and European integration: remaking the Celtic periphery*, University of Wales Press, Cardiff, 141–51.

Morton, H.V., 1929, *In search of Scotland*, Methuen, London.

———— 1933, *In Scotland again*, Methuen, London.

Munro, N., 1906, *The Vital Spark*, Blackwood and Sons, Edinburgh.

Murray, G., ed., 1988, *Art in the garden: installations, Glasgow Garden Festival*, Graeme Murray, Edinburgh.

Murray, Hon. Mrs, 1799, *A companion and useful guide to the beauties of Scotland, to the lakes of Westmorland, Cumberland, and Lancashire; and to the curiosities of the district of Craven in the west riding of Yorkshire — to which is added, a more peculiar description of Scotland, especially that part of it, called THE HIGHLANDS*, London.

Nairn, T., 1975, *The break-up of Britain: crisis and neo-nationalism*, New Left Books, London.

Neill, W., 1992, 'Re-imaging Belfast', *The Planner*, 78(18), 8–10.

Newburg, V.E., 1976, 'The literature of the streets', in H.J. Dyos and M. Wolff, eds., *The Victorian city: images and realities*, vol. 1 'Past and Present/Numbers of people', Routledge and Kegan Paul, London, 191–209.

Newby, P.T., 1981, 'Literature and the fashioning of tourist taste', in D.C.D. Pocock, ed., *Humanistic geography and literature: essays on the experience of place*, Croom Helm, London, 130–41.

Newte, T., 1791, *Prospects and observations on a tour in England and Scotland*, London.

Nicolson, J.R., 1975, *Beyond the Great Glen*, David and Charles, Newton Abbot.

Nock, O.S., 1950, *Scottish railways*, Thomas Nelson, Edinburgh.

NTS (National trust for Scotland), 1992a, *A children's guide to the Culloden Exhibition*, National Trust for Scotland, Edinburgh.

———— 1992b, *The Battle of Culloden*, National Trust for Scotland, Edinburgh.

O'Barr, W.M., 1994, *Culture and the ad: exploring otherness in the world of advertising*, Westview, Boulder, Col.

O'Dell, A. and Walton, K., 1962, *The Highlands and Islands of Scotland*, Thomas Nelson, Edinburgh.

Orr, W., 1982, *Deer forests, landlords and crofters: the western Highlands in Victorian and Edwardian times*, John Donald, Edinburgh.

Otté, J., 1858, *Landscape photography: or a complete and easy description of the manipulations necessary for the production of landscape pictures*, London.

Ousby, I., 1990, *The Englishman's England: taste, travel and the rise of tourism*, Cambridge University Press, Cambridge.

Owen, R., 1821, *Report to the County of Lanark*, Glasgow.

Ozouf, S., 1988, *Festivals and the French Revolutions* (trans. A. Sheridan), Harvard University Press, Cambridge, Mass.

Patmore, J.A., 1983, *Recreation and resources: leisure patterns and historic places*, Blackwell, Oxford.

Pattison, I., 1992, *More Rab C. Nesbitt scripts*, BBC Books, London.

Pearce, D.G., 1987, *Tourism today: a geographical analysis*, Longman, London.

Phelps, A., ed., 1869, *Writings, speeches etc. Leaves from the journal of 'Our life in the highlands' from 1848 to 1861*, London.

Philo, C. and Kearns, G., 1993, 'Culture, history, capital: a critical introduction to the selling of places', in G. Kearns and C. Philo, eds, *Selling places: the city as cultural capital, past and present*, Pergamon Press, Oxford, 1–32.

Pittock, M.G.H., 1991, *The invention of Scotland: the Stuart myth and the Scottish identity, 1638 to the present*, Routledge, London.

PKDC (Perth and Kinross District Council), n.d., *Falls of Bruar: a visitor's guide*, Leisure and Recreation Department, Perth and Kinross District Council, Perth.

Plamenatz, J.P., 1970, *Ideology*, Pall Mall Press, London.

Plumb, J.H. and Weldon, H., 1977, *Royal heritage: the story of Britain's royal builders and collectors*, British Broadcasting Corporation, London.

Pope-Hennessy, V., 1932, *The Laird of Abbotsford: an informal presentation of Sir Walter Scott*, Putnam, London.

Prebble, J., 1989, *The king's jaunt: George IV in Scotland 1822, 'one and twenty daft days'*, Fontana, London.

Purvis, T., and Hunt, M., 1993, 'Discourse, ideology, discourse, ideology, discourse, ideology …', *British Journal of Sociology*, 44, 473–99.

Quigley, H., 1936, *The Highlands of Scotland*, Batsford, London.

Reed, P., 1993, 'The post-industrial city?', in P. Reed, ed., *Glasgow: the forming of the city*, Edinburgh University Press, Edinburgh, 187–201.

Reid, D., 1994, 'Foreword', in J.M. Fladmark, ed., *Cultural tourism*, Donhead, Wimbledon, ix–x.

Reiss, T.J., 1982, *The discourse of modernism*, Cornell University Press, Ithaca, NY.

Revill, G.E. and Watkin, C., 1994, 'Educated access: National Forest Park guides', paper presented at annual conference, Institute of British Geographers Rural Geography Study Group, Nottingham, September.

Richards, J.M., 1958, *The functional tradition in early industrial buildings*, Architectural Press, London.

Ritchie, L., 1835, 'Scott and Scotland', in G. Cattermole, ed., *Heath's picturesque annual*, Longman, Rees, Orme, Brown, Green, Longman, London, whole issue.

Robbins, K., 1983, *The eclipse of a great power: modern Britain, 1870–1975*, Longman, London.

Robertson, J.L., 1904, *Scott: poetical works*, Oxford University Press, London.

Rojek, C., 1993, 'Disney culture', *Leisure Studies*, 12, 121–35.

Rouillé, A., 1986, 'Exploring the world by photography', in J.-C. Lemagny and A. Rouillé, eds, *A history of photography*, Cambridge University Press, Cambridge.

Rumble, P., 1989, 'Interpreting the built and historic environment', in D. Uzzell, ed., *Heritage interpretation*, vol. 1 'The natural and built environment', Belhaven Press, London, 24–32.

Runte, A., 1976, 'The west: wealth, wonderland and wilderness', in J.W. Watson and T. O'Riordan, eds., *The American environment: perceptions and policies*, John Wiley, London, 47–62.

Sadler, D., 1993, 'Place-marketing, competitive places and the construction of hegemony in Britain in the 1980s', in G. Kearns and C. Philo, eds, *Selling places: the city as cultural capital, past and present*, Pergamon Press, Oxford, 175–92.

Said, E., 1978, *Orientalism*, Random House, New York.

Schudson, M., 1984, *Advertising, the uneasy persuasions: its dubious impact on American society*, Routledge, London.

Scott, P.H., 1994, 'The image of Scotland in literature', in J.M. Fladmark, ed., *Cultural tourism*, Donhead, Wimbledon, 362–73.

Scott, W., 1820, *Lochiel: or the Field of Culloden*, 3 vols., G. and W.B. Whittaker, London.

———— 1829: 1972, *Waverley*, Penguin, London.

———— 1904, *Scott's poetical works, with the author's introduction and notes*, Oxford University Press, London.

———— 1962, *Rob Roy*, Dent, London.

Scrope, W., 1938, *The art of deer stalking, illustrated by a narrative of a few days' sport in the Forest of Atholl*, London.

───── 1843, *Days and nights of salmon fishing in the Tweed, with a short account of the natural history and habit of the salmon*, Simpkin, Marshall, Hamilton, Kent and Co., London.

Selwyn, P., 1979, 'Johnson's Hebrides: thoughts on a dying social order', *Development and Change*, 10, 345–61.

Shaw, G. and Williams, A.M., 1994, *Critical issues in tourism: a geographical perspective*, Basil Blackwell, Oxford.

Shepherd, G., 1988, 'The kailyard', in D. Gifford, ed., *The history of Scottish literature*, vol. 3 'Nineteenth century', Aberdeen University Press, Aberdeen, 309–18.

Shields, R., 1991, *Places on the margin: alternative geographies of modernity*, Routledge, London.

Shoard, M., 1982, 'The lure of the moors', in J.R. Gold and J.A. Burgess, eds., *Valued environments*, George Allan and Unwin, London, 55–73.

Simons, H.W., ed., 1988, *Rhetoric in the human sciences*, Sage, London.

Smiles, S., 1986, 'Samuel Palmer and the pastoral inheritance', *Landscape Research*, 11(3), 11–15.

Smith, A., 1776, *The wealth of nations*, Edinburgh.

Smith, L.M.H., 1983, *The road to the Isles: the Hebrides in lantern slides*, Loanhead.

Smout, T.C., 1969, *A history of the Scottish people, 1560–1830*, Collins/Fontana, London.

Squire, S.J., 1994a, 'Accounting for cultural meanings: the interface between geography and tourism studies re-examined', *Progress in Human Geography*, 18, 1–16.

───── 1994b, 'The cultural values of literary tourism', *Annals of Tourism Research*, 21, 103–20.

Stafford, F.J., 1988, *The sublime savage: James Macpherson and the poems of Ossian*, Edinburgh University Press, Edinburgh.

STB (Scottish Tourist Board), 1993, *Scotland: where to go and what to see*, Scottish Tourist Board, Edinburgh.

STCG (Scottish Tourism Co-ordinating Group), 1992, *Tourism and the Scottish Environment*, Scottish Tourist Board, Edinburgh.

Stephenson, T., ed., 1946, *The countryside companion*, Odhams Press, London.

Stevenson, R.L., 1886, *Kidnapped: being the memoirs of David Balfour in the year 1751*, Henderson, London.

───── 1889, *Edinburgh: picturesque notes*, new edition, Seeley and Co., London.

Stewart A. and Birt, A., 1990, *A tramp around the City of Culture*, Lochar Publishing, Moffat.

Stewart, D.G., 1822, *Sketches of the character, institutions and customs of the Highlands of Scotland, Edinburgh*.

Sulivan, R., 1780, *Observations made during a tour through parts of England, Scotland and Wales in 1778. In a series of letters*, T. Becket, London.

Sutherland, K., 1985, 'Introduction', in W. Scott *Redgauntlet*, Oxford University Press, Oxford, vii–xxxi.

SWHC (Scottish Whisky Heritage Centre), n.d., *The story of scotch whisky*, Scottish Whisky Heritage Centre, Edinburgh.

Thornton, T., 1896, *A sporting tour through the northern parts of England, and a great part of the Highlands of Scotland, including remarks on English and Scottish landscapes and general observations on the state of society and manners*, Sportman's Library, London.

Thubron, C., 1975, *Journey into Cyprus*, Heinemann, London.

Towner, J., 1985, 'The grand tour: a key phase in the history of tourism', *Annals of Tourism Research*, 12, 297–333.

Trevor-Roper, H., 1983, 'The highland tradition of Scotland', in E. Hobsbawm and T. Ranger, eds, *The invention of tradition*, Cambridge University Press, Cambridge, 15–41.

Tuan, Y.F., 1974, *Topophilia: a study of environmental perception, attitudes, and values*, Prentice-Hall, Englewood Cliffs, NJ.

Turner, G., 1990, *British cultural studies: an introduction*, Unwin Hyman, London.

Turnock, D., 1970, *Patterns of highland development*, Macmillan, London.

——— 1982, *Railways in the British Isles: landscape, land use and society*, Adam and Charles, London.

Urry, J., 1990, *The tourist gaze: leisure and travel in contemporary societies*, Sage, London.

Våge, J., 1993, 'Farm buildings in Norway', in M. Fladmark, ed., *Heritage, conservation, interpretation, enterprise*, Donhead, Wimbledon, 93–100.

Victoria, 1968, *Our life in the Highlands*, William Kimber, London (republication of two volumes originally published in 1868 and 1884).

Wallace, G., 1987, 'Compton Mackenzie and the Scottish popular novel', in C. Craig, ed., *The history of Scottish literature*, vol. 4 'The twentieth century', Aberdeen University Press, Aberdeen, 243–57.

Walsh, K., 1992, *The representation of the past: museums and heritage in the postmodern world*, Routledge, London.

Ward, S.V., 1988, 'Promoting holiday resorts: a review of early history to 1921', *Planning History*, 10(2), 7–11.

——— 1994, 'Time and place: key themes in place promotion in the USA, Canada and Britain since 1870', in J.R. Gold and S.V. Ward, eds,

Place promotion: the use of publicity to sell towns and regions, John Wiley, Chichester, 53–74.

——— 1996, *Selling places: past and present*, Spon, London (in press).

Ward, S.V. and Gold, J.R., 1994, 'Introduction', in J.R. Gold and S.V. Ward, eds, *Place promotion: the use of publicity to sell towns and regions*, John Wiley, Chichester, 1–17.

Ward Lock, 1947, *Inverness, Strathpeffer and the north of Scotland*, Ward Lock and Co., London.

Warnock, M., 1976, *Imagination*, Faber and Faber, London.

Watson, J.R., 1970, *Picturesque landscape and English romantic poetry*, Hutchinson, London.

Weir, T., 1971, *The Kyle Line*, Famedram Publishers, Gartocharn.

——— n.d., *The Mallaig Line*, Famedram Publishers, Gartocharn.

Wernick, A., 1991, *Promotional culture: advertising, ideology and symbolic expression*, London, Sage.

WFS (Walker, Fraser and Steele), 1914, *The Scottish register of grouse moors, deer forests, salmon fishings, mansion houses and mixed shootings to let and for sale*, Walker, Fraser and Steele, Glasgow.

Whitbourne, R., 1623, *A discourse and discovery of New-found-land. With many reasons to prove how worthy and beneficial a plantation may there be made, after a better manner than it was. Together with the laying open of certain enormities and abuses that trade to that country, and the means laid downe for reformation of*, London.

WHR (West Highland Railway), 1894, *Mountain, moor and loch, illustrated by pen and pencil on the route of the West Highland Railway*, Sir James Causton and Sons, London.

Whyte, I. and Whyte, K., 1990, *On the trail of the Jacobites*, Routledge, London.

Williams, Lord, 1981, *A heritage for Scotland*, HSMO, Edinburgh.

Williams, R. 1980, 'Advertising: the magic system', in R. Williams, *Problems in materialism and culture*, Verso, London, 170–95.

Williamson, J., 1978, *Decoding advertisements: ideology and meaning in advertising*, Marion Boyars, London.

Willis, D., 1991, *The story of crofting in Scotland*, John Donald, Edinburgh.

Wilson, R.B., 1970, *Go Great Western: a history of GWR publicity*, David and Charles Newton Abbot.

Winsberg, M.D., 1992, 'Walt Disney World, Florida: the creation of a fantasy landscape', in D.G. Janelle, ed., *Geographical snapshots of North America*, Guilford Press, New York, 350–3.

Withers, C., 1992, 'The historical creation of the Scottish Highlands', in I. Donnachie and C. Whatley, eds, *The manufacture of Scottish history*, Polygon, Edinburgh.

Witt, S.F. and Moutinho, L., eds, 1989, *Tourism, marketing and management handbook*, Prentice-Hall, Englewood Cliffs, NJ.

Woodsworth, N., 1994, 'Clear the Highlands again!', *Financial Times*, 5/6 November, xiii.

Wormald, J., 1991, *Scotland revisited*, Collins and Brown, London.

Wright, P., 1985, *On living in an old country: the national past in contemporary Britain*, Verso, London.

———— 1991, *A journey through the ruins: the last days of London*, Radius, London.

WTO (World Tourist Organisation), 1991, *Tourism to the year 2000: qualitative aspects affecting global growth*, World Tourist Organisation, Madrid.

Wylson, A. and Wylson, P., 1994, *Theme parks, leisure centres, zoos and aquaria*, Harlow: Longman.

Yates, N., 1988, 'Selling the seaside', *History Today*, 38, August, 20–7.

Youngson, A.J., 1973, *After the Forty-Five: the economic impact on the Scottish Highlands*, Edinburgh University Press, Edinburgh.

———— 1974, *Beyond the Highland line*, Collins, London.

Zube, E.H. and Galante, J., 1994, 'Marketing landscapes of the Four Corners States', in J.R. Gold and S.V. Ward, eds, *Place promotion: the use of publicity to sell towns and regions*, John Wiley, Chichester, 213–32.

Zube, E.H. and Kennedy, C., 1990, 'Changing images of the Arizona Territory', in L. Zonn, ed., *Place images in the media: portrayal, meaning and experience*, Rowman and Littlefield, Savage, MD, 183–205.

Index

Abbotsford 64, 74, 76, 104, 131, 138
Aberdeen 38, 39, 53, 93, 114, 122, 131, 133, 145, 146
accessibility 5, 12, 13, 40, 43, 57, 61–2, 91, 92
accommodation, tourist 12, 20, 40, 41, 179, 180
advertising 2, 4, 8, 11, 12, 14, 16, 23, 24, 27, 33, 99, 132, 142, 184–5, 187, 189–91, 197–202
aesthetics 33, 63, 70
Albert, prince 79–83, 87, 103, 111, 177–8
American tourists 20, 64, 76, 89–92
angling 5, 6, 81, 99, 106, 110, 112, 115, 195
antiquarianism 62, 64, 78, 108
architecture 2, 11, 80, 131, 180, 191
Arnol (Isle of Lewis) 142, 153–4
Arnold, Malcolm 1
Auchindrain township 154–5
audiences 10, 15, 22
authenticity 10, 12, 14, 22, 34, 36, 54–5, 59, 67, 78, 83, 144–5, 158, 194
aviation 123–4, 138, 187
Ayr 97, 131
Ayrshire 12, 20, 63–4, 123, 164

bagpipes 1, 5, 6, 77
Ballater 122, 132
Balmoral 76, 77–8, 79–83, 103, 111, 145
Banks, Iain 119
Barra, Isle of 120, 152
Barrie, J.M. 89
Batsford, B.T. (publishers) 13, 132, 133–5
Baxters Foods 4, 170–1
Beckwith, Lilian 119
Betjeman, John 132, 139
boosterism 12, 18, 34, 104, 186, 196
Borders, the 6, 7, 76, 104, 109, 163, 199

Boswell, James 42, 44, 45–7, 58
Bramer 77, 104, 114, 122, 131–2
British Tourist Authority 5, 25, 182, 187
Buchan, John 119, 120
Burns, Robert 1, 12, 43, 48–9, 58, 60, 62, 63–4, 83, 84, 119, 131
Burns Societies 1
buses 126–8
business conferences 7–8, 22

Cairngorms 9, 31, 138
Caledonian Societies 1
Callander 114, 120
canals 61, 132, 163, 175
caravanning 116–18
Celtic Revival 63, 179
censorship 75
Central Lowlands 5, 8, 36, 38, 43
Chicago 18, 178
chivalry 52, 54, 83, 195
Cities of Culture, European 14, 186–90, 192, 196
clans 1, 39, 74, 77, 85, 142
Clyde, River 47, 160, 167, 185–6
estuary 20, 62, 97
coaches, horse-drawn 40, 61, 123
motor 116, 118, 123, 126–8
coal mining 160, 164
Cobbett, William 167, 184
colonization 12, 17–18, 34
commodification 4–5, 8, 159, 196
communication, processes of 10–11, 15, 22–7, 142
cotton industry 165–9, 175, 192
country dancing, Scottish 6
Crockett, Samuel R. 89, 119
Cronin, A.J. 119, 120
crofting 6, 39, 147–8, 151, 153–4, 192
Cuillins (Skye) 69, 118
Culloden, Battle of 36, 39
battlefield 36, 39, 136–7
cultural studies 28

cultural tourism 63, 176–93
Cuthbertson, D.C. 130

Dale, David 165
deer stalking 106, 109–12, 115
deindustrialization 160, 162
depopulation 6, 40, 41
discourse 11, 12, 16, 28–9, 31, 34, 116, 189
distilleries 6, 171–2, 174
Disney, Walt 2, 21, 175
Donizetti, Gaetano 1, 60, 75
Dumfries 7, 127, 131
Dundee 38, 164, 175
Dunrobin Castle (Golspie) 147–51

Ealing Studios 2, 120
economic development 7–9, 12, 17, 18–19, 22, 34, 39, 146, 155–6, 184–91
Edinburgh 5, 14, 36–8, 40, 45, 50, 63, 72–4, 76, 87–9, 91, 93, 96, 102, 103, 104, 125, 126, 128, 130, 131, 133, 161, 169, 176, 178–9, 186, 192, 195
   Castle 6, 36, 72, 88, 142, 200
   emblematic landscapes 2, 6, 7, 198, 200
   Festival xi, 14, 180–83, 191, 192
   Military Tattoo 182
   Royal Visit (1822) 60, 72–4, 177
   Waverley Station 6, 97, 106
Enlightenment, Scottish 45, 194
engraving 69, 104
excursions 97, 99, 103, 114
exploration 43, 47

fairs 177, 191
ferries 6, 40, 96, 125, 127
film 2, 11, 23, 119, 120, 179, 181–2
fishing industry 5, 6, 146–7; *see also* angling
'fly-drive' holidays 13, 124
folklife museums 13, 152–6
food-processing industry 2, 4, 8, 14
Forestry Commission 24, 29, 31, 33, 130
forestry parks 24, 29, 31, 33, 130
Forsyth, Bill 120
Forth Rail Bridge 91, 93, 100, 198

Fort William 79, 96, 97, 125, 128, 131
forts 39
Foucault, Michel 28, 35
Freed, Arthur 2

Gaelic 39, 44, 53, 58, 59, 70, 71–2, 75, 192
Galloway 7, 199
Garden Festivals 185–6, 192–3
gender 5–6, 31
George IV, King 60, 64, 72–4, 79, 177
Gilpin, William 47–8, 55, 57, 58, 59
Glasgow 5, 38, 62, 91, 93, 96, 102, 103, 104, 114, 125, 131, 133, 138, 161, 169, 175, 176, 196, 201
   Docks 123, 160
   European City of Culture 186–8, 189
   Garden Festival 185–6, 192
   Great Exhibitions 178, 179–80
   industrial landscapes 163–4, 165
   re-imaging 14, 184–91
Glencoe 41, 131
globalization 7, 21
golf 6, 13, 24, 99, 106–7
Grand Tour, the 20, 41
Great Exhibitions 14, 102, 103, 169, 177–80, 186, 196
guidebooks 9, 12, 13, 20, 21, 24, 26, 28, 31–2, 40, 44, 58, 87, 97, 104, 122, 128, 135, 149, 153–4, 167, 170, 195
guides, human 44

heritage 8, 13–14, 28, 79, 136–8, 140–78, 196
Highland Folk Park 155–6
Highlands, Scottish 1, 2–7, 12, 13–14, 32, 35, 38–58, 61, 64–85, 91, 93, 96, 97, 99–101, 106, 109–12, 120, 124, 125, 127, 131–5, 144, 145–59, 195, 196–202
   cattle 6, 14
   Clearances 38, 89, 147–52, 158
   dress 73–4, 77
   games and gatherings 1, 5, 6, 77, 124, 142, 145
Highlands and Islands Development

Board 35
hill walking and rambling 5, 11, 106, 107, 112, 118, 125, 138
hire cars 124, 127, 128
Historic Scotland 142, 153–4
horse transport 41, 87
hospitality 16, 41, 43
hotels 8, 20, 97, 122, 124, 127, 138, 145
hunting 13, 29, 35, 39, 77, 80, 109–12

ideology 12, 16, 31, 32, 34, 115, 118, 144, 147–52, 170, 177, 194
identity xi, 19, 42, 73, 83, 152, 159, 180, 182, 202
industrial archaeology 14, 161–5
industrialism 62, 194
industrial heritage 8, 14, 160–75, 196
industrial tours 14, 169–74
interpretation 13–14, 24, 136–7, 140–44, 146, 156–8, 162, 168, 174, 195
itineraries, tourist 5, 40, 44, 49–53, 61
Inverness 38, 40, 45, 93, 114, 123, 131

Jacobite uprising (1745) xi, 12, 36, 38, 39, 65, 78, 136, 174
Jacobites 70, 72, 78, 87
Johnson, Dr Samuel 42, 44, 45–7, 54, 57, 78, 131, 194

kailyard 89–90, 119–20, 202
Katrine, Loch 68, 69, 76, 84, 104

Landseer, Sir Edwin 1, 74, 83, 119, 149
landownership 32, 39, 72, 111, 119, 149
landscape gardening 48
lantern slides 90
literary tourism 12, 54, 57, 63–4, 68, 76, 84, 90, 106, 167, 195
literature 1, 28, 60, 63, 64–85, 119, 120, 184
lithography 26
Loch Ness Monster 1, 14, 156–7, 159
Lomond, Loch 62, 102, 127, 131

MacCaig, Norman 198–9, 200
MacGregor, Alasdair Alpin 130, 139
Maclaren, Ian 89
Mackenzie, Compton 119, 120
Mackintosh, C.R. 187
Macpherson, James 53–8, 194
Mais, S.P.B. 119, 135
maps 12, 13, 39, 40, 41, 49–53, 57, 128
marketing 8–9, 22–3, 84, 135, 142
Marxism 30, 184
mass tourism 10, 13, 21, 107
media 9, 10, 12, 15, 16–35, 86–90, 119, 196
medievalism 62
media content 10–11, 12, 22, 25–7
melancholic landscapes 47, 81, 119
Mendelssohn, Felix 1, 54, 104
migration 1, 27, 38, 89, 152, 179
military roads 39–40, 50
modernism 119
modernity 2, 13, 34, 39, 55, 93, 198
monumentality 79, 151
Morton, H.V. 130–32, 139
motoring 13, 24, 112, 116–39, 146, 186
mountaineering 5, 13, 106, 107
museums 28, 181, 186, 197, 200–201
music 28, 181, 186, 197, 200–201

Nairn 98, 99, 107, 114
National Trust for Scotland 130, 136–7, 141, 142
nationalism 42, 151, 152, 159, 177
New Lanark 14, 163, 165–9, 174–5
Nesbitt, Rab C. 1, 189
newspapers 2, 16, 19, 20, 26, 33, 130
nostalgia 2, 14, 43, 119, 135, 197, 201
novelists 1, 11, 70–71, 72, 77

Oban 93, 97, 104, 114, 132
oil industry 120, 122, 137, 147
opera 64, 181, 186
Ordnance Survey 40
Orientalism 35
Orkneys 142, 145
Ossian 12, 36, 42, 53–7, 60, 75, 83, 101, 104, 112, 194
Owen, Robert 14, 165, 175

package holidays 26, 124
packaging places 13, 145–7
pageants 12, 73, 80
painting 1, 11, 43, 64, 69, 83, 119
pastoralism 62–4, 84
Pennant, Thomas 44
Perth 4, 39, 55, 98, 106, 114, 125, 131
Phelps, Sir Arthur 87, 100
photographic tours 108–9
photography 1, 5–7, 26, 69, 90–91, 99, 104, 106, 108–9, 132, 133, 149
Picturesque, the 45, 57, 58, 62, 71, 131, 144
picturesque tourism 43, 47–9, 104
pilgrimages 19, 57, 76
place promotion 7–9, 11, 12, 13, 16–35, 135–6, 142, 170, 184–91, 195–202
poetry 12, 53, 60, 64, 67–70, 200
popular culture 1, 10, 90
posters 9, 11, 16, 19, 23, 25, 26, 28, 33, 122, 187
postmodernism 14, 159, 185, 187
Prestwick Airport 123–4
producers (communicators) 11, 22, 23–5
product advertising 2, 33, 201
product packaging 2, 4
promotional gifts 23, 26
publicity 8, 9, 14, 19, 24, 170, 184–91, 192

radio 23, 119
railways 6, 13, 20, 26, 83, 86–111, 120, 122–3, 163, 177, 179, 195
rallying, motor 124–5
regalia, royal 72
reimaging 14, 19, 184–91, 192
rhetoric 12, 16, 32–3, 34, 116–39, 145, 147, 151, 162, 182, 196
road networks 13, 39, 40, 61–2, 116, 124–6, 139
romanticism 5, 50, 54, 58, 62–4, 71, 74, 78, 79, 80, 87, 194, 201
Rossini, G.A. 1, 75

St Andrews 106, 131, 133
Scott, Sir Walter 1, 12, 38, 60–85, 86, 97, 101, 103–4, 112, 119, 131,

138, 180, 181, 194–5
Scottish Office 25, 159
Scottish Photographic Society 108, 141
Scottish Tourist Board 14, 25, 35, 197–202
seaside resorts 20, 21, 97
Shell County Guides 13, 132–3
Shetland 145, 151
shipbuilding 160, 163, 164, 170, 184
shipping
  coastal 13, 91, 102, 120
  oceanic 13, 61, 90, 91, 123, 180
shooting 13, 87, 99, 106, 112, 115, 195
skiing 9, 24, 112, 119, 139
Skye, Isle of 63, 69, 131, 132
souvenir views 90
spa resorts 19–20, 96, 127
Staffa, Isle of 55, 97, 103, 104
steamships 12, 13, 62, 84, 91, 96, 102, 116, 123, 180, 187
Stephenson, Tom 116–18
stereoscopic photographs 90–91, 92
stereotypes 5–6, 17, 120, 184
Stevenson, R.L. 1, 86–9, 119
Stirling 5, 68, 125, 131
Stonehaven 133, 146
Strathpeffer 96, 127
Stuarts 12, 15, 38, 70, 72, 78, 79, 84, 89, 174
Sublime, the 48, 53, 56, 194
supernatural phenomena 42, 132–3
Sutherland 40, 118, 147, 149, 150–51

tartanry 2, 4, 5, 6, 77–9, 81, 85, 100, 119, 120, 152, 181, 182, 202
Tayside 7, 75, 201
television 11, 14, 16, 19, 22, 23, 26, 33, 119, 120, 197–202
theatre 28, 64, 67, 73, 74–5, 181
theme parks 21, 155–8, 159, 168, 175, 185
Thomas Cook and Son 13, 20, 101–4, 112, 127–8, 139, 177, 180, 196
tourism, defined 10
tourist 'experiences' 8, 142, 168–9, 172, 174
town guides 35
tradition, invention of 1, 12, 60, 64–84

trails 79, 84, 145, 151, 157, 168, 172
travel, defined 10
travel agents 5, 16, 26
travel brochures 5–7, 9, 11, 14, 16,
    19, 23, 25, 26, 28, 33, 136
travel writers 2, 11, 22, 23
travellers' tales 11, 12, 36–59
Trossachs 63, 68, 69, 103, 114, 127,
    132
Turner, J.M.W. 1, 63, 69, 71, 74

urban and regional development, *see*
    economic development
urban regeneration 184–91
urban tourism 176–93, 196

values 8, 11, 12, 30
Victoria, Queen 75, 79–83, 87, 100,
    111, 112, 131, 184
videos 19, 23, 26

Western Isles 6, 45–7, 55, 61, 63, 69,
    97, 103, 104, 120, 131, 152
whisky 4, 5, 8, 11, 14, 15, 99, 154,
    171–4, 175
Wilson, George Washington 91
Wordsworth, Dorothy 41, 55, 63,
    167
Wordsworth, William 41, 55, 56, 57,
    63, 167